Cloud
Security

D0731842

A Wiley Brand

Cloud Security

by Ted Coombs

A Wiley Brand

Cloud Security For Dummies®

Published by: **John Wiley & Sons, Inc.,** 111 River Street, Hoboken, NJ 07030-5774, www.wiley.com

Copyright © 2022 by John Wiley & Sons, Inc., Hoboken, New Jersey

Published simultaneously in Canada

No part of this publication may be reproduced, stored in a retrieval system or transmitted in any form or by any means, electronic, mechanical, photocopying, recording, scanning or otherwise, except as permitted under Sections 107 or 108 of the 1976 United States Copyright Act, without the prior written permission of the Publisher. Requests to the Publisher for permission should be addressed to the Permissions Department, John Wiley & Sons, Inc., 111 River Street, Hoboken, NJ 07030, (201) 748-6011, fax (201) 748-6008, or online at http://www.wiley.com/go/permissions.

Trademarks: Wiley, For Dummies, the Dummies Man logo, Dummies.com, Making Everything Easier, and related trade dress are trademarks or registered trademarks of John Wiley & Sons, Inc. and may not be used without written permission. All other trademarks are the property of their respective owners. John Wiley & Sons, Inc. is not associated with any product or vendor mentioned in this book.

LIMIT OF LIABILITY/DISCLAIMER OF WARRANTY: WHILE THE PUBLISHER AND AUTHORS HAVE USED THEIR BEST EFFORTS IN PREPARING THIS WORK, THEY MAKE NO REPRESENTATIONS OR WARRANTIES WITH RESPECT TO THE ACCURACY OR COMPLETENESS OF THE CONTENTS OF THIS WORK AND SPECIFICALLY DISCLAIM ALL WARRANTIES, INCLUDING WITHOUT LIMITATION ANY IMPLIED WARRANTIES OF MERCHANTABILITY OR FITNESS FOR A PARTICULAR PURPOSE. NO WARRANTY MAY BE CREATED OR EXTENDED BY SALES REPRESENTATIVES, WRITTEN SALES MATERIALS OR PROMOTIONAL STATEMENTS FOR THIS WORK. THE FACT THAT AN ORGANIZATION, WEBSITE, OR PRODUCT IS REFERRED TO IN THIS WORK AS A CITATION AND/OR POTENTIAL SOURCE OF FURTHER INFORMATION DOES NOT MEAN THAT THE PUBLISHER AND AUTHORS ENDORSE THE INFORMATION OR SERVICES THE ORGANIZATION, WEBSITE, OR PRODUCT MAY PROVIDE OR RECOMMENDATIONS IT MAY MAKE. THIS WORK IS SOLD WITH THE UNDERSTANDING THAT THE PUBLISHER IS NOT ENGAGED IN RENDERING PROFESSIONAL SERVICES. THE ADVICE AND STRATEGIES CONTAINED HEREIN MAY NOT BE SUITABLE FOR YOUR SITUATION. YOU SHOULD CONSULT WITH A SPECIALIST WHERE APPROPRIATE. FURTHER, READERS SHOULD BE AWARE THAT WEBSITES LISTED IN THIS WORK MAY HAVE CHANGED OR DISAPPEARED BETWEEN WHEN THIS WORK WAS WRITTEN AND WHEN IT IS READ. NEITHER THE PUBLISHER NOR AUTHORS SHALL BE LIABLE FOR ANY LOSS OF PROFIT OR ANY OTHER COMMERCIAL DAMAGES, INCLUDING BUT NOT LIMITED TO SPECIAL, INCIDENTAL, CONSEQUENTIAL, OR OTHER DAMAGES.

For general information on our other products and services, please contact our Customer Care Department within the U.S. at 877-762-2974, outside the U.S. at 317-572-3993, or fax 317-572-4002. For technical support, please visit https://hub.wiley.com/community/support/dummies.

Wiley publishes in a variety of print and electronic formats and by print-on-demand. Some material included with standard print versions of this book may not be included in e-books or in print-on-demand. If this book refers to media such as a CD or DVD that is not included in the version you purchased, you may download this material at http://booksupport.wiley.com. For more information about Wiley products, visit www.wiley.com.

Library of Congress Control Number: 2022930200

ISBN: 978-1-119-79046-4; 978-1-119-79047-1 (ebk); 978-1-119-79048-8 (ebk)

Contents at a Glance

Table of Contents

Introduction

L earning about cloud security is a bit like going to the dentist: It has to be done, but who wants to do it? This book will make the process painless and perhaps even enjoyable. Though the information in this book will be useful to everyone who has data, uses the cloud, or lives on the planet, it will be most useful to people who are responsible for the management of company data security — particularly, when that data is stored in the cloud.

Cloud security is data security. Books about cloud security tend to focus on only the aspects of using the cloud. But this book could have been titled *Data Security Even When You Use the Cloud For Dummies*. But that was too long. This book covers emerging information security topics, such as DataOps and AIOPs, that, though not cloud specific, are important topics to know about when your company manages sensitive data or develops applications to manage critical data. They are more than technologies — they are *philosophies* that will help you create a strategy for managing information security. If you're in the infosec business, you know it's a lot like herding cats — and those cats are having kittens, like, every day!

You'll learn about technologies that range from AI to key fobs that will assist you in getting the job done right. Most of all, you'll learn that your biggest concern isn't hardware or VPNs or cryptographic strength. It's people. (Remember *Soylent Green?* Maybe not. It depends on your weakness for early 1970s sci-fi.)

In any event, people are the highest risk in any effort to protect data. Putting it in the cloud just makes it particularly hard to protect because it lies outside your local network security and firewall.

Some people will try to hack into your system and steal your data. It happens millions of times a day, most of which are automated attempts to find weaknesses in your data security or to find areas of the applications you use that can be exploited. Even scarier than protecting your data from people trying to hack into your systems is protecting your data from the people who have authorized access. They may not mean any harm, but if they're careless or uninstructed in the proper ways of The Force (information security), they can unwittingly hand over the keys to the kingdom.

There are also so many different ways that your data is threatened today. One of the biggest threats now facing companies is ransomware. World leaders are meeting at this very moment (well, at the moment I wrote this paragraph) to discuss what can be done about this terrible threat to economic stability. Add to that the gigantic breaches that happen many times each year, revealing personally identifying information and financial data, and you have a data security nightmare.

Armed with this book, you can find new approaches to protecting your information, particularly when it's stored in the cloud. You'll learn about how virtual environments make your job a challenge as you try to keep up with the fluid environment that makes the cloud so powerful. There are also different kinds of clouds, not just different brands. You need to know about topics such as public, private, and hybrid clouds and how to manage data as it moves between them.

One of the keys to modern information security is good encryption. Though this book is a bit forward-looking, it doesn't attempt to deal with the challenge of post-quantum encryption. However, you will learn about different types of encryption as well as some of the ways to manage encryption keys, your company's deepest secrets.

About This Book

Books in the *For Dummies* brand are organized in a modular, easy-to-access format that lets you use the book as an owner's manual. Because cloud security isn't about just a single application, you can think of this book as a handbook or guide to the many technologies and efforts to bring about information security, particularly in the cloud. This book's chapters are organized to first explore basic concepts and then move to more complex solutions. Still, it's not critical that you read the book completely through. You can head right to concepts that interest you the most, though there's a chance you might need to jump back to earlier chapters to review basic ideas or gain context. The first part of this book is best used by companies first starting on their journey into the types of information security practices that include using clouds as part of the IT environment. If you're further down that path, you will find more advanced topics in Parts 2, 3, and 4.

Web addresses appear in monofont. If you're reading a digital version of this book on a device connected to the Internet, you can click a web address to visit that website, like this: www.dummies.com.

Foolish Assumptions

The ideas, information, and details about cloud security are relevant to nearly every business that manages data. I'm assuming, if you're reading this book, that you have some background in managing or working directly in the information security field. This book is meant as a primer, so some readers may find the information more of a review while others see some of these topics for the first time.

Icons Used in This Book

As you make your way through this book (if that's how you're reading it), you see the following icons in the margins:

TIP

The Tip icon marks bits of information you will find particularly helpful. When you're skimming the book, these tips should pop out to give you a quick grasp of the topic.

REMEMBER

Remember icons mark information that is important to keep in mind. Some of them review topics from earlier in the book that are relevant to the information being presented.

TECHNICAL STUFF

The Technical Stuff icon marks information of a technical nature that is more important to someone working in the field and might need a bit more depth.

WARNING

The Warning icon points out bits of information you can use to avoid issues you might encounter.

Beyond the Book

Because cloud security is an evolving and complex field, there's no single source or best place to go for more information. Every business has a unique need when protecting their private information, so throughout this book, I've done my best to include URLs to further information about both products and frameworks that will evolve as the information security challenge evolves.

In addition to what you're reading right now, this book comes with a free, access-anywhere Cheat Sheet that gives you an overview of some of the major cloud security topics I discuss in greater detail in this book. To find this Cheat Sheet, visit www.dummies.com and search for *Cloud Security For Dummies Cheat Sheet* in the Search box.

Where to Go from Here

Get started reading Chapter 1 to help you understand some of the responsibilities required of someone taking on the job of cloud security. Chapters 2 and 3 dive into cloud-specific resources and basic techniques for protecting data. Chapter 4 is specifically for companies that develop their own software. (If your company doesn't do software development, you might want to skip this chapter.) Chapter 5 might be the most important chapter, dealing as it does with restricting access to your cloud resources. The rest of the book talks about security applications and complying with security regulations, and then ends with a chapter pointing to some of the more important applications you might want to use in your fight to keep your information secure.

1

Getting Started with Cloud Security

Chapter **1**

Clouds Aren't Bulletproof

All the great innovators have been known to "have their head in the clouds." Now it's your turn. Cloud computing is one of the greatest innovations of modern computing since the Internet, but with all its many benefits come certain responsibilities. One *vital* responsibility is the management of security. You can think of clouds as Infrastructure Elsewhere, but the security of all infrastructure must be managed. In this chapter, I spell out the basics of getting to know your business so that you can best create a security plan, which is the first step toward optimal application and data security when using clouds.

REMEMBER

For the most part, whenever I mention clouds in later chapters, I'm talking about public clouds, like AWS and Google Cloud. I reserve Chapter 9 for a more detailed discussion of private and hybrid clouds.

A word to the wise: When the responsibility for cloud security falls in your lap, don't panic. You'll soon find out that, with the right plan and the right tools, the task can be easily managed. To get started, you have to get to know your business. You may *think* you know it, but in order to provide truly successful security, you have to know it *in detail*, beyond just knowing the name of the person manning the front desk.

Knowing Your Business

It's great to know exactly what your business sells, whether it's widgets or services, but when it comes to cybersecurity, you need to know your business a bit more intimately. This new insight into how your business runs not only allows you to create a rock-solid security plan but also may help you innovate by better understanding how things get done. One of the first steps is knowing what you want to protect.

Discovering the company jewels

It's time to gather your first thoughts about cloud security into an actionable strategy, by understanding which assets you're trying to protect. This becomes the most important part of your plan. Depending on the size of your company, the strategies will start to differ. If you're thinking that cloud security doesn't differ much from everyday cybersecurity, you're absolutely correct. Getting cloud security right means you have a plan for all your cyberassets — wherever they live and operate.

TIP

Create an inventory of all your assets. Later in this chapter, I offer some suggestions for creating the right team. It's best to rely on them when creating an inventory of assets rather than try to noodle it out yourself.

Initiating your plan

Small companies can start their plan in a spreadsheet. You could probably get away with using a simple yellow legal pad, but then it's not so easy to share with others, and *that* is the part of the plan that comes next. Create a spreadsheet or database if you're more comfortable with it and start to list all applications used by your company. (It's easier said than done!). Many departments use applications that are hidden from the IT department. These *siloes* are towers of applications and data that are cut off from the other parts of the company — for example, accounting applications that are in use only by Accounting or sales tracking applications used only by Sales. This single exercise can be an eye-opener. You may look at the list and think, "Who is watching all this stuff?" That's why you start here.

REMEMBER

All your applications are creating and using data. Each application on your list should also include information about the kinds of data it creates or uses.

Automating the discovery process

Larger organizations might use automated discovery applications that can help you create a basic list of applications, networks, and data. This is a particularly important first step when migrating to the cloud. For example, Amazon Web Services (AWS, for short) has an application called the AWS Application Discovery Service. (More about that service in the next sections.)

AWS Discovery Service

The AWS Discovery Service collects and documents information about the applications in use within your company and then stores that information in an AWS Migration Hub. This vital data can then be exported into Excel or certain AWS analysis tools. This is the data that underlies your ultimate cloud security plan!

TIP

AWS also has APIs (application programming interfaces) that allow you to store performance data about each of these applications. (Save room for storing the risk level information I talk about later in this chapter.)

There are two ways to gather information using the AWS Discovery Service:

>> **Agentless:** This system collects data by gathering it from your VMWare application. If you have not deployed virtual machines at this point in your migration to the cloud, this system won't be useful. If you choose AWS as your cloud service provider, you'll find that AWS and VMWare are intricately interconnected.

>> **Agent-based:** Deploy this application on each of your servers, both physical and virtual. The system then collects a variety of information, including the number of applications currently running on the server, the network connections, the performance metrics, as well as a listing other processes currently running.

Google Cloud Discovery Service

This particular discovery service is built into the Google Cloud. If you've already gotten started using the Google Cloud for your applications, you can make use of instance metadata, which is great for obtaining information on elements such as an application's IP address, the machine type, and other network information.

The project metadata collected by the Google Cloud Discovery Service tracks the same kind of information but includes applications that may still be running in your (physical) data center. When you're ready to tackle collecting instance and project metadata, check out the following link to Google documentation on storing and retrieving this kind of information:

`https://cloud.google.com/compute/docs/metadata/overview`

Knowing Your SLA Agreements with Service Providers

A *service level agreement*, also known as an SLA, spells out the performance and reliability levels promised to you by your cloud service provider. Though performance isn't technically part of cloud security, it's part of the overall availability of your applications and data. Your company's IT department likely has SLA agreements in place with the departments it serves. These SLA agreements depend on the cloud service providers doing their part, and they give you an idea of what they promise. For example, you can't promise 99.99 percent uptime if the cloud service provider offers only 99.5 percent. Some SLA agreements might also include references to the security they provide.

REMEMBER

One main benefit of using the cloud is that some of the security responsibility for your applications is handled by the cloud service provider. This normally includes physical security and some, but not all, antimalware security. They may additionally offer security services for hire.

Here are links to the many SLA agreements offered by some of the top clouds. Though this list is by no means complete, it gives you an idea of what's being offered and what you might expect from the cloud service provider you select or have selected:

- » **Amazon:** https://aws.amazon.com/legal/service-level-agreements
- » **Google:** https://cloud.google.com/terms/sla
- » **Oracle:** www.oracle.com/cloud/sla

These service level agreements cover issues such as guaranteed uptime, disk operation efficiency, domain name system (DNS) integrity, email delivery, and more. Most of these are guaranteed at levels approaching 100 percent. Because nothing is perfect, they usually guarantee 99.99 percent or 99.95 percent for the unforeseen failures that can and do happen, but I wouldn't lose sleep over it. Statistically, you're safe with these services.

Where is the security?

One promise that's hard to track down in a cloud service provider's SLA is one concerning security. Security isn't guaranteed — just implied. Cloud service providers protect your data and applications to the limit of their ability, including issues such as physical security and some degree of malware detection by a 24/7 network operations center.

Because security is a shared responsibility, you often find that, in discussions about their security, cloud service providers talk about how they can help you create a secure cloud experience. Many of them have tools for these tasks:

>> Encrypting data

>> Monitoring for malware attack

>> Remediating catastrophic failure

Some of the applications that perform these tasks are third-party products and services that interoperate with the cloud service provider. You generally find the partner companies listed on the cloud service provider's website.

Explore the security and service offerings of companies that are partnering with your selected cloud service provider. These companies are usually certified and provide a seamless software experience.

Knowing your part

When it comes to cloud security, the ball is primarily in your court. It's up to you to decide whether you have the company resources needed in order to provide the necessary security services. You can also choose to contract with a third-party service provider. They generally offer security monitoring and in some cases also provide applications for identity and login management.

Consider using an artificial intelligence (AI) security framework. Chapter 7 goes into more detail about how using artificial intelligence for IT operations (AIOps, for short) can help you integrate your cloud security into your overall cybersecurity using big data to recognize data intrusions and speed up resolutions.

Building Your Team

One part of security planning that's often overlooked involves the important step of building a security team. The people on the team don't need to be security or cloud experts, but they need to understand the kinds of applications and data that your company is running in the cloud. Your success depends largely on putting together the right team, so this section talks about putting together that team.

Finding the right people

It's true that data security issues normally cross boundaries within a company: Different departments or groups run different applications, have different security requirements, and possibly follow some different legal data protection requirements. For cloud computing environments, this is even more true — cloud computing not only spans the various parts of your company but is also, in most cases, hosted outside of your company's data center. This increases the responsibility of managing the security of the various parts of your cloud environment.

The people you want on your team will help build your security plan and later make sure that it's implemented within their neck of the woods. Because these team members will work closely with the people using the cloud applications and associated data, it often becomes their responsibility to do the housekeeping to make sure their coworkers are following the best security practices. They don't just wander around looking for "sticky notes" with passwords stuck to monitors — they educate, they do some of the policing, and they further the objectives of the plan they help create. This strategy spreads the responsibility for cloud security throughout the entire company.

Including stakeholders

When talking about stakeholders, you might have a tendency to look around the room during a meeting to spot people you think may be interested in being responsible for cloud security. Choosing the right stakeholders is a bit of an art. Getting the right people on your team is important for maximum success. There are a number of stakeholders you might not have imagined that can be involved when using cloud services, including these:

>> **Cloud service providers:** These are the companies providing the actual cloud services, such as Infrastructure as a Service (IaaS), Software as a Service (SaaS), and Platforms as a Service (PaaS).

>> **Cloud carriers:** These are the telecom companies providing access to the cloud services. They are often forgotten but are quickly remembered whenever their systems fail. Cloud service providers can promise you 99.99 percent uptime, but if the cloud carrier fails, the promise is moot.

>> **Cloud brokers:** These companies provide value added services on top of cloud service providers. You can think of them as packagers. They're important because the value added services they provide can cover areas such as security and identity management applications.

>> **Cloud auditors:** This one is exactly what it sounds like — third-party services that audit your systems to make sure you're complying either with items such as your SLA agreements or with regulations safeguarding your data.

>> **Cloud consumers:** This one consists of you and the people in your company. You and your company's end users are an important part of developing your security plan.

Find a contact, within the organization, from each of the various cloud service providers you use and make them part of your team.

When selecting company stakeholders, you might be tempted to choose only department heads to be on your security team. In many situations, they are not the people most familiar with the applications and how they're used. For example, department heads might not know which external applications are being accessed via an API, and they may not be up to speed on the level of security involved in managing the credentials used to gain access to the API.

Find the people who are using the applications and data — the *actual* stakeholders, in other words — and put them on your team. This strategy does two things:

>> It involves the people most likely to be impacted in creating and knowing the security plan. That way, it's not handed down to them in a memo that gets "filed." Instead, they have a personal stake in making the plan work.

>> It lets the employees who are most familiar with the applications and data they use every day know who needs what level of access to which applications.

Hold group meetings (Zoom is just one option) and select your stakeholder team members based on their level of interest, excitement, and knowledge.

Creating a Risk Management Plan

After you've put together your team, it's time to get to work. After the obligatory icebreaker "What's your name, which department do you work in, and where's your favorite lunch restaurant?" the real work of creating a security plan starts.

You can't begin protecting something when you don't know what you're protecting and how much protection it needs. Not all applications and data are created equal. Some may require access limitations to only a few people and need special encrypted communications, whereas others may require a simple username and password for access. Get started by creating a simple diagram, as shown in Figure 1-1, that will give you an idea of where your risks may be lurking. This section covers some of the basic strategies for creating a risk management plan.

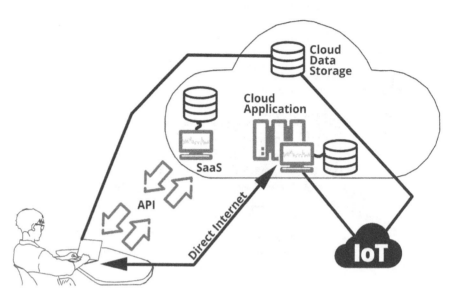

FIGURE 1-1:
Map applications,
APIs, data
storage, and
IoT devices.

Identifying the risks

If your relatively small business is looking to document the security risks you're facing, you can probably start with just a simple spreadsheet. If you have many assets, you might consider either having your developers put together a database application or use one of the commercial asset management applications.

REMEMBER

Asset management applications differ from configuration management database applications. Although they can overlap in some areas, their focus is quite different. Asset management applications deal with *assets* — anything that has value, in other words (admittedly, a fairly broad definition). A configuration management program manages configuration *items*, or CIs — those items one uses to successfully complete the much narrower task of delivering an IT service. So, CIs are assets, but not all assets are CIs. An asset might be a knowledge base, but not be important enough to be managed as part of an IT service. Configuration *management database* applications (also known as CMDBs) are covered in greater detail in Chapter 7. Spoiler alert! CMDBs are cooler than asset management programs because they track how various systems interoperate with one another. When it comes to risk management, knowing how stuff works together is the key.

TIP

Most configuration management systems (CMSes) can generate a service map showing dependencies between systems. It's pretty cool.

For now, put together a list of the assets that are critical to your operation. You can worry later about what kind of software program manages them.

To get started, list all your assets, including these:

>> Cloud data storage

>> Local data storage

>> Cloud applications

>> Local applications

>> Data repositories accessed via APIs

>> Computers, mobile devices, IoT devices

>> Other compute devices

TIP

When documenting your assets list, it helps to list the location where each device might be found. This includes specifying whether it's a local physical location or in the cloud. (And, if it's in the cloud, be sure to say which one.)

Assessing the consequences of disaster

No one wants to think about consequences, but in order to prepare for eventual catastrophes, you must know what potential events might occur. Carefully think about the risk involved for each asset. Ask yourself questions such as, "If this device were compromised, or destroyed by malicious hackers, what would do I stand to lose?" Put this assessed risk into a column or database field.

TIP

Assigning a numeric value to the potential risk allows you to create some useful visuals, as covered later in this chapter.

Pointing fingers at the right people

After you have an idea of the risk involved with each asset, you should assign that risk to the team member best capable of managing that risk. Spell out the roles and responsibilities involved with managing the risk.

TIP

Don't dump all the responsibilities on one person, or even on a couple of people. Spread them out so that no one gets overwhelmed, particularly if things start going wrong. You don't want one person trying to manage a potential catastrophe.

Create a role-based responsibility matrix. That term sounds like a mouthful, but it's simply a list of responsibilities, a description that lays out both what's involved in the responsibility and who's assigned to manage it. They may also have people on staff who ultimately take on the assigned tasks.

REMEMBER

Perhaps the most important step in creating the plan is to figure out how not to fail. Think of the things you need to do to prevent, to the best of your ability, bad things from happening. Perhaps this strategy involves limiting data access or ensuring that access occurs only by way of an encrypted tunnel.

Disaster planning

If all the steps you take to avoid disaster are successful, you might never need to implement contingency plans — but you should have such plans on hand anyway. What will you do if the nightmare becomes real and you're faced with a situation such as a ransomware attack, where all your data is locked up and the bad guys are asking for millions in Bitcoin? Maybe a hot backup with different security protocols running in the background that you can quickly switch to can do the trick. Maybe not. The thing is, you simply have to be creative in coming up with a solution that you know will work, given your particular circumstances.

REMEMBER

Keep in mind the old saying "No risk, no reward." Risk is something that should be managed — few things come without risk.

In your risk assessment plan, meet with the stakeholders and talk about the information you've put together so far and decide how much risk you can actually live with. The first solution you suggest — a hot backup, for example — may be too expensive or too much work to be feasible, but stakeholders need to be aware that, without it, there is higher risk. And neither is it the case that a shutdown is all you have to deal with. Customer trust can fly out the window if all their personal financial details are released to the world, or at least to the world of people trying to exploit it.

REMEMBER

Managing risk isn't a one-time endeavor. It's a challenge that you have to constantly focus on because risks change. New exploits are created. Staff turnover can create new risks if the new hires are uneducated in the security procedures you've put in place.

When Security Is Your Responsibility

When you finally have worked out the details of your cloud security plan, you still have to put that plan into action. Being responsible for cloud security is a bit like being a circus ringmaster: You're sure to have irons in many fires at a time, and a bit of juggling may be going on.

REMEMBER

Your security plan is not a dead document. It's meant to be enhanced, revised, and ignored on weekends. (Okay, maybe not the last one.) Revisit the plan often to make sure that your asset list is up to date and that you have an accurate understanding of the risk level of your various assets.

Determining which assets to protect

Earlier in this chapter, I suggested breaking out a spreadsheet and creating an application tracking your applications by entering them into the spreadsheet, but in the end it's probably more cost effective to just use an automated asset tracking tool. These tools allow you to keep your list of assets up to date daily — something you probably couldn't do manually, or at least wouldn't want to.

These are the assets you track:

>> Software applications

>> Computer hardware, including mobile devices

>> Networks, both hardware and software based

>> Internet of Things devices or other technology devices

Using an automation tool

An *IT asset management* tool (also known as an ITAM because everything IT needs its own acronym) is a software tool that allows you to track all your company's technology assets. It's a bit like the spreadsheet I describe earlier — but one on steroids.

ITAM tools track detailed information such as the purchase price, maintenance costs, repair costs, and device manufacturer. This is important information, particularly as part of a disaster recovery plan.

You have to know where everything is at any given moment. Because people are the greatest threat to security, you want to know where all those employee laptops and mobile devices are and what condition they're in. Do they have the latest security patches? Are all the licenses up to date? Are passwords being changed regularly?

Contractual information is also tracked in an ITAM tool. You can track warranty information, licenses, support agreements, and any terms and conditions for use, particularly for software assets.

Letting ITAM help you comply

Many companies must work within different security compliance regulations. For example, SOC 2 compliance can give your company an edge when working with sensitive customer information. (For more on SOC 2, see the nearby sidebar, "SOC 2 in a nutshell.")

SOC 2 IN A NUTSHELL

SOC 2, the number-2 variety of system organizational control, is a best practices audit to make sure that your business-to-business (B2B) services are secure and trustworthy. Becoming SOC 2 certified lets the businesses you work with know that they can depend on you to secure their information. The trust service criteria include the ones described here:

- **Security:** Securing access to information
- **Availability:** Making sure your systems are up at least 99 percent of the time.
- **Process Integrity:** Maintaining data change authorization
- **Confidentiality:** Keeping sensitive information safe
- **Privacy:** Securing data lifecycle management

Becoming SOC 2 compliant isn't an overnight process. It can take up to a year to get your policies and procedures in place to guarantee the level of security SOC 2 requires. This is more than just a piece of paper: When you do business with a company that is SOC 2 certified, you can have a high degree of confidence that its leaders have done the hard work of making sure your data remains safe.

Applications designed to manage and protect your company's assets

Spreadsheets and databases can be great risk assessment tools for smaller business, but if you have a larger company with many assets, you may want to get started immediately using an automation tool to automatically discover your assets, and update your CMDB or asset tracking system, and then manage assets with greater visibility. You can also find applications that will assist you in discovering vulnerabilities in the overall *attack surface* — all the points an attacker might gain entry into your system — and alert you to fixes or, in the case of AI deep learning systems, will automatically repair the problem before it even rears its ugly head.

This list details a few of the major applications, to get you started:

>> **Qualsys** (www.qualys.com): Here's a company offering a whole suite of applications for asset tracking, cloud and IT security, and regulation compliance. The (free) asset tracking app does global IT asset inventory and discovery. Its goal is to make everything visible. Qualsys also offers several applications for threat detection, a CMDB for configuration item tracking, an inventory of digital certificates, and a cloud security monitoring app, among others. The cloud security monitoring app continuously monitors cloud assets and resources for misconfigurations and nonstandard deployments.

>> **Ivanti** (www.ivanti.com): With Ivanti's tools, you can use AI to discover problems with your cloud assets. In fact, you can automagically discover and fix problems before they even become an issue. That's the great thing about deep learning and AI; Ivanti tools comb through massive amounts of data in order to spot things that are acting out of the ordinary and then either alert you or automatically fix the problems. This is the essential use of AIOps.

>> **Tanium Asset** (www.tanium.com/products/tanium-asset): Visibility is a vital part of managing complicated cloud environments. Automating asset discovery and being able to see your assets and how they're performing is critical to efficiency and success. The Tanium Asset application is up to the task, even feeding real-time information to your CMDB so that you have the most up to date configuration information available.

>> **Tenable.io** (www.tenable.com/products/tenable-io): Tenable is a risk-based vulnerability management SaaS application. As such, it gives you a view of where vulnerabilities might exist and the risks they pose. After scanning your entire network, it can suggest ways for you to shore up weak points. It also integrates with a CMDB — without having to use scanners or agents. Their vulnerability assessment can provide information as short-lived resources scale up and down, something often missed during normal vulnerability scans.

>> **Detectify** (https://detectify.com): This suggestion isn't an asset management application per se, but it still helps you protect one of your most important assets. One point of weakness for many companies is the website. Though this isn't the number-one asset weakness, it's likely number two — and it's public-facing. One thing you can do to test your website for vulnerabilities is to *pen*etration-*test* it (known as *pen-testing*). Many software applications out there can assist you with this process — Detectify is one of the better apps out there. It scans your public-facing websites, looking for vulnerabilities, and offers suggestions on how to overcome them.

Knowing your possible threat level

When figuring out the risk for each of your assets, set up a standardized threat-level metric that works for you. You can also use the standard shown in Table 1-1, if it's easier.

TABLE 1-1

Risk Levels

Risk Level	Asset Type
Low	Public data, such as an informational website
Low	Easily recoverable systems that contain no confidential information or critical services and are not networked to higher-risk networks
Low	Runs noncritical services
Medium	Contains confidential or internal-use-only data
Medium	Network-connected to other medium risk networks
Medium	Provides important services or information important to business operations, but not enough to stop or severely damage the business
High	Contains secret, financial, personally identifying information
High	Contains data restricted by compliance regulations, such as medical records or financial and credit card information
High	Provides business-critical services
High	Networked to other high-risk networks.

REMEMBER

It's easy to overlook systems, servers, or devices that may not contain any confidential information or critical services themselves but are networked to systems that are higher risk and contain risky information. The seemingly low-risk system may act as a gateway for unauthorized access to the higher-risk information.

TIP

Different regions of the world have varying restrictions on privacy and different compliance regulations. The European Union is a good example of an area with higher privacy regulations and "the right to be forgotten." Companies that maintain public information, like Google for instance, are required to remove private information at the request of the person to which it refers. In other words, if you don't want to appear in a search, you can have that searchable information removed, maintaining your privacy.

Van Gogh with it (paint a picture of your scenario)

A picture is worth a thousand words. Making your risk assessment simple to read and easily understood by those responsible for protecting systems is best done with a heatmap.

A *heatmap,* with colors from green to red, allows you to quickly assess the risk and dangers involved with each possible security breach or system failure. Figure 1-2 gives you an idea of the color scheme you might use in creating a heatmap. Even here with the scenarios laid out, you can see that the deep red is reserved for only the riskiest scenarios and represents a lower percentage of overall risk.

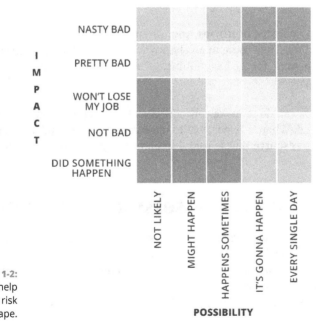

FIGURE 1-2: Color maps help visualize your risk landscape.

Giving each color a numeric value allows you to do things like sort your spreadsheet based on overall risk. You can see in Figure 1-3 that the values show the highest risk quickly and easily. Giving each risk a numeric value also allows you to export this data to other applications that will help evaluate and monitor your risk.

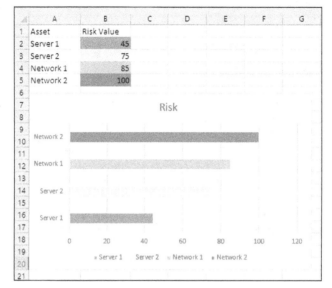

FIGURE 1-3:
Simple
spreadsheet
heatmap shows
the highest risk.

TIP

For more complicated heatmaps, you can use an off-the-shelf heatmap generation application. They come in all shapes and sizes, including ones you can integrate into a map for geopositioning. (Check out Balbix at `www.balbix.com/insights/cyber-risk-heat-map/`.)

Whatever you can do to make concepts visual makes them simpler for your team to understand. When it is possible to have your heatmap updated automatically, you'll have a resource that is useful in an ongoing way, rather than just a planning tool.

Setting up a risk assessment database

Determining what to do when things go wrong is one of the most important steps you can take to fend off a true disaster. The most important question you need an answer for is, "What happens when confidentiality is lost?" This loss might be caused by hackers, an accidental data release from a program error, or the inadvertent publishing of data to the web.

TIP

More damage is done by trying to cover up a data breach than by the breach itself. It's a difficult task to own up to this kind of security failure, but it's the right thing to do.

Confidential data loss

You should make a plan to deal with confidentiality loss, even though it may seem like trying to close the barn doors after the horses have escaped. The loss will have generated an impact that might be felt for a long time. The good news is that if you work to shore up your security after a failure, trust can be rebuilt. Rarely do companies go out of business for this kind of a security breach. If the information was of a personal nature, it may be more difficult for people to secure a new credit card, protect themselves from identity theft, or prevent bad actors from trying to steal money from their bank accounts.

Integrity loss

Whenever critical infrastructure has been compromised, whether it's a server or a network, it temporarily loses its ability to host services and data in a trusted manner. Luckily, this is the simplest problem of all to overcome.

Make sure you have applied all the security patches and increased security on the devices that were involved in the breach. Recover any lost data from backups. Monitor the regenerated system or systems like crazy. Be aware that some of the data that may have been compromised can contain information that makes it easier for a hacker to gain access to the newly regenerated system.

Data access loss

Many scenarios can lead to data loss. Data theft might have occurred, or data may have been encrypted during a ransomware attack, or the data storage device may have been attacked or simply failed. Part of the risk assessment must include the plan for dealing with these kinds of catastrophic losses and a plan to recover from them.

Data access loss can also be temporary, caused by network failure such as the one caused when the cloud computing company, Fastly, went down. That failure took down some of the largest Internet businesses for an hour in June of 2021.

Access to data can also be lost to a software failure such as the database management system's failure to respond or the hardware hosting the data failing or degrading. Hackers can also block access to data through exploits such as denial of service (DoS) attacks.

When you build the risk assessment database, you want to track fields such as these:

>> The prospect that the negative event will occur

>> The possibility of a confidentiality breach

>> The impact of integrity loss

>> The impact of loss of availability

With each of these items, you should include the *security level* (high, medium or low) and the *mitigation plan* — in other words, instructions for what to do when things go wrong and you haven't had your morning coffee yet.

TIP

The good news is that much of the hard work of developing a cloud security framework has already been done for you by somebody else. You can make free use of the following established frameworks:

>> **NIST risk management framework:** https://csrc.nist.gov/Projects/risk-management

>> **CSA CCM framework:** https://cloudsecurityalliance.org/research/cloud-controls-matrix

>> **ISO 27017/18 framework:** www.iso27001security.com/html/27017.html

>> **ISO 27701 framework:** www.iso.org/standard/71670.html (Privacy information management)

Avoiding Security Work with the Help of the Cloud

Using a cloud for your applications or data storage doesn't completely free you from the duties of cybersecurity, but it does move *some* of the responsibility to the cloud service provider. This section talks about what those responsibilities are and how you can best work with your cloud service provider to implement the best security plan.

Having someone else ensure physical security

Physical security in a data center can be a costly and time-consuming headache. Badges, biometrics, physical barriers, and closed circuit camera systems are all part of the physical security you may need to maintain around your server equipment. Okay, you might have your server in a repurposed utility closet with a cooling fan, but if you're serious about protecting direct access to the server, you need a great deal of infrastructure, continued maintenance, and personnel to manage it all.

By the way, that server running in the closet just may have data on it that you'd rather not let out into the wild. Part of the risk analysis will reveal just how much protection you should have around this device and deciding whether the data and applications should live in the cloud is part of that assessment.

One benefit of using the cloud for your services and data storage is that the cloud service provider is ultimately responsible for maintaining physical security around the hardware hosting your stuff.

Making sure providers have controls to separate customer data

Cloud service providers generally host many customers on the same hardware. This is known as multitenancy. When malware infects one tenant, it may allow access to the hypervisor that controls the virtual machines on the device, potentially allowing unauthorized access to other virtual machines belonging to other cloud customers. There is no simple fix other than to guard against malware. It's important to understand that multitenancy is one of the risks of doing business in the cloud.

Recognizing that cloud service providers can offer better security

Let me give you an example — here are some of the things Amazon Web Services does to guarantee the security of your applications and data:

>> **Geographic site selection** to reduce risk from natural disasters such as earthquakes, hurricanes, and flooding

>> **Multiple data centers** that provide a redundant backup and failover mechanism

- >> **Services** such as business continuity plans and pandemic responses

- >> **Restricting physical access** to approved employees and contractors

- >> **Monitoring and logging all data center access** as well as providing security guards, CCTV cameras, and sensor-intrusion detection systems

- >> **Monitoring data centers** for fire, water leaks, climate and temperature, and electric power with backup

- >> **Carrying out security and risk review** internally and by third-party companies to evaluate ongoing security risks

As you can see, these measures are more than most businesses — even large businesses — will want to take on by themselves. You literally rent all this security when you begin using a cloud service provider.

REMEMBER

These measures aren't unique to AWS. All major cloud service providers have these kinds of security measures in place. Some of them even surpass these measures with antipersonnel plants, such as creeping juniper and other noxious or thorny plants, around the building, antitank barriers that can be raised by security, and even oxygen-free server rooms.

Chapter **2**

Getting Down to Business

I n Chapter 1, I set the stage for your cloud security rollout. Armed with a plan, you can now get busy with the details of securing your private and cloud computing environments. In this chapter, you gain an understanding of your responsibilities when using the cloud, learn about the various services offered by cloud service providers, see how security is shared between you and the cloud service provider, and manage your environment by restricting access and managing the plethora of connected devices.

Cloud security can be easily overlooked or taken for granted. A few years ago, pro wrestling fans woke up to find out that their personal information had been exploited when the WWE data stored on an Amazon Web Services server had been hacked. The personal information of over 3 million fans was leaked. Though hackers gained access through an apparent database vulnerability, the hack may never have happened if the WWE had been better prepared. You must understand your part in the world of cloud security — and collecting the information into systems that give you an overview of your environment is one of the most important steps you can take. Without this overview, security planning is like slogging through mud.

Negotiating the Shared Responsibility Model

Each cloud service provider adheres to a model of shared security (also called *shared responsibility*). This model outlines which security areas they're responsible for and what areas are your responsibility. This differs, depending on which cloud service provider you decide to go with, or in some cases your company may use multiple cloud service providers.

REMEMBER

Different departments in a larger company commonly set up their own cloud computing environments, which is often the easiest way to gain access to applications unique to their department or a quick-and-easy way to set up remote data storage. These departments likely fail to consider the security responsibilities they've taken on when they set up their cloud service. It then becomes the responsibility of the person in charge of cloud security to check the shared responsibility between your company and the cloud service provider.

The responsibility varies depending on the type of service you're making use of. These service types are covered in greater detail later in this chapter. Table 2-1 gives you an idea of how responsibilities are different, depending on the service. Read further to learn the details of Software as a Service (SaaS), Platforms as a Service (PaaS) and Infrastructure as a Service (IaaS).

TABLE 2-1

Responsibilities per Service

Responsibility	SaaS	PaaS	IaaS	Your Business
Devices	YOU	YOU	YOU	YOU
Data	YOU	YOU	YOU	YOU
Identity accounting*	YOU/THEM	YOU/THEM	YOU	YOU
Computer applications	THEM	YOU/THEM	YOU	YOU
Virtual networks	THEM	YOU/THEM	YOU	YOU
Operating systems	THEM	THEM	YOU	YOU
Physical servers	THEM	THEM	THEM	YOU
Physical networks	THEM	THEM	THEM	YOU
Physical data center	THEM	THEM		YOU

Some cloud service providers offer identity accounting services as an add-on or via a third party.

Coloring inside the lines

You must pay attention to the details of how your data security is shared with a cloud service provider. Much of the security is your responsibility. "Coloring inside the lines" (see the section heading) means that you should use a guide to make sure you're following industry best practices. You can use an industry standard guide that can be downloaded for free. Here are a couple different downloads:

>> **CIS Controls Cloud Companion Guide: (**www.cisecurity.org/white-papers/cis-controls-cloud-companion-guide)

This document highlights some of the basic service models covered later in this chapter.

>> **NIST Cybersecurity Framework Policy Template Guide:**

(www.cisecurity.org/wp-content/uploads/2020/07/NIST-CSF-Policy-Template-Guide-2020-0720-1.pdf)

The NIST Cybersecurity Framework is the industry standard you will want to follow for your IT security.

TIP

Make sure all your security keys are secure and up to date. These are the keys that are the foundation of your encryption, and it's the encryption that keeps your data safe, whether stored or in transit to and from the cloud. Chapter 11 goes into more detail about managing your keys.

Learning what to expect from a data center

When you contract services from a cloud service provider, it will have one or more data centers that provide various kinds of security. Because that security policy essentially becomes yours, you should review it carefully. Here are some items that call for special attention:

>> **Physical security:** Basic physical security for a data center first involves ensuring that there are only a few access points. That means the building generally has no windows and few doors and that the few doors that exist are manned by security guards who monitor the number of people entering and leaving. The people passing through security machines usually need to enter some type of digital access information, whether it's a security card or biometric information such as a handprint, fingerprint, retinal scan, or facial ID. In some cases, a *man trap* is used. A person enters a door, sometimes unlocked by a security guard watching on a camera, entering a small space (sally port), and a second door must then be unlocked, either by a guard or some other form of biometric like a handprint or eye scan.

- >> **Virtual security:** Virtual security is best known as malware detection. Just as you might do this kind of virus and malware checking on your own personal computer, data centers have a huge responsibility to check data for tampering and malware. when it resides in, or is transferred in and out of, its data center. This real-time monitoring of data provides good but not perfect security, because new exploits are created every minute.

  Data centers must also monitor attempts to gain unauthorized access by hacking network connections and public-facing devices. Firewalls, port scanners, and AI-based network analysis tools are used to monitor against attack. *Honeypots* are caches of fake data serving no purpose other than to alert network administrators if someone accesses them.

- >> **Redundancy:** Knowing that things break or fail, data centers must have redundant systems, whether it's in the form of data storage devices or items such as cooling systems. Servers generate a lot of heat and quickly fail if cooling systems go down. Another type of infrastructure that must be redundant is the physical Internet connection, whether it's a fiber bundle, T3 line, or any other connection to the outside world. It happens that trunk lines are cut accidentally by crews digging in the street, which is often the cause of massive Internet outages. Network systems must be ready to route traffic over backup lines when this happens.

- >> **Power continuity:** Emergency generators and battery backup systems can provide continuous electricity during a power outage. Many large data centers have more than one redundant power system in the event of an emergency. There is one caveat to this — power to the servers may remain turned on with backup power, but your connection to the servers may disappear because of power outages locally at your facility or with Internet service providers that connect you to cloud services.

- >> **Disaster preparedness:** Storms, floods, earthquakes, volcanic eruptions, tsunamis, hurricanes, tornadoes, and fires — oh, my! These events certainly happen, and data centers must be prepared to withstand any of these or have a backup site that's ready to take over if the site is lost or severely damaged. Some data centers are built to withstand nuclear warheads.

REMEMBER

Though every precaution might be taken, disastrous situations transcend any human ability to keep your services live. The best anyone can do is make sure that plans are in place to manage the likely disasters. These preparations can be costly and cumbersome and beyond what your company could possibly manage on its own within onsite data centers, so putting your resources in the cloud is often the best choice to avoid disasters.

Taking responsibility for your 75 percent

You cannot run away from the fact that, in the long run, you're the one responsible for your data security. Though shared responsibility is great, and a benefit of using the cloud, you can't just relax, thinking that half your job is done. (See the matrix diagram of these responsibilities later in this chapter, in Figure 2-1.)

SaaS, PaaS, IaaS, AaaA!

The IT world is full of acronyms and abbreviations, and cloud computing is no different. All the services seem to have a double *a* in the middle of their name — perhaps a clue that what follows next is that this service involves cloud computing.

SaaS

SaaS, or Software as a Service, is a popular way to use software applications hosted in the cloud rather than on your desktop or even your local data center. Chances are high that your company uses some of the popular ones, like Salesforce for tracking customers and sales leads, Dropbox for saving and sharing files, Shopify for ecommerce, or Zoom — which needs no explanation.

The advantage of using SaaS is that the service provider — usually, a software vendor hosting its application using a cloud service provider — takes responsibility for updates and delivery. This is helpful because IT departments trying to roll out software updates to individual computers can be a major pain. It's also great for the software company because changes can be made quickly, and if security issues pop up, they can be dealt with immediately. This definitely fits the agile model of software development: *Release often.* The other benefit is that these software vendors usually take advantage of the cloud's ability to distribute applications geographically nearest to where they are being used, known as *edge computing* or *edge delivery.*

Another great feature of using a SaaS application is that the problem of how various members of your organization can access the same application and the same data is solved. Connecting to applications in the cloud does away with older and more cumbersome technologies such as Remote Desktop connections.

REMEMBER

The world has changed in so many ways. Working from home is now the norm. Working from anywhere in the world is also common. SaaS solves the complexity of shared applications.

SaaS security

When setting the risk assessment of using SaaS applications, you want to consider the types of data being handled by the application. If you're using Google Docs, you might be writing classified documents. When using SaaS accounting systems, bad actors can have access to your financial info and customer list, and to the vendors you use to make widgets or provide your services. Consider the security needs of each application.

Though the security responsibility ultimately falls on you, SaaS providers usually take on the responsibility of managing user login identification. But back to you now. Persuading your fellow employees to use strong passwords that are changed frequently and are unique to the application is no simple task. Consider implementing a password manager, a type of vault that stores the passwords unique to each application. That way, if one password is hacked, the attackers don't have carte blanche to every single one of your accounts.

One technology that is sometimes used is single sign on (SSO). Systems such as Imprivata (`www.imprivata.com/`) allow users to use one set of credentials to access many applications without having to maintain a different user ID and password for each one.

WARNING

Don't think that just because companies are huge, they must somehow follow awesome security practices that are sure to keep your identity safe. In 2020, Zoom announced that 500,000 user passwords had been stolen and put up for sale. Though having hackers attend your Zoom meetings for you might appear to be an easy way out of all your commitments, it does little for corporate security.

PaaS

PaaS, or Platforms as a Service, is a cloud-based service that allows software developers to easily write code using tools provided by the PaaS service provider in a virtualized environment. This means that the applications you use are shared only with the people on your development team. It's a bit like having your own server, except that the server is virtual and may actually be on the same machine as other virtual servers.

PaaS servers generally provide development tools, storage, databases, and, of course, the operating system for which you might be developing — normally, either Linux or Windows. This is a slick idea because your developer can be using a Windows machine and be connected to a virtualized Linux platforms for development.

Here are some benefits of using PaaS:

>> Able to develop from anywhere

>> Can easily include developers from around the world

>> Able to provide a highly secure development environment

>> Rapidly scalable

PaaS security

The PaaS provider handles most of the security, and it's not unlike all other forms of cloud or standard IT security, where authentication of the user is the key to guard against unauthorized access to your development environment. When you reach the point of selecting a PaaS provider, take the time to see what types of authorization they require. Most of them are username- and password-based. Check to see the level of complexity they require in a password and whether they offer two-factor authentication, biometrics, or other security measures. Because these services are generally provided via a web-based environment, the whole login process is encrypted using secure sockets layer (SSL) protocol.

When you're satisfied that the level of security provided by the PaaS provider is sufficient, your developers will be in a position to focus on application security, making certain that the programs they develop can withstand hacking attempts.

IaaS

IaaS, or Infrastructure as a Service, provides computing resources, networking, and data storage on demand. Not only can you get started almost immediately with as much or as little infrastructure as you need, it's generally also provided on a pay-as-you-go basis. This makes using cloud-based servers and networking affordable for even the smallest company.

In the old days (before some of you were even out of grade school), you could conceivably rent a server or co-locate a machine in a data center, but you were responsible for nearly 100 percent of the security and if you needed more capacity, it was a long-and-involved process to get another server up and running. Virtualization changed all that, and now infrastructure providers can quickly spin up a new server for you and —when you no longer need it — make it go away.

TIP

When you need access to underlying hardware, it's possible to take advantage of BMaaS (no, that's not a joke). Bare Metal as a Service has all the benefits of cloud computing, such as pay-as-you-go, but additionally gives you hardware access. Of course, you lose some of the benefits of virtualization with this option.

IaaS security

Sometimes, you need more security than is generally provided by a typical IaaS environment. This is when you might want to look into a *logical network*, a virtualized network that appears to the end user like a hardware network. it gives you the ability to create a private network within a public cloud. This level of security may be required in order to meet compliance requirements or simply to provide higher-level security for your high-risk data or applications.

Larger cloud service providers will have tools for creating virtual private clouds. These services allow you to

>> Set your own IP address

>> Create subnets

>> Configure routing tables

Amazon Web Services (AWS), for example, even allows you to store your data on its Simple Storage Service (Amazon S3) and then restrict access so that it's only accessible by applications from within your virtual private cloud.

FaaS

When you create functionality on infrastructure managed by the cloud service provider, this is Function as a Service, or FaaS. It's also known as *serverless computing*, which is a shortcut way to build functionality without the hassles of an IaaS environment. The cloud service provider takes care of everything else, and all you have to do is provide the functionality. When it comes to simplicity and scalability, FaaS is the way to go.

SaaS, PaaS, IaaS, FaaS responsibilities

To easily see how each service type stacks up when it comes to who takes responsibility for managing the individual components, such as applications, servers, and networking, check out Figure 2-1.

REMEMBER

The responsibility for security ultimately falls on you, whether you provide it or make sure someone else is adequately providing it.

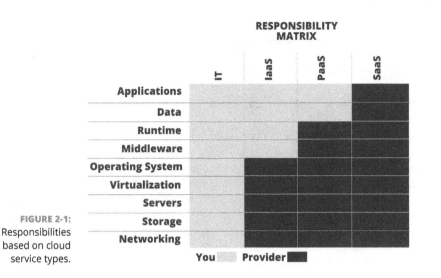

FIGURE 2-1:
Responsibilities
based on cloud
service types.

Managing Your Environment

The first and most important step in managing your environment involves cataloging your assets to best protect them. In a large organization, finding all the assets and maintaining an accurate and current inventory is no simple undertaking. You need to use a discovery tool along with a log management tool, usually required for most scenarios involving compliance requirements.

There are two basic types of discovery tools:

>> **Active:** These software programs ping devices on the network to see whether they're connected. Some active discovery tools log in to the devices to catalog applications being run on the devices. One downside to using an active discovery tool is that it can be bandwidth intensive. In other words, it can slow your network with its constant pinging and possibly returning application inventories. It also requires a bit of complicated security to allow traffic in both directions between devices and the discovery tool.

>> **Passive:** These software applications act as listeners, waiting for devices to send information about themselves known as *system logs,* or *syslogs.* This approach uses far less bandwidth and is easier to configure for firewall security. Using log management software to return syslog data allows both active or live data as well as archival logs to be used for identifying connected devices. The downside of using a passive discovery tool is that each device must be able to send syslog data, and not all devices are configured to do that — particularly, IoT devices.

Here are some discovery tools:

LogicMonitor: www.logicmonitor.com/ (Active)

Spiceworks: www.spiceworks.com (Passive)

OpenNMS: www.opennms.com (Passive)

TIP

I also want to mention DHCP (Dynamic Host Configuration Protocol) logging, which can track the devices trying to log on to your network. DHCP is the network program that hands out IP addresses to devices that aren't configured to have dedicated IP addresses. Auditing tools are available to track DHCP access and, most importantly, changes over time. This way, you or an AI can determine, when possible, that you might be under attack. You can find many of these tools — select one depending on the operating system you require.

Restricting access

Allowing only authorized access to each one of your assets is one of your greatest responsibilities in a shared security model, such as the one you share with your cloud service provider. Chapter 5 covers restricting access and authentication in considerable detail.

Briefly, data has associated risks that range from "Whatever — who really cares?" to "If that ever gets out, we're dead." You must take the time to manage who has access to data at each level. Applications are a bit like people in this regard. When applications create data that needs to be restricted — or merely have access to restricted data — they may prove tempting targets for potential attacks.

Make certain that machines with restricted data are networked in a way that prevents access at lower restriction levels. Data access restriction is like the multi-headed monster, Hydra: You cut off one head, and more pop up.

REMEMBER

People are the weakest link in the security chain. Making sure your coworkers use strong passwords and practice safe computing practices is your concern.

Assessing supply chain risk

Restricting access to data and resources for employees of your company is only part of the task. Managing risk and controlling logins to those third parties, vendors, and suppliers who also need access to your data is known as supply chain security risk management.

Depending on how your company does business, this supply chain can include a global and diverse set of service providers. This situation is common now for companies supporting lean development, where a great many of your company's services may be outsourced.

For example, you may have hired programmers from around the world using one of the popular freelancing sites. You've probably done some research or testing to find out what skills they have, but you don't really know who they are or what risks they might pose. They might not even be risks personally, but the site itself might have a weak security infrastructure, or the system might be vulnerable because of a previous hack.

Security risks exist not only within the freelancing market — medium and even large businesses on which you rely may also have weak IT security. In fact, the larger the size of the third-party vendor, the greater the risk landscape.

REMEMBER

Don't make some of the common mistakes of assessing the risk of third parties only when you first contract their services. These risks change over time and should be evaluated on an ongoing basis. People change, and corporations change a lot! Another common mistake is ignoring the small guy. Normally, a great deal of focus is placed on your top suppliers, meaning that the individual freelancers are often forgotten. It's true that it's more work, but every person matters when it comes to evaluating security risks. Sometimes the risks of supply chains often seem to outweigh their usefulness. Of course, only an IT manager sees it this way.

You must consider three main risks in the management of supply chain security:

>> **Data leaks:** Data can leak from both internal and external sources. Data leakage occurs when your private or confidential information is unintentionally released to the public, such as on the Internet. This can happen intentionally when someone steals and exposes your data, or unintentionally due largely to configuration errors. For example, someone checks their account on your web page, and the data of thousands of users suddenly appears.

>> **Supply chain breaches:** Hackers gain entry into part of your supply chain and cause havoc. In some cases, malware can be installed in your products during the manufacturing process. The idea is that the malware, entered in a less-secure process causes further damage farther down the supply chain, kind of like a time bomb.

>> **Malware attacks:** Recently, the worst kind of malware attack has been ransomware — someone encrypts or blocks access to your data and then demands a payment to release it back to you.

Managing virtual devices

As if tracking physical devices weren't complicated enough, in the increasingly complex environment created by mobile devices, and IoT thingies there is an even more labyrinthine environment — that of virtual devices. A program called a *hypervisor* creates virtual devices, most often servers, with specific operating systems and software ready to go the minute they're spun up (created).

One complex part of tracking virtual devices is that they tend to be ephemeral. They are spun up when needed and then disappear (they're destroyed) when they aren't. Not all virtual devices are ephemeral, and some store and use sensitive data. Obviously, knowing where these devices exist and the risks they pose is important.

Other virtual devices include virtual networks and even virtual clouds. Virtual clouds are usually private clouds hosted within a public cloud. Chapter 9 goes into greater detail on private, public, and hybrid cloud configurations.

Application auditing

After you've used one of the discovery tools that shows you a list of devices connected to your network, you should catalog the applications that run on them. Cataloging applications allows you to control application versions, software patches (covered later in this chapter), the types of data and risk levels associated with each application, types of users (roles) that are allowed access to the applications, and (finally) license expirations. Many of the discovery tools manage this task for you, not only letting you know which machines are connected but also polling the device to discover which applications are running on them. This strategy sometimes includes information such as installation dates and version numbers.

Many stand-alone asset discovery applications have been discontinued in favor of smarter applications that use artificial intelligence to track the data flowing through these applications, looking for situations that fall outside of an expected range and alerting you to problems before they even happen. (The acronym here is AIOps, which is short for *artificial intelligence for IT operations*.)

HERDING CATS (MANAGING THE GROWING CHAOS)

One thing you can expect in any technological environment is that it will grow and become more chaotic. This statement is true for so many reasons. One is that the number and types of devices connecting to your network and using data expands every day. Though everyone knows that mobile phones and Internet-connected smart speakers are just one of those ways, now smart glasses, which have gotten a slow start, have started to mature, creating a whole new device type that connects to your cloud applications and uses your data. Also, a new wave of security devices and remote video cameras is on the forefront.

One company at the forefront of providing security at the device level is Deep Instinct, a firm that uses deep learning and other AI techniques to predict potential threats and prevent them on mobile devices. Check out Deep Instinct at www.deepinstinct.com.

Managing Security for Devices Not Under Your Control

Often, certain devices that store and manage important information aren't connected to your company network. These devices generally don't appear in automated asset discovery systems because they don't send log data to a log management program or use DHCP to log in to a network. You can easily overlook these kinds of devices. Some of them appear in the supply chain mentioned earlier in this chapter.

Inventorying devices

Manually inventorying these devices can be critical to your company's information security. Most larger companies put bar code plaques on devices for tracking. Though most of these are for the physical inventory of assets, you can take advantage of those bar codes and manage devices that way. Use these physical tags to tie your devices to a risk management system where more detailed digital tags describe things such as the risk associated with this machine, owner information (and risks about the owner), the expected physical location of the device, and much more. If this sounds like something you would want to pursue, check out www.myassettag.com.

TIP

Use asset inventories when managing periodic device risk assessments. Don't get caught doing one and then never doing them again.

REMEMBER

When you use the cloud, the servers in the cloud aren't under your control. The good news is that when data is stored in the cloud, it isn't as vulnerable to attack as it might be when stored locally. Humans are easy prey for all sorts of social engineering attacks that allow breaches in local security. This is not a flaw shared by data stored in the cloud, which tends to have more robust security.

Using a CASB solution

A *clouds asset security broker* (CASB, for short) brokers transactions between your users and the cloud. It can be implemented in either hardware or software, and locally or in the cloud. Unlike firewalls that control basic access, a CASB offers fine-grained control over access and can discover unusual user activity. They are used to

>> Manage cloud security risk

>> Comply with privacy restrictions

>> Enforce local security restrictions

A CASB is particularly good at managing security across diverse cloud environments in a unified way. It provides visibility into what is taking place that may be evading your attempts at management. This statement is particularly true when departments are using unsanctioned applications, creating a situation known as shadow IT. Though shadow IT is common in large organizations, it poses a security risk. Using a CASB solution helps you manage those risks.

You can choose from various methods for employing a CASB solution:

>> **Using an API:** With this option, your choices are limited to what's allowed by your SaaS provider.

>> **Using a forward proxy:** Forward proxies grab data headed to an application in the cloud and forward it to the CASB for checking before forwarding it to the application. This can be tricky in situations where there's a fluid number and/or types of devices.

>> **Using a reverse proxy:** Here, data is directed to a federated identity system that manages a user's identity across multiple identification systems and then sent on to the SaaS application. This method is the most versatile of the options listed here.

One of the easiest CASB solutions to use is Netskope, which follows the data-centric approach of following data wherever it goes. Check it out at www. netskope.com.

REMEMBER

Many CASB solutions are on the market. You need to figure out which one meets your needs and your budget. For example, Netskope isn't the cheapest option on the market, but it gets high marks from Gartner, Inc., a leading global research and advisory firm.

Applying Security Patches

This might seem to be a no-brainer but applying security patches in a timely manner is often the most overlooked part of securing your applications, whether they're running in the cloud, in your data center, or on individual compute devices. Yes, your phone (unless it's a flip phone) is a compute device and needs security patching.

You probably know where I'm going here — there's an app for that! Yes, rather than try to manually manage all your security patches or, worse just blowing off this task, you can use a patch management application.

What you're replacing when you use a patch management application is the chaos that's created whenever you rely on each different software application to update itself. Half the time they don't, or else you don't have it configured correctly or the phone wasn't plugged in or the computer was turned off or the Internet went down. Avoid all that nonsense. Make life easier and use one of the following applications:

>> **GFILanGuard:** This application is good for businesses running machines with different operating systems. It has releases for Windows, Mac, and Linux, and it updates more than 80 different applications.

>> **ManageEngine Patch Manager Plus**: This excellent business patch management tool has Windows, Mac, and Linux versions. More than 350 applications are covered by this program, and it's free for up to 20 computers and 5 servers.

>> **Chocolatey:** Admittedly, it's Windows-only, but this software updates more than 7,000 different programs. For a Windows shop, this is a must-have program, even if it is a bit work intensive.

WARNING

Poorly configured patch management software can trip you up by letting you download the wrong security patches or older patches that have been superseded.

Looking Ahead

Now that all your devices and applications are secure, the next chapter begins the discussion of data and how you secure it. After all, that's the heart of any cybersecurity strategy, though you can find some exceptions that prove the rule. Devices connected to and in control of factory equipment, medical devices, and utility command-and-control systems deal with more than just data as such and hacking them can have serious repercussions. For example, in 2021 Colonial Pipeline was hacked by a ransomware attack, shutting down oil delivery in its four main pipelines serving the eastern and southeastern United States. Millions of dollars in cryptocurrency were paid to regain control of these services.

In the case of Colonial Pipeline, according to the company's CEO, hackers exploited an unused, and probably forgotten, virtual private network (VPN). You can see how accessing a VPN that likely wasn't listed as an asset that needed to be protected yet was networked to high-risk assets was the weak point in their cyberdefense system. It's not clear how the hacker got the credentials to exploit the VPN, but it's likely that social engineering was involved. This is where someone pretending to be a trusted person convinces someone else to grant them access. That's why a robust user access system is critical.

The Colonial Pipeline hack is a perfect example of the security issues discussed in this chapter. This lone exploit not only cost Colonial tens of millions of dollars but also impacted the national security and economy of the United States. And all because of old VPN — it's certainly something to think about.

Chapter **3**

Storing Data in the Cloud

I n January of 2021, hackers gained access to over 250,000 Microsoft Exchange servers worldwide. The hack they used to break in was an unknown exploit in the email server software. Because this was an unknown problem, there was no way that anyone could have anticipated the attack. The problem is that the exploit revealed an amazing amount of confidential information from some of the largest companies in the world. Once the hackers gained access, the data was there for the taking.

Sometimes, despite your best efforts, hackers weasel their way into your systems. The goal then becomes making the information they have access to worthless to them because it's encrypted or sequestered in impenetrable systems. Data security, especially for data stored in the cloud, is an extremely important concern. This chapter talks about finding the data in your organization and then tracking it and protecting it. Data might possibly be your company's greatest and riskiest asset.

Dealing with the Data Silo Dilemma

One of the considerable hurdles to excellent cloud security is locating all the data that needs protecting. A silo, like the one you might see along the road when driving past rural farmland, holds grain. Grain goes in and grain goes out, but it stands alone, as shown in Figure 3-1. It's not connected to other siloes, near or far. Data can be accumulated and stored in the same fashion. Cloud computing has made this easier than ever because it's now simple for each department in a company to have its own cloud computing resources.

GATHER ALL THE DATA INTO THE BARN

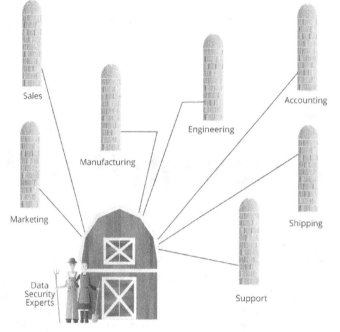

Sales

Accounting

Engineering

Manufacturing

Marketing

Shipping

Support

Data Security Experts

FIGURE 3-1:
Gather all the data in silos into a central repository for safekeeping and better utilization.

You don't want your data sequestered from the main corporate data the way kids are made to dine at the card table at holidays and parties sometimes so that the adults can be seated at the main table. Sequestered (siloed data, in other words) is at higher risk because it's more difficult to track by systems looking for vulnerabilities.

One of the great challenges of silo creation is Software as a Service (SaaS). A silo is created when your company contracts to use applications stored in the cloud and the resulting data is stored with the same service provider. Data stored with the service provider is stored in a silo and not always visible to the IT department, or to other groups in the company that may find the data useful or important.

One way to overcome data silos like the ones shown in Figure 3-1 is to use an integration tool. The Tibco Cloud Integration tool creates connectivity throughout your business by allowing you to connect data, devices, and processes located anywhere. Check them out at www.tibco.com/products/cloud-integration.

As if you needed another acronym, the Tibco product is known as an Integration Platform as a Service (iPaaS).

TECHNICAL STUFF

Cataloging Your Data

You can find many reasons to install a data catalog. To give you an analogy, it would be like trying to stream your favorite TV shows without a guide. Instead, guides to your programs provide pictures, descriptions, ratings, and reviews so that you can decide whether a program is truly one you want to watch. Data catalogs do exactly the same thing for your data.

People within your company will be able to quickly and efficiently find the data resources they need. Along the way, they're also able to see whether it's the data they need, whether they have the security rights to that data, how others might be using it, and so much more.

The catalog also serves as the single point of truth about the data within your company. It helps prevent duplicate data and missing data and assists you in knowing the importance of data so that it can be protected appropriately.

There is no getting around it. Setting up a data catalog takes some real work — something poor Pinocchio's Blue Fairy clearly understood:

Laziness is a serious illness and one must cure it immediately; yes, even from early childhood. If not, it will kill you in the end.
—CARLO COLLODI, *THE ADVENTURES OF PINOCCHIO*

The reward for your hard work is the creation of new and important assets for your business.

Data catalogs allow you to treat your data like real assets. Often data is thought of as an afterthought or just something that gets created. Treating it like an asset means that it gets used like an asset when building big data applications or used by departments that may not have had earlier access. It also means that it will be given the protection that such an asset deserves. Simply put, a *data catalog* is a rich and extensive library where data is indexed, organized and stored.

Data catalogs contain other useful information about the data, such as its history. How did the data originate? How did it change over time? How is it being used now? You can think of it a bit like an online store for your data where people with the right access can shop for data resources they may never have known existed and make use of it. Such powerful data catalogs are an important part of any data governance program.

REMEMBER

To protect something, you must know it exists.

Selecting a data catalog software package

Because so much of the data we humans generate today is valuable for use with big data AI systems, you might consider using the ultimate data cataloging system: IBM Watson Knowledge Catalog (www.ibm.com/cloud/watson-knowledge-catalog). This package specializes in gathering information that's important to AI deep learning programs. It also assists with preparing for security audits and compliance requirements.

Another option is the Google Cloud Data Catalog (https://cloud.google.com/data-catalog), a data discovery and metadata management service. It creates tags for your business data, making finding the data that much simpler. This program uses the same search technology used in Gmail.

Finally, there's Collibra Data Catalog (www.collibra.com/data-catalog), a machine-learning-based data cataloging system that helps you find and catalog siloed data, giving your company access to all its trusted data and enabling better insights and smarter business decisions. Use a Google-like search to find the data you need or view graphs that show data quality, its history, and statistics about its use.

Three steps to building a data catalog

After you've selected a data catalog program, you will want to initiate the following three-step process. (Don't worry! Most of what follows is automated by the programs I just described.)

1. **Indexing**

   The data catalog software indexes the metadata that describes your data, whether stored within a database management program (DBMS) or in file format.

2. **Organizing**

   This step is a bit like adding marketing data: You write out descriptions about what the data is and how it's used, and details about tables and structure. This is to create meaningful searches for data. You're "selling" data, whether monetarily or not, so you want to present it in ways that make it valuable to someone.

3. **Tracking**

   Tracking your data assets will store information about the data's origin, its analysis, and its key performance metrics.

Controlling data access

Now that your data is in a catalog, it's time to protect your data by adding a data access control system. One popular method of controlling access is with the help of Microsoft Active Directory, an identity control system built on the Microsoft Jet Database. It has been around a long time, and its success has led to the development of alternatives designed to cope with the complexity of the typical cloud environment. One such alternative is JumpCloud (`https://jumpcloud.com`), a system that creates secure and vendor-neutral connections to devices and resources. The advantage over using Microsoft Active Directory is that it connects with macOS, Zoom, Slack, and Google Workspace.

When compliance issues are a concern, an excellent control system is Auth0, a recognized user control system for HIPAA- and PCI-compliant systems (`https://auth0.com`). Auth0 allows you to

>> Control access to applications and APIs

>> Manage users

>> Handle login management and authentication issues

>> Ensure security

TECHNICAL STUFF

When something is *HIPAA-compliant,* that means it abides by privacy standards, set down by the Health Insurance Portability and Accountability Act (HIPAA) of 1996, that were designed to protect sensitive patient health information from being disclosed without the patient's consent or knowledge. A PCI-compliant system is committed to following standards, set down by the payment card industry (PCI), designed to reduce the likelihood of credit card data being compromised.

Controlling access using Amazon Web Services (AWS)

When your data resources reside specifically in an AWS cloud, you can make use of some of Amazon's native tools to control access. AWS offers a data access control system for data lakes stored in its cloud system. (A *data lake* is a repository for all your data, both structured and unstructured data types.)

Data access control is particularly important when you want to allow third parties only partial access to your data. (The idea here is to restrict what they have access to so that you aren't giving them access to all your data.)

The person who administers your data lake is the one who restricts data specifically down to the database column or field level. Giving someone access to columns of information that contain no personally identifying information (PII) is known as *pseudoanonymization*. The information still resides in the data, so it's not truly anonymized, but limiting access gives the same types of protection without the overhead of anonymizing your data. (I talk about data anonymization in more detail later in this chapter.) Pseudoanonymization is not at quite the same safety level as true anonymization, because hackers gaining access see the PII, but for most purposes it should prove adequate.

The AWS data lake software allows you fine-grained control over access via permissions and policies. These can be set at the column level, as just described, or at the database table level or over the entire database.

Using Immuta for access control

Immuta (www.immuta.com) is another fine-grained data access control application. It gives data analysts access to data without creating role based access. The no-code policy builder allows you to control access to data all the way to the column and row level.

Immuta can control access to data by way of dynamic data-masking, a way of anonymizing data so that it remains useful while hiding private information. You have a number of options for masking data, including these:

>> **Hashing the data**

>> **Regular expression masking:** This uses a regular expression, <regex>, to turn data into a complex string of characters.

>> **Rounding:** Rather than giving exact amounts that can lead to the identification of specific accounts, rounding allows for data analytics without revealing identifying information.

>> **Conditional masking:** This database feature allows data to be hidden or shown based on specific conditions, including who is viewing the data.

>> **Replacing data with a null or constant value:** When data is queried, you can specify that certain fields or columns of data are replaced with zeros or some other nonsensical value, hiding the real contents but still showing that the field exists. This is important when queries require a certain number and set of fields, but you only want to release some of the data.

>> **K-anonymization:** This technique makes it less likely that people can be identified by linking one dataset with another, therefore re-identifying data that has been previously anonymized — in other words, figuring out the secret. K-anonymization requires that "k" number of individuals in the dataset have similar attributes. The higher the value of k, the harder it is to match data from one set to another. For example, at least 12 people should have the same birthday and live in the same zip code.

WARNING

K-anonymization is susceptible to several types of attacks, including the Homogeneity attack and the Background Knowledge attack. Users in a database may share both a common ID (Homogeneity) as well as common sensitive information. Learning the cohort or common ID can reveal the sensitive information. Background Knowledge attacks reveal sensitive information by narrowing the field of possibilities. For example, knowing that heart attacks occur more often in Japanese patients could help narrow the range of values revealing a patient's possible disease.

Working with labels

One goal of good data management is to make it accessible to the greatest number of users. Using data labels makes this possible, even if the process itself is tedious and time consuming. Trust me: After it's done, the benefits are many.

There are two kinds of data labeling:

>> **Data annotation:** Adding a brief text description of the data

>> **Tagging:** Adding a word or phrase describing the data

Although data labeling can be done by your team, certain companies offer data labeling services. You can also use AI applications to label your data. The Scribe Data Labeler (www.clarifai.com), for example, automatically creates annotations for text data as well as images and videos. This can shortcut your data labeling tasks immensely.

REMEMBER

When using a data labeling service, you're giving a third-party access to your potentially sensitive data.

Developing label-based security

Database applications, such as Oracle, have features that allow for security based on labels. In the case of Oracle, a column is added to a table where the security label is added. The data, once labeled with a security label, is matched against the security label of the user trying to access the data. With the help of this feature, you can create extremely fine-grained access.

TIP

Data labeling is the key to good machine learning AI systems.

Applying sensitivity levels

Adding labels to data allows you to apply any number of risk levels, depending on how sensitive the data may be. You can use text labels such as "death to all who enter" like the old pirates once did, or you can use numbers, like 1 = Open to anyone, 2 = Poker tips, closed to poker partners, 10 = Death to all who enter. You can apply these sensitivity labels to your data.

Some applications, such as the Microsoft 365 applications, have features for applying sensitivity labels. Your administrators can create and modify such labels that the people in your company can use to apply specific protections to a document, such as Public, General, Confidential, or Highly Confidential. Only licensed users identified as having the right clearance level can view the document. (Be aware that this feature often requires a special license.)

Assessing impact to critical functions

Data labeling and sensitivity levels require that you take the extra step of determining how sensitive the data truly is by considering the impact of losing the data or — much worse — having it end up as a TikTok video set to the song *Deleter*, by Grouplove.

Begin the process of assessing the impact of lost or stolen data on critical functions by first knowing what the critical functions of your business are. What functionality would cripple your business if it suddenly disappeared or — worse — was stolen?

Though sometimes overlooked as critical data, the company accounting system houses a great deal of confidential information. Most accounting systems will have a list of all your customers, what they bought, how much they owe you, and more. Additionally, lost or stolen vendor information can negatively impact an organization. Your financial data, which is normally backed up, would be difficult to re-create if it were to be lost.

REMEMBER

Trade secrets are often underprotected. It is a task in and of itself to find and protect your trade secret information, which can include

>> Source code with unique and protectable code

>> Plans and drawings for products

>> Patent applications that have not been filed

>> Internal communications that discuss designs and protectable secrets. (A protectable secret may be a company trade secret, like the recipe to Coke.) Revealing company trade secrets or confidential designs that may not have reached the patent stage is extremely important.

After you've made a list of the critical functions that can be harmed by an unauthorized data release or data loss, you next need to figure out how you're going to protect that data. It all begins by taking the time to classify it. Read on to find out how that's done.

Working with Sample Classification Systems

It helps to have an example of how data should be classified. Your company may well have different types of data, but these examples should get you started. These classifications will hold true whether your data is stored locally or in the cloud. When planning for cloud security, a good data classification system is vital.

Restricted

Restricted data should be maintained under the highest level of data protection. Failure to protect data under this classification can carry criminal and civil penalties. When managing data at this level, it's most likely covered under a compliance requirement and may require that a third party audit your systems for compliance.

Here is a list of some of the more common compliance standards:

>> **Credit card information:** Payment card brands and financial institutions typically required PCI compliance as part of their contracts with merchants. When your systems aren't PCI compliant, you can use the services of a credit card processor that maintains that level of compliance. Though the credit card information is restricted, you should also make sure that personally identifying information stored about your customers also remains restricted. Consider tokenizing the data, which I cover later in this chapter.

>> **Health record information:** Health record data is covered by HIPAA compliance. People really don't want their health information made public, and it should be protected with great caution.

>> **Federal contractor data:** The federal government requires that the data you collect be protected. The standards are set down in the Federal Information Security Management Act (FISMA) of 2002.

>> **Attorney/client data**: You've heard of attorney-client confidentiality. It doesn't mean much if the data your attorney collects is not protected under the strictest measures.

High

Data in the High category, if leaked, can cause significant harm to your company or to individuals. Oftentimes, this data also carries legal and civil consequences whenever a breach occurs.

>> **IT security credentials:** Passwords and encryption keys are examples of data that should carry with it strict protections. Depending on the harm to your company or employees if it's released, this information can also be classified as Restricted.

>> **Employee records:** HR information contains sensitive data that, if discovered, can cause severe harm to your employees and to your company's reputation.

>> **Banking information:** You might think that banking information such as your checking account number and the routing number of your bank should be protected with the same level of security as a credit card number, and you may want to treat it as such because it never hurts to be overly cautious, but modern banking normally requires two-factor authentication and has fraud safeguards that can protect bank accounts in ways that credit cards are not.

>> **Social security numbers:** "Hmm," you say? Yes, social security numbers were once treated with great privacy restrictions. The confidentiality of a social security number has not decreased; only public disregard for the dangers

involved with release of this information has done so. Social security number breaches are the basis for most identity theft. Knowing these numbers can grant access to credit agency reports, which reveal a lot of personal information.

TIP

Find other ways to identify people — whether patients, customers, or employees — rather than by using social security numbers.

Moderate

Data classified as moderate could cause some harm to the company or individuals if hacked. Release of this information can also carry civil liability, as explained in this list:

>> **Intellectual property documents**: Intellectual property — in particular, trade secrets — should be protected carefully because its release can damage a company irreparably. Many types of intellectual property can be protected by protections such as patents and copyrights, but even those merely serve as a license to sue, and don't constitute protection at all. Trade secrets are the family jewels (so to speak) of your company. They are also often overlooked, and often not even identified. You might consider an audit, particularly if your company writes source code, to determine what kinds of code comprise "the secret sauce" and might need extra layers of protection. The most famous secret (besides Area 51) is the Coca-Cola recipe: It's highly guarded because recipes are unprotectable as intellectual property. Depending on the damage if it's released, you might consider a higher classification for this type of data.

WARNING

Trade secret information is often poorly protected, or in some cases never identified, until someone makes off with it.

>> **Immigration documents:** Visas and work permit information carries with it vast amounts of personal details, including social security numbers where applicable. Release of this data can cause someone great difficulties.

>> **Student records:** Student records are private, and protections are covered under compliance restrictions set down by the Family Educational Rights and Privacy Act (FERPA) of 1974. Student record information allows someone to know not only potentially embarrassing information but also personally identifying information, such as an address.

>> **Building plans:** Building plan information is restricted for a number of reasons, including terrorism concerns and potential theft planning. Though you may post partial building plan information on the wall for emergency exits, actual building plans include electrical, security, layout, plumbing, and other vital support information. These should remain protected.

Low

Information classified as low risk will have little or no impact on your company or individuals if released. Standard data protection should be enough to manage the protection of this information. You should regularly revisit data classified as low, to make sure that the risk has not changed over time.

WARNING

Be aware of how networks impact your data risk classification. Often, data considered low risk is on a network that's linked to higher levels of confidentiality.

Tokenizing Sensitive Data

One way to increase the number of people or programs who can make use of your data without releasing sensitive information is to obscure the information while still giving access to the important parts. You can think of it a little like seeing redacted government reports where all the sensitive names and places are blacked out by a marker.

Defining data tokens

One way to maintain the ultimate level of data security is not to store your sensitive data where it can be hacked. Instead, sensitive data is replaced by a *token*, a type of pointer back to the sensitive data without revealing anything about the data it points to. Between the tokens and your secured sensitive data sits a tokenization system.

You can think of tokens, in their simplest form, as coins. Coins were created from cheap metals to represent a value in a valuable metal like gold. You were protecting the valuable material with something of little intrinsic value.

The original token system was written to protect credit card transactions. Credit card information was entered into the credit card processing software, which returned a token, a randomized account number. This token could then be used in the future to process transactions on this card without the need for the end user to retain any of the cardholder's private information or credit card details. Notice in Figure 3-2 that the token is the same length as the credit card number. Systems designed to handle credit card numbers can then handle a similarly sized token.

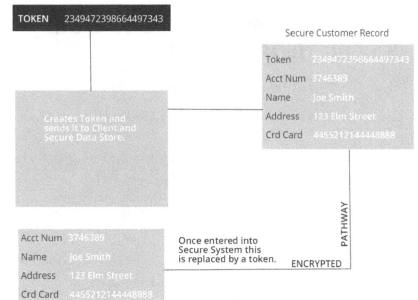

FIGURE 3-2:
A tokenization
system replaces
the credit card
number with a
token of identical
length.

Isolating your tokenization system

It stands to reason that the tokenization system should not be accessible by the application that created the sensitive data. It must be secured in such a way that hackers can't gain entry, because then the entire system would be insecure. Your tokenization system must be isolated from other devices on your network, and access must be limited to authorized team members.

Accessing a token system

Allowing access to a token system requires an additional level of security. It should require, at minimum, two-factor authentication. Curious about two-factor authentication? Check out the nearby sidebar, "What's up with two-factor authentication?"

WHAT'S UP WITH TWO-FACTOR AUTHENTICATION?

In a nutshell, these three things can authenticate you:

- **Something you know:** It might be a password or a PIN number or being able to answer a question for which you've previously provided answers.

- **Something you have:** This item can be an ID card, a smartphone, or a credit card that identifies you.

- **Something you are:** This type of authentication is biometric, using personal identifiers such as fingerprints, retinal scans, and now — popular with mobile phones — your face.

Each one of these items is an authentication factor. So, a combination of two of these is what constitutes two-factor authentication. In many cases, after you type your user ID and password, the system attempts to send you a text message. These are the first and second factors in the list.

Segmenting Data

Segmenting data means grouping it into subsets based on how it will be used and how sensitive that data is. When you segment out data, you don't have to protect all of it at the same security level. The idea here is that if someone hacks into your server and encounters segmented data, they may not have access to all the data — only a portion of it. Though that's not necessarily a good thing, it's better than access to all the data, as in nonsegmented data.

Group together your most sensitive data so that this group becomes the focus of your protection — your protect surface, in other words. This should be done whether your data is supersensitive or not. Group information such as your customer data, accounting data, correspondence, and all other low- and medium-level security information. You can group information based on the classifications you've decided to use.

Anonymizing Data

The most important thing to remember about data is that you want it to remain useful. Data analytics can use data that may have all the personal and private information replaced with fake or obscured data. The data that remains unobscured can be used for analysis. For example, if you have sales data and you replace the customer's name and contact information with fake data, the sales transactions still remain, allowing you to see your sales volume over days, weeks, months, and years without revealing any of your customer information.

Data anonymization is often used in storing log data, allowing you to view logs without revealing information such as an IP address, which can be used to locate someone. As for anonymization techniques, you have a number to choose from. The next few sections look at a few in greater detail.

k-Anonymity

This technique for making data anonymous attempts to make each record indistinguishable from k number of other records. An example of k-anonymized data is when you have a dataset with two attributes: city and birthday. The number following k, such as k-1, means that at least one other record has the same city-and-birthday combination. Of course, as the number following k increases, the higher the level of anonymization and security. More than 85 percent of Americans can be identified by simply using a combination of their birthday, zip code, and gender identity. Gender identification becomes a little more obscure as gender becomes more fluid.

k-anonymity uses properties assigned to the data attributes. Each property type requires that a different action be taken on the data, as shown in Table 3-1.

TABLE 3-1   **K-Anonymity Attributes**

Type	Property	Data Examples	Required Action
Key	Directly identifiable	Name, phone number	Obscure data.
Quasi-identifier	Identifiable by linking to other data	Zip code, birthdate, gender	Generalize.
Sensitive	Sensitive information	Medical diagnosis	Completely unlink from identifying information.

ℓ-diversity

Because k-anonymity has proven vulnerable to different types of attacks where information can be derived by way of a logical series of assumptions, ℓ-diversity provides greater anonymity by requiring that there are ℓ different sensitive type values for each combination of quasi-identifiers. This discussion is highly technical — just know that whether you use the less private k or ℓ methods of anonymizing your data, you still need to add obscurity. The next section talks about some of those methods.

Obscuring data

Replacing data with information that will obscure it ("fuzzify" it — yeah, I made it up) will make your anonymized data more private. Here are some of the ways this is done:

>> **Hiding:** Data is replaced with values such as O's (zeroes) to hide sensitive data that is no longer needed for data analytics.

>> **Hashing:** A hashing algorithm changes the data into a new value. Hashing doesn't always create a unique value, but it's rare that it's not unique. This is useful if you want to also hide the length of your data, because the hash won't match the original length.

>> **Permutating:** This maps the data to a new value that can be mapped back to the original value by way of a translation table. This is useful when meaningful data is needed for analytics but you don't want to reveal the true values.

>> **Shifting:** This changes the data — usually, numerical data — by shifting the values to new values. It can sometimes seem obvious and doesn't fool people for long.

>> **Enumerating:** This process changes the data — usually, numeric — by changing the value without changing the order of the data so that analytics can still evaluate the order of values.

>> **Truncating:** This one sounds like an elephant joke, but it just means cutting off part of the data, leaving just enough for analytics or recognition while hiding the entire value. You see this concept all the time when you're asked for the last four numbers of your social security number.

You can hide data in other ways, but this list describes the most common.

Encrypting Data in Motion, in Use, and at Rest

Encrypt, encrypt, encrypt! Whether your data is sitting in a database or being used or being sent to or from its storage location, you want to encrypt it so that prying eyes have a more difficult time reading the data. You can choose from different strategies for protecting data, depending on whether it's being stored somewhere or is in transit. This section covers some of those protection mechanisms.

Securing data in motion

Data in motion is the information traveling to and from your applications running in the cloud. The most common way data in motion is protected is by using Transport Layer Security (TLS), a modern version of Secure Sockets Layer (SSL). TLS is the encryption technology that provides security for the web by having web browsers and web servers negotiate a secure connection before data is transferred between the two.

WARNING

TLS isn't perfect, because of exploits such as man-in-the-middle attacks and DNS exploits where spoofing makes it seem that the recipient is who they say they are when they are not.

When greater security is needed, you can create an encrypted tunnel between the two ends of the communication.

Encrypting stored data

When your data is stored in the cloud (data at rest), it's like honey to bears. Data at rest is protected initially by all the normal security devices, such as firewalls. With sensitive data stored in the cloud, an additional level of security is needed. Your sensitive data stored in the cloud must be encrypted so that when hackers gain access they are confronted with gobbledygook (encrypted data). (*Note:* Gobbledygook is not a technical term.) Some compliance regulations, such as those covering credit card and healthcare data, require that data at rest be encrypted.

Cloud storage providers will sometimes encrypt stored data automatically. Google Cloud, for example, always encrypts data stored on the cloud before it's written to storage. Cloud service providers like Google offer additional ways to encrypt your data using your own encryption keys. User supplied keys allow for additional levels of encryption on top of the base encryption Google does on its own. Amazon Web Services (AWS) requires that you take the additional step of configuring your data to be encrypted.

Another option is to have your cloud service provider create keys that you manage using a cloud key management service. These keys are then used in the same manner as user supplied keys, creating an additional level of encryption on top of the basic encryption.

REMEMBER

When using encryption on top of the basic encryption, regardless of whether user supplied keys or user managed keys are used, you're responsible for managing those keys. Almost worse than having your keys discovered is losing your encryption keys. Without these, your data is unrecoverable gobbledygook.

TIP

Encrypt your data before sending it to the cloud so that when it's encrypted a second time by the cloud storage provider, you get added protection. This is effective for added security if the cloud service provider's keys are discovered.

Protecting data in use by applications

Now that you're certain that your data at rest is encrypted, you need to take a closer look at your applications and the data that is being processed. Data being processed generally must be decrypted so that the application can perform any processing, such as updates or searches. That makes data in use by applications the most vulnerable, and extra precautions must be taken to protect it.

Because applications are using decrypted data, anyone logged in to those applications can read, copy, or steal that data without the hassle of stealing encryption keys. You need to employ strong access rights that govern who is given access to your sensitive data.

Monitoring systems that watch user behavior are important when protecting secure data. For example, when a user has too many failed login attempts, the account needs to be disabled. Many rule-based behavioral systems flag any suspicious behavior — some of the worst hacks can come from disgruntled employees who have been granted access but then begin a crash-and-burn behavior pattern.

TIP

Applications often create *scratch,* or temporary, files while working on your data, and these files are commonly unencrypted, creating a risk that the data can be discovered. To protect buffers, scratch files, and cache used by applications from prying eyes, take advantage of the encryption capabilities of the operating system you're using.

REMEMBER

Applications using temporary data are slowed down while performing encryption-decryption operations. You may have to weigh your security concerns against application performance if you intend to encrypt temporary files.

Creating Data Access Security Levels

After your data has been organized and secured, it's time to start granting access to people and applications that need to operate on this data. When granting access, you have to consider data security levels. I introduce this idea of data security levels in Chapter 1, where I talk about these three levels:

>> **Low:** Risk to the company if data is lost is minimal because you're dealing essentially with public information.

>> **Medium:** When confidential information is involved, the consequences to the company if the data is lost or stolen may be bad but not catastrophic.

>> **High:** It's an end-time scenario of catastrophic proportions if this data is lost or stolen.

Revisit your data risk assessment regularly. Data changes and so can its risk level.

REMEMBER There are three things you want to consider when classifying data security levels: confidentiality, data integrity, and availability. In other words, you want to know that the data is safely protected from unauthorized access, that it won't be corrupted or wiped out, and that the infrastructure can deliver it to applications or users requesting it.

Controlling User Access

In a world where people are spending less time at a desk in an office with other people, cloud computing has made it possible to work from anywhere in a secure and simple manner. In the past, to work from home meant logging on to a corporate network via a virtual private network (VPN) that encrypted communications to corporate applications or maybe even to your desktop. With applications living in the cloud, simple access via encrypted websites makes working elsewhere simple — but it also increases security risks. That means that, for some access, extra precautions need to be taken to restrict who can gain access.

Restricting IP access

One of the simplest ways to restrict access to content is by allowing only specific IP addresses to access content. One type of restriction is known as *outbound IP whitelisting*. Your firewall can be set up to allow, or *whitelist*, specific cloud applications.

Another type of restriction is *inbound IP whitelisting*. This type of restriction is normally set up within the cloud application, allowing only inbound connections from specific IP addresses.

REMEMBER

IP addresses can be spoofed. IP addresses are placed in the data packets sent over the Internet. It's possible to change (spoof) these addresses, making them appear to be from an invalid source (essentially hiding the sender) or to *impersonate* the source — making them appear like they are coming from a trusted source, like your bank.

Limiting device access

Great attention has been paid to limiting access to your cloud resources, but equal or greater attention should be paid to limiting access to devices— and for an important reason: Devices can be hacked, stolen, or compromised. Of course, the same is true for people — at least when it comes to being hacked or compromised — but devices are more vulnerable. Getting this right means you've found the balance between applying device restrictions while still allowing people to work remotely.

In many of the cloud security management programs available on the market, you can apply tags to devices as well as to people as a way of identifying their risk levels. In today's world, most people are carrying smartphones, which, in the world of network security, are known as *unmanaged* devices. The IT manager responsible for network and cloud security has no control over these devices, and security must be handled on the back end by setting up access control policies.

WARNING

Allowing unlimited access from smartphones or other personal devices can be a recipe for disaster.

One example of handling the security of unmanaged devices is to take care of the easy stuff first. Many phones are now used to access and edit Microsoft 365 documents. SharePoint is a Microsoft collaboration platform that allows you to put limits in place. Here's the range of available SharePoint limits:

>> Allow full access from desktop apps, mobile apps, and the web

>> Allow limited web-only access

>> Block access

These create a conditional access policy. If you use Microsoft Teams, access to Teams is also impacted by this policy.

Moving on to cloud app security, Microsoft has Microsoft Cloud App Security (MCAS), a system that gives you fine-grained control over how apps are accessed. You can connect your AWS cloud to MCAS by configuring it in the AWS Web

Services console. The complete instructions for making this happen are available online at `https://docs.microsoft.com/en-us/cloud-app-security/connect-aws-to-microsoft-cloud-app-security`.

Building the border wall and other geofencing techniques

When your organization operates within specific geographic locations, you can limit where in the world people can log on to your network and cloud resources. You can identify someone's location in several ways. The older and most common technique is to use the IP address of the device logging in. IP addresses are distributed in specific geographic areas, allowing you to know to some degree where in the world the device is located. This system is far from perfect, because systems like Tor can mask a true IP address and location by bouncing the connection through a series of Tor-connected devices.

Another way of identifying location in mobile devices is to use the GPS on the device. This one is harder to spoof but can easily be turned off so that no GPS data is sent.

Despite these issues, location based access control (LBAC) can be an effective access control tool. This method is normally done by the cloud customer rather than by the cloud service or application provider.

An example of how this is set up in a cloud configuration is Microsoft Azure, which has a Conditional Access setting within its configuration settings. There you find a Block Access by Location option. Using this setting, you specify a range of IP addresses that identify a specific region or country.

TIP

In the Azure portal, you can also create a Conditional Access policy based on user identity.

Geofencing is a practice whereby GPS or RFID data is used to physically locate a device geographically. Geofencing then uses location data in a few ways. You can use smartphone GPS data to determine whether someone trying to log in is physically located where you might expect them to be. This is a type of two-factor authentication. You can use geofencing for marketing and communications purposes as well. On a macro scale, location information could identify specific products of interest to a user, like a snowblower in Wisconsin. On a smaller scale, it is possible to locate someone within a store and send them a message letting them know that power tools are now on sale.

Getting rid of stale data

One problem area that is often overlooked involves data that may contain sensitive information but is no longer used and is simply stored for no good reason. Such data should be deleted as soon as possible. This list describes the types of data that fall into this category:

>> **Log files:** Your computers and server machines maintain log files of transactions. Log files may contain information that should be protected. Reading them to find sensitive information probably isn't a good use of your time. Instead, consider creating a policy that deletes log files after a specified period.

>> **Temporary storage:** TMP files and other temporarily stored information that is no longer of use should be deleted regularly. Like log files, they may contain sensitive information, and deleting them is a great idea.

>> **Communications:** It's so easy to let email pile up for years at a time. After a few years or shorter, those messages are probably no longer important to you and — out of an *over*abundance of caution — should be deleted. The messages may contain private and personal information.

>> **Financial data:** Businesses are required to maintain financial information for a set number of years. According to the IRS, this period can be from three to seven years. After that, except for some statistical information that can be summarized in reports, there's no reason to keep detailed records.

After your data is secure, you can move on to securing your software development. Secure software is important to the overall security of your system and you can put many procedures and applications into place. (Chapter 4 gets you started in the right direction.)

IN THIS CHAPTER

» Implementing cloud security with DevOps and DataOps

» Building a DevOps environment for your data

» Moving away from waterfall development

» Adding security to your applications

» Automating your testing

Chapter **4**

Developing Secure Software

C loud security often focuses on user authentication and not enough on other security holes, such as the ones that often remain during software application development. This chapter covers issues in secure software development and how it impacts cloud security. Simplistically, cloud security involves people, applications, data handling, and hardware. Though there are many ways to build secure software, this chapter begins by focusing on DevOps and DataOps, two methodologies for application development that not only increase development speed but also offer built-in ways to ensure the security of applications and how they handle data.

Turbocharging Development

Technology and IT requirements to manage cloud security are increasing every day. Even though the rapid growth of technology, like tentacles into every part of our human lives, continues to increase at breakneck speed, we need to find ways to bring it to heel. One of the challenges we face when trying to enforce security and governance is finding the balance between enforcing security and promoting agility.

Often overlooked, application development contains one of the great risks in computing and in particular cloud computing. IT development struggled to find just the right path forward in finding the right balance between planning, developing, testing, and implementing code and the ability to be agile. This path forward is known as *DevOps,* which are the guiding principles applied to code development that allow for agility *and* maintain order and control.

DevOps uses principles and tools that maintain software code in repositories that make developers check in code and check out code, a little like checking your coat at a theater or museum. One benefit of this process, which you don't get when you do a coat-check, is that you can roll back code in the event of a failure. To stick with the same analogy, if you check out your coat and spill a drink on it, you can simply trash that coat, go back to where you initially stored it, and get your coat back again — as though nothing had happened.

These are some of the other features of DevOps:

>> Encapsulated and reusable code

>> Agility

>> Distributed development (when developers are in different geographical locations)

>> Automated testing (particularly important for cloud security)

These features, among others, have made DevOps now the go-to way professionals use to develop applications. These principles — ones that revolutionized software development — are now being applied directly to how we use and develop with data. After all, when you develop applications, the chances are high that they will operate against a dataset.

No more waterfalls

The agile method of software development bypasses a lengthy planning process where you have everything thought out before the first line of code is written, as in the *waterfall* model, a methodology dating back to 1956. In fact, the waterfall model often includes the step of first writing the program in pseudocode and later translating it into whichever programming language you've opted to use. The *agile method,* however, starts the developer writing code immediately after the requirements have been developed and a simple plan laid out. (See Figure 4-1.)

Agility is gained by putting applications quickly into the customer's hands and then letting the customer "bang on it" and then figuring out where it needs to be fixed or enhanced and then having the developer get busy again on the next version. Whew! This strategy became quite popular when web development started. Nonprofessional programmers just started banging out code because everyone wanted a web page immediately, and the programmers could then finesse the code as needed. It soon became clear that this was a faster and easier way to get things done.

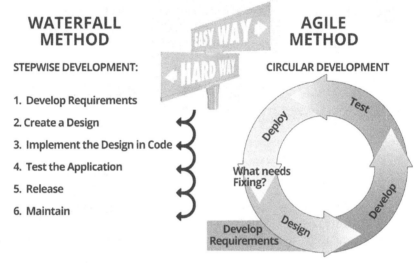

FIGURE 4-1:
Comparing the
waterfall and
agile software
development
methods.

Agile development depends on these components:

>> Incremental code delivery

>> Team collaboration

>> Continual planning

>> Continual testing (which increases cloud security)

>> Continued learning

Development for data analytics has all the same challenges, and so it benefits from this same circular development pattern of designing, delivering incremental code releases, and testing on the fly.

Older methodologies just aren't up to the task of meeting 21st century requirements. To meet these growing needs, making the switch to the agile method of software development is a no-brainer. Agility comes with continuous delivery, planning, learning, and improvement. You might think that revving up the speed might be cause for increased security concerns, not rushing software to market. Switching to the agile method doesn't mean that you sacrifice dependability or making sure that security is built into the program, however. It just means that testing for security issues is simply interwoven into the process rather than stuck at the end. This leads to evolutionary improvement.

REMEMBER

Fulfilling delivery dates in weeks or months is a thing of the past because users now expect same-day delivery by the IT department. Haste can lead to security holes, particularly when using the cloud.

CI/CD: Continuous integration/continuous delivery

Continuous integration (CI) and continuous delivery (CD) are a combined way of delivering software faster, in which one or more programmers check their changes into a central code repository several times a day.

When code has been checked in, it triggers an automated testing process. This rapid test is quickly delivered, sometimes in less than 10 minutes, so that the developer can make any necessary corrections and then continue with development.

Shifting left and adding security in development

The concept of shift-left comes from the waterfall method, where security considerations were part of the testing that was scheduled just before a final release. Once the product was released, development teams normally collected user error reports. Edits to the code were completed and saved in a pre-release version until a large software update release was planned. Rather than benefit from small, incremental fixes and updates, users often had to wait months or even years for fixes. Figure 4-2 shows the linear and cumbersome steps in the waterfall method. Moving the testing phase into the coding step so that they are both done continuously is "shifting it left."

Linear Left to Right Waterfall Method

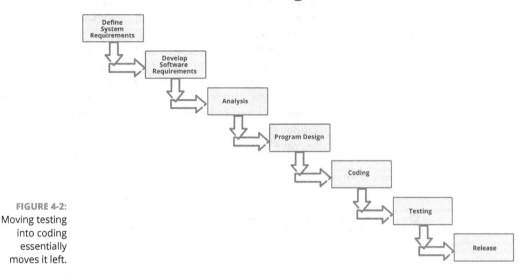

FIGURE 4-2:
Moving testing into coding essentially moves it left.

Tackling security sooner rather than later

Shifting testing left means that security also moves left in the overall pipeline of software development. Addressing the operational parts of software development, such as applications running in the cloud, should come earlier rather than later. You may have heard this old saying:

"He who fails to plan is planning to fail."

This quote has been attributed to both Winston Churchill and Benjamin Franklin. Both were smart enough to come up with the phrase and, regardless of who originally said it, what was said was absolutely correct. By shifting left the planning for security, you get to prepare much earlier in the development process for issues related to running your application in the public cloud.

TIP

Don't bolt on security — make security a planned part of development.

Making security part of the development plan early on will save you headaches later. You won't achieve truly secure software by simply throwing tools at the problem — it takes a comprehensive plan that covers every part of the development cycle, from inception to release.

Because all software is different, there is no clear picture of what must be done, because security concerns differ based on what the program is intended to do, the level of security needed to protect its data, and the risk associated with flaws in the program. Step one: Build a team that extends throughout your organization. You hear this advice time and time again because, in today's world, the division lines between an IT department and other company departments or groups has nearly disappeared, or, more accurately, the lines have become more intertwined. In the past, during the development phase, you would talk to the customer, ascertain their needs, create a plan, have the customer sign off on the plan, write the program, and then deliver the program. Development teams now include the stakeholders. They remain an integral part of the process because continuous delivery requires continuous input and feedback. This way, the program evolves into exactly what they were hoping to receive.

Organizational commitment to security is the key!

REMEMBER

Putting security controls in place first

Before you begin a program design or write one word of code, it's a good idea to have your team put some security controls in place first. If you start with security, it becomes, from the beginning, an integral part of the plan. In Chapter 1 of this book, I introduce the idea of doing a risk assessment for your company. Doing the same thing before the software has been written gives you a clear path forward. Once you know the risks, you can plan for them ahead of time.

After you've identified the risks you might encounter with your application, you lay out the types of security measures you'll need to put in place to secure the application. This might include straight encryption or the use of encrypted communication tunnels or special measures to protect memory so that the application, running in the public cloud where it might share hardware with other applications, is protected.

Your team should include all the people who might have a say in how security is managed. In larger companies this may include a compliance team that's responsible for making sure the applications comply with government and industry security regulations. You can see how setting out a plan to meet compliance is easier on the front end than trying to shoehorn it in later.

Circling back

A continuous delivery cycle is circular, such that most of the development phases are repeated. Part of that cycle should be to review the security plan and the details your team has put together and then make certain they have all been accomplished for each cycle. Don't make a plan and then never check to see whether it was followed.

TIP

Make a simple spreadsheet of the steps to meet each of the risk factors and review this list during each testing phase. To make this task easier, you can automate security testing with the help of DevSecOps. (More on that topic in the next section.)

Implementing DevSecOps

Tools to automate security testing can be used to not only speed up the process but also make it more efficient by checking each of the requirements you've laid out in your plan. Here are some of the programs that can help you make sure that your applications are following best practices:

>> **Microsoft Azure Advisor** (https://azure.microsoft.com/en-us/services/advisor): It's like having a best practices expert in your pocket. This application allows you to focus on the critical operations that will ultimately save you time and money. Prioritize your efforts by picking which changes to make now and which you can put off until later.

>> **Prisma Cloud** (www.paloaltonetworks.com/prisma/cloud): Using a shared dashboard with your entire development team, this application scans servers and VMs in in order to secure applications, data, and infrastructure. Great for developers because it integrates with most popular development IDEs.

>> **Gauntlt** (http://gauntlt.org): This tool helps facilitate testing and communication between the groups involved in the development process. Communication between everyone involved is critical to success.

>> **Veracode** (www.veracode.com): You definitely want an application that scans your code to look for security holes. Veracode has a suite of applications for testing that target static analysis, software composition, vendor analysis (for testing third-party applications), and web application scanning.

Automating Testing during Development

With a rapid development cycle, you need the advantages of automated code testing. Manual code testing simply takes too long. You will pay dearly in person-hours to save a few dollars on a good testing application. Rest assured that adding automated testing allows you to be thorough while maintaining an efficient development cycle that doesn't impact your development schedule. Not doing the testing, or trying to do it manually, will likely have a significant negative impact on your schedule, particularly if you have to go back and fix errors in your code that are found later during a software audit, or worse, after release.

REMEMBER

Software audits have long been a necessary part of the development cycle, but if you're finding significant problems in the audit, you likely have done no automated testing along the way.

Using static and dynamic code analysis

Static code analysis automates what in the past would have been a manual code review. What you're looking for is weakness in the code that can lead to vulnerabilities that can and probably will be exploited by hackers. This strategy is particularly important when your code is running in the cloud, where it has a large potential threat landscape.

Static code analysis happens early in the development cycle. This catches potential code weaknesses early so that they aren't overlooked later. Also, when you're releasing code as quickly as possible, you want these errors caught early and fixed.

TIP

Static code analysis helps you comply with industry standards or government oversight by checking the code for specific flaws.

Dynamic code analysis happens later in the development phase, when a program is unit-tested. Most applications are built of component parts, or units, which are individually tested. Though this type of code analysis catches many types of problems, it often overlooks the kinds of errors normally caught by static code analysis.

TECHNICAL STUFF

The big difference between static and dynamic code analysis is that static code analysis finds fundamental flaws in the code that will cause crashes — the ones you might find in a manual code review such as memory leaks and more — but doesn't catch problems when code doesn't do what you expect functionally. That is the job of dynamic code analysis. Dynamic code analysis shows how an application responds in real life to user input.

The value of using a static code analyzer is threefold:

>> **Speed:** Automated code reviews are significantly faster than manual reviews.

>> **Depth:** Static code analyzers can check every single code path.

>> **Accuracy:** Automating code review takes out the chance of human error.

These are a some of the more popular static software testing tools:

>> **Sonarqube (www.sonarqube.org/):** This application is open-sourced software developed by SonarSource. It performs continuous inspection of your code, detecting bugs and security vulnerabilities in more than 20 different programming languages.

- » **Coverity (`www.synopsys.com/`):** An excellent, scalable static software code analysis tool. Not only does it find vulnerabilities in your code but also manages risk by ensuring that your apps comply with all security and coding standards.

Here are a couple of the popular dynamic software testing tools to check out as well:

- » **Accunetic (`www.acunetix.com/`):** This application automates testing of web applications. It discovers your applications, scans them for vulnerabilities, and then lets you know the exact lines of code that are causing the issues.
- » **Netsparker (`www.netsparker.com/`):** This tool scans your discovered applications for vulnerabilities and even assigns tasks to developers for code repair when vulnerabilities are found.

Taking steps in automation

Automating software testing is a bit like teaching a child: You start with the simple concepts first. Beginning with simple tasks, such as checking database interactions, helps you be thorough and efficient, taking care of the easy fixes first and then moving on to more difficult challenges.

REMEMBER

Include all repetitive tasks in your automation. It's the mundane and boring tasks that are often either overlooked or prone to error because humans eventually screw up while performing the same action again and again. Taking repetitive tasks into account not only saves you a great deal of time but also increases the likelihood of finding security flaws.

Combing through large amounts of data is another area that cries out for automation. Doing it manually is time consuming, often repetitive, and prone to human error. This is an area where automated testing procedures truly excel.

Once your application reaches a release stage — something you should expect to happen often in a continuous delivery cycle — you use automated tools to check for security flaws not caught throughout the development process. Because many applications are now web-based, check out tools such as the ones described in this list:

- » **Burp Suite (`https://portswigger.net`):** A very popular suite of testing tools. Check out the CI/CD driver in the Enterprise Edition. The suite has a huge library of add-ons. A bit on the expensive side but worth it.
- » **OWASP Zap (`https://owasp.org/www-project-zap`):** A free set of testing tools that has many of the features of Burp Suite and more.

Leveraging software composition analysis

Software applications are now rarely written completely from scratch. The idea of code reusability has reached a level of maturity to allow applications to now be developed using many third-party components and code written by freelance coders, as shown in Figure 4-3. Software composition analysis (SCA) will:

>> Search your code for the use of any open-source components.

>> Checks open-source components to make sure that they comply with license requirements.

>> Verifies the quality of the component's code

>> Evaluates the software security of the component.

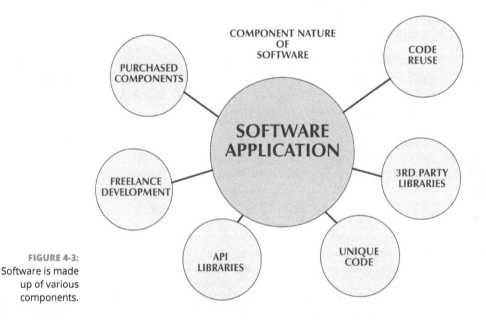

FIGURE 4-3: Software is made up of various components.

Security holes in open-source code

Open-source code has become part of almost every modern web application. Libraries such as Bootstrap (used to make applications mobile-ready) are often used, and JavaScript component libraries like jQuery and jQueryUI are almost must-have items. No one develops these components from scratch. Visual components that display elements such as buttons and icons are also common with libraries like FontAwesome.

Though it makes perfect sense to use as many labor-saving components as possible, each one you add presents a possible security hole. The components I just mentioned are less likely to contain security flaws because they have been tried and tested in millions of websites. Other open-source component libraries may not have been as thoroughly vetted as these.

Have a Plan B. Depending on the size of a particular open-source development community, vulnerabilities may take considerable time to correct. This is particularly true when direct support of a component is unavailable and you must either rely on your own programmers to fix the problem or wait for community developers to come to the rescue.

TIP

Check out license types of the open-source software you're using, to ensure compliance with its license. (Some licenses require that you release your source code to the public.) Check to see that your security profile allows that kind of release. Software composition analysis will discover your licenses.

Synopsis www.synopsis.com is a popular software composition analysis tool. This tool checks your package managers used in software development, source code, binary files of compiled applications, container images and any other types of files on which your application relies. It checks these components against the National Vulnerability Database found at nvd.nist.gov.

Dependency tracking

Dependency tracking is an automated tool that performs component analysis. This relies on a *software bill of materials* (BOM), which is a list of all components that make up a software package. (It's not unlike a dinner recipe.) This idea was originally created to bring about software transparency. The BOM plugs into your DevSecOps monitoring system for continuous monitoring of the components and then spits out any problems it finds. This gives you the power of continuous delivery, continuous insight, and continuous transparency.

Security holes and how to plug them

Plugging potential holes or security flaws begins with an understanding of how much open-source and third-party-developed software is being used in your applications. Many companies have a longstanding policy about the use of open-source software, based on the need for support. It was understood that privately developed applications came with support — either free or pay. Open-source applications tended to come with community support and may not be as reliable as privately written, closed source applications.

Develop an audit to determine and document the use of open-source components in your software. This can help send up flags if or when security flaws are discovered in a component. You can then swap out the component for a fixed version or choose to replace it with one that's more secure.

REMEMBER The decision to use open-source components should be part of your security plan when you first begin your application plan. Weigh any vulnerabilities these components may have against your risk tolerance.

TIP Using GitHub (https://github.com) as your source code repository helps, because the site makes vulnerability searches through code in the repository and alerts you to any issues. For tips on how to extract data from GitHub and load it into your cloud-based data warehouse, check out this description of Snowflake at https://github.tosnowflake.com.

Proving the job has been done right

These are the two most important reasons for making sure your security measures have been effective:

>> You don't want people hacking your system.

>> You may have to provide proof of your success in order to be in compliance with security and privacy regulations.

Your cloud service provider maintains logs of what occurs in your environment. It's up to you to do something with that information. Automating the monitoring process is always the best way to go.

Logging and monitoring

One of the most common ways of monitoring security is logging who has had access to your cloud environment. This type of monitoring is still fairly new to many cloud service providers — therefore, their expertise in this area is a factor to consider when selecting a cloud service provider.

What you need are some tools to do the monitoring. Certain cloud service providers can route event information and allow you to build some basic security policies that will monitor events. If you're using AWS for your cloud service provider, check out the AWS CloudTrail, CloudWatch, and GuardDuty apps. They can get you started on monitoring your security.

You may opt to use a third-party monitoring tool like DynaTrace, at www. dynatrace.com. This particular application monitors metrics, and logs, in addition to user experience data. In an agent-based system, all you need to do is install the OneAgent component. This AI-based engine alerts you when problems are found and directs you to the root cause.

Another way to monitor security is to route your event traffic to a big data security analysis system such as Splunk for further analysis. Splunk www.splunk.com, a leader in cybersecurity products, claims that it can help companies reduce data breaches by 70 percent. (I talk more about Splunk later in this chapter, when I discuss AIOps.)

REMEMBER

Not monitoring your cloud environment means you're operating with zero visibility into potential problems. Waiting for disasters to happen is the wrong approach.

Ensuring data accountability, data assurance, and data dependability

The job of a data analyst is complex and has largely been a manual one involving data integration, the assembling of data pipelines assemblage, testing, managing production development and, of course, creating documentation. This level of demand creates slow processes that are time consuming and forever error prone. This makes it difficult to keep up with user demand and same-day expectations.

Beyond simply keeping up with demand, you also have the increased burden of showing that you're doing it right. To accomplish this, there must be *change control* (making a trackable list of the changes you've made) and an audit trail of who was responsible for the changes providing accountability, assurance, and dependability.

In addition to an audit trail, a key requirement for assurance and dependability is testing. Testing at every stage before code is moved into the software repository provides positive assurance. In this way, your code base serves as your source of truth.

With the increased burden that comes with complexity, meeting user expectations, increased governance, and increased testing, the only way forward is to do more with less. One way to accomplish that is to free data teams from the tasks that provide no direct value (drudgery, in other words).

As with many IT challenges, the answer to complex testing is automation. Testing is an example of a laborious and mundane task that needs to be automated. Without automation, the task of testing would be not only a laborious chore, often overlooked, but also one that is prone to errors and would definitely take too much time in a DataOps delivery schedule.

Once your data has been tested to eliminate as many future problems as possible, it then behooves you to include automated monitoring to catch problems before the user does. These systems check the quality of your production data, analytics processes, and new code releases.

Consider using a tool such as Aunalytics (www.aunalytics.com) to automate your data validation and monitoring. FirstEigen (https://firsteigen.com) uses AI to perform data quality testing. As a machine learning tool, its ability to spot errors and data use habits grows over time.

You can automate tasks like traceability and issue tracking with continuous code releases. Automating the day-to-day tasks of testing and monitoring increases the efficiency and agility of the entire data analytics process.

In addition to freeing your team from mind-numbing tasks, automation has a direct impact on the TCO — or total cost of ownership — which includes the ongoing cost of maintaining your code.

A popular DataOps tool that seems to have all the functionality you'll need — and more — is DataKitchen (https://datakitchen.io). This is an enterprise-level DataOps platform that automates end-to-end data workflows to help you coordinate your data analytics teams, people, projects, and testing.

Running Your Applications

Once you've developed an application that actually runs in the cloud, you need to host it there. You have lots to consider when deciding which hosting provider to choose. Cost is usually factor number one, followed closely by the number and kinds of services that are provided by the cloud service provider.

In addition to cost and services, think about where the company has servers around the world. If you have an international customer base using your application, you'll want to make sure that the cloud service provider has servers where your customers live, if for no other reason than connection speed and network lag time considerations.

Because the choice you make is one you will likely live with for years to come, and one that may impact your business competitively, you need to select a provider that you believe will have longevity, flexibility, and the ability to develop new services that will support your application over time.

Another approach to consider is one where you develop your application to run on more than a single provider, known as a cloud agnostic approach. (More on that in the next section.)

Taking advantage of cloud agnostic integration

More than 80 percent of companies that use cloud services use more than one cloud service provider. (Chapter 9 talks more about the various cloud strategies you can take.) When developing applications that run in the cloud, one important consideration is being able to run your application in more than one cloud environment — being cloud agnostic, in other words. Cloud agnosticism is similar to the old days of Java programming, when the idea of write once, run anywhere first became a reality.

Even if your company uses only a single cloud service provider, developing applications that will run on several platforms without changing the code ensures that you don't get stuck with a single-provider scenario. Though it seems that some of the larger cloud service providers are too big to fail, anything can happen. If for no other reason than price comparison, you want the ability to either make the switch or add cloud service providers. There are hundreds of different cloud service providers, but AWS, Google, Alibaba, and Microsoft control over 50 percent of the market.

Another reason you might choose a cloud agnostic approach is to avoid situations where one cloud service provider runs into technical difficulties. It happens to the best of them. In certain huge outages, trunk lines have been accidentally disrupted during excavations. Other providers, such as Nirvanix in 2013, simply went out of business and gave their customers a couple of weeks to migrate. Imagine how much simpler things would be if the applications hosted there could simply begin running on a different provider. There is probably no greater concern for most companies than reliability.

Track when cloud services are up and down by using Downdetector (https:// downdetector.com).

Cloud service providers are more than just hosting sites. Part of what makes them attractive as services are the applications that are part of the offering. You may decide that the applications of another vendor are preferable to what you're getting now, and you may want to switch to take advantage of new services. Or, when services go bad (see the later section "Understanding That No Cloud Is Perfect"), you may need to switch to another provider to avoid catastrophe.

In any case, you want to position your company to take advantage of the flexibility of a cloud agnostic approach. Companies that have been taking advantage of a cloud infrastructure for years may not have had the advantage of creating applications with a cloud agnostic strategy and may now be stuck with vendor lock-in.

Recognizing the down sides of cloud agnostic development

So, with all the upside of a cloud agnostic approach, the downside is that the initial development cost increases because more aspects must be taken into consideration. There may be a learning curve for the developers and team when incorporating some of the newer technologies. Moving from a monolithic development strategy to a more distributed and manageable microservices model is one that requires a new way of thinking about design and an understanding of the underlying technologies.

Feature specificity — the unique features one cloud offers over another — can become an issue impacting your decision to use more than one cloud service provider. When one of the providers offers a solution not offered by others, or when the solution is so much better in one cloud service provider than what the others provide, it may be difficult to move away from a service you enjoy. This is particularly true when selecting cloud-provided database management systems. Some of them are easier, faster, and more powerful than others.

Experience is also a consideration. Quite often a development team will have experience working with a particular cloud service provider and be expert at developing in line with their unique set of tools and specifications. Moving outside their comfort zone might be too high of a cost or risk. Go with what you know might be the best strategy in this case.

TIP

Create a pros-versus-cons assessment when considering a cloud agnostic approach before starting development. You may want to select only a few platforms to support, because it's virtually impossible to write code that runs on all of them equally well. Select the platforms that provide these features:

>> Reliability, dependability, and durability

>> Services you need

>> Global coverage

>> Security (of course!)

>> The right price

>> Ease of use

Developing a matrix of the cloud service providers and how they stack up in these various areas makes it easier to select the right ones to develop for.

Getting started down the cloud agnostic path

There are several different methods and technologies to consider when choosing to develop your application with a cloud agnostic approach. Make sure you follow good methodologies to achieve the best outcome. Here's a look at the basic approaches:

>> **Automate like crazy:** This chapter has laid out the advantage of a DevOps approach to development. Using a continuous delivery strategy requires that many of the steps along the way need to be automated.

Cloud agnosticism means that the workload in a DevOps development cycle will increase, because you must make certain that the code you develop runs equally well on the platforms you want to support.

>> **Design using a microservice modules approach:** Gone are the days when every application had a monolithic architecture. Applications can now be developed using a microservice architecture, where functionality is broken into small units, or modules. This style of architecture structures an application into a form that is

- Easily maintained
- Easily tested
- Structured around business functions
- Developed by a team that has responsibility for that module

This architectural style enables the delivery of complex applications in a component form that fits well into a continuous delivery environment. Elements of an application are broken down into units based on their function. Having a team responsible for a specific microservice unit makes them easier to develop, maintain, and test. It also makes for great code reuse.

REMEMBER

When building an application as cloud agnostic, you can more easily manage the application when it's broken into smaller units. When moving between cloud services, you might find it easier to match services to microservice modules.

>> **Use a service mesh:** As your application becomes more complex as the number of microservices grow, you'll want to employ *a service mesh* — a dedicated infrastructure layer that enables service-to-service communications

using a proxy. Service mesh applications enable more than simple interservice communications — they also enable security, observability, workflow, and more.

Istio (`https://istio.io`) is an open-source service mesh that layers over the top of applications, providing communications, load balancing, traffic behavior, and automatic metrics, logs, and traces. Istio runs on top of Kubernetes (`https://kubernetes.io`), an open-source container-orchestration system.

>> **Containerize:** Containers are lightweight and stand-alone executable software packages that let you run applications in a virtual environment that includes all of the system tools, libraries and application settings necessary to run. One of the more popular container applications, Docker (`www.docker.com`) does exactly that, making it simple to move a Docker container from one cloud to another. It's easy to see how using Docker containers would simplify the development of a cloud agnostic application.

Docker containers are different from virtual machines because Docker containers do not virtualize the machine and rather share the operating system kernel with other applications. Having said that, it's important to know that Docker containers are well isolated, so they present a low risk when sharing the OS with other containers.

REMEMBER

The goal of cloud agnostic development is to make it easy to move your application from one cloud type to another with a minimum amount of effort.

This is just a brief introduction into technologies that each requires a book. The idea and technologies are still new and maturing. There is no single sure way to make sure your applications are cloud agnostic. Employing some (or all) of these technologies, such as containerization and a service mesh, moves your application into the next level of capabilities and increases the ability to manage a complex, or even distributed, application.

Like DevOps but for Data

Data stored in the cloud is definitely an important consideration in cloud security, but there is another, and maybe more important, factor: the development of those data analytics capabilities that make use of that data on a daily basis. Data simply stored away is useless, whereas today's companies are more data-driven than ever.

As with software development, your data analytics team also faces a growing demand to provide insights from your data with increased speed and efficiency and without sacrificing security. To achieve the same kinds of development speed, you can borrow from the proven ability of DevOps to get the job done quickly and efficiently.

The principles of DevOps applied to data are known as *DataOps*, short for *data operations*. Though the principles are similar, allowing for factors such as check-in and check-out of data, and evolutionary, continuous delivery, DataOps is more than DevOps applied to data. The principles are similar, but the challenges met by DataOps are somewhat different. The important aspects of DataOps that mirror what you see in DevOps includes things such as agile code development, version control systems, and automated testing.

A DataOps application development environment generally involves the use of a pipeline that manages the various development steps in this agile and rapid delivery scheme. One tool you might consider using to manage the huge amounts of data involved is Genie (`https://netflix.github.io/genie`), a federated big data orchestration-and-execution engine developed by Netflix and released as open source. Another large and complex business, Airbnb, developed Apache Airflow, a workflow tool that was also released as open source: `http://airflow.apache.org`.

The agility of the DevOps principles transfers well to the concept of DataOps. This enables faster results when developing applications for data analysis. Companies are demanding immediate access to insight from the data it owns. Efficiency and reliability in providing those insights is the goal.

Source code control using a source code control system such as Git (`https://git-scm.com`) allows you to check in and check out code. This not only allows multiple developers in various locations to work together but also gives you the ability to roll back code — and it creates an automatic audit trail of development. Git also allows for *branching* your code, which allows for different versions of an application to be created that stem from an "original" version of the code. In the world of DataOps, this also means creating a new branch of data. The data used in this manner allows for similar features such as rollback of data and audit trails. With branched data, you can create a development sandbox for trying things out rather than jumping right in to work on production data.

I talk earlier in this chapter about writing reusable and maintainable code. Creating modularized code in the form of microservices gives you an application that is easily maintainable and easily testable. You can think of this concept as building a car: Over time, cars have become more complex and at the same time more modular, with parts easily plugged in. This arrangement has made cars easier to troubleshoot and repair and has also lowered their overall cost. Modularized code development is much the same as a car: Cars have idiot lights that alert you to problems and easily point repair people in the right direction. Well-written code does exactly the same thing.

Branching data, in much the same way as code through version control systems, has revolutionized development. You no longer need to operate on production data nor on copies that quickly become stale and outdated. In the past, creating feature branches of data was difficult because of the size and complexity of large datasets. They call it big data for a reason! DataOps takes a different approach by building, changing, and destroying environments automatically, a concept taken from virtualization.

The version control system provides the type of audit trail most governance requires. Because governance is part of the initial development plan, a DataOps development plan employs *privacy by design* (software development with privacy in mind) and *governance by design* (keeping governance requirements at the fore-front while creating your applications). When changes are made to a data project, every modification is tested for security and code errors.

TIP

Automate or die! Keeping up with the competition in a rapidly changing environment requires that you automate. It's not really a choice.

Automated testing allows you to scale development. Scalability is one of the key benefits of DataOps or DevOps or any of the Ops. Part of the process of continuous delivery and delivery, automating your application testing greatly increases the speed with which you can release new code. "Greatly increase" is a bit of an understatement, though: When it comes to testing, if it's not done in an automated fashion, it's likely to be overlooked, which leads to the desperate situation of "hope" projects, where you release a project and just hope it works.

The ability to rapidly test code and data is one of the limiting factors to growth. There is no reason not to implement an automated testing tool that can catch most of, if not all, the errors. Rapid testing and deployment enable large, data-heavy companies to code and deploy updates at a rate commensurate with industry demands.

Testing, 1-2-3

Testing occurs in both the innovation pipeline (where data is fixed and code changes) and the value pipeline (where code is fixed and data changes). Testing in the innovation pipeline validates that the code is producing the expected results. Testing in the value pipeline is looking for *outliers* — data that falls outside the statistical norm. For this reason, both code and data tests are required to continuously monitor the health of the data application.

Data analytics is not just an exercise. In the real world, data drives critical business decisions. DataOps requires that data returned from a data product be valid for decision-making.

REMEMBER

Automated testing of data can lead to greater assurance and quality.

Is this thing working?

In addition to testing, monitoring after release is important. With monitoring, errors that were uncaught previously may be caught, or new errors in the data will be caught by the monitoring system. This way, errors are quickly caught — hopefully, before they cause a problem — and corrected. (Dynatrace, at www.dynatrace.com, has an all-in-one system monitoring tool that works well in a DataOps environment.)

If you're building data applications, you may also want to build an application that can spot outliers in your data as an alert mechanism.

Working well with others

DataOps has a core principle that collaboration is the key to success. Collaboration between members of a team and across disciplines leads to creative solutions and better results. Including the end user in your discussions is important because this person has the best idea of what they need from a data project. Also, feeling heard, they will be much happier along the path to the end result.

Developing in isolation leads to problems such as heroism (trying to do it all yourself) and poorly understood (or an inability to meet) changing requirements. After all, DataOps embraces change. In a simple example, when operations team members discuss how a project impacts them and then data scientists (concerned, as always, with accuracy) add their feedback, the iterative nature of agile development allows for a continually improved end-product and happier end users. This is also how governance and agility are kept in balance.

Modern data development should lead to the idea of creating data products rather than simply developing for a single need. These products and data pipelines can be simply reused, either as is or modified through the principles of inheritance borrowing from object-oriented programming. When certain aspects of a pipeline are reusable, they can be refined into a new data product in a fraction of the time it took to create the original product. The result is also more reliable and better trusted.

Baking in trust

Beyond creating better security, DataOps also increases user trust in the data on which your business relies daily. Data analytics provides the insights that businesses rely on to make important decisions. Nothing is worse than trying to use data that is full of errors. The resulting insights from that kind of data are simply wrong — in other words, useless.

Not only is user trust at stake in managing your data correctly, but government oversight also requires that the data be reliable. The big balancing act is to provide better data reliability without sacrificing efficiency and speed.

Developing in a cycle where testing is an integrated part increases the chance that errors are caught early and more often. (Take another look at Figure 4-1 to see how testing is part of the DevOps development cycle.)

Part of developing trust is making all the stakeholders part of your testing plan. After the users of the data understand what has been tested, they feel ownership in the quality of the data. (This is especially true if their input was requested in developing a test plan.)

REMEMBER

Data changes. Users will trust it until they can't, so data testing and monitoring must remain a continuous effort.

DevSecOps for DataOps

There are so many Ops it's sometimes hard to keep them all straight. DataSecOps is the extension of DevSecOps for the data analytics world. The DevOps philosophy proposes that you create a working relationship between all stakeholders while developing applications and that they continue working closely together during the cycles of continuous delivery resulting in well-tested and secure applications. This same idea is applied to the applications developed by data scientists and data analysts that bring forth the insight from the terabytes of data your business has collected and stored over the years. Figure 4-4 shows how teams of data engineers, heads of security, governance, risk, and compliance as well as data stewards and data owners work collaboratively to bring about secure data analytics applications.

REMEMBER

Having all the stakeholders, security, and development teams working together is the key to making this streamlined DevOps-like method of development efficient and secure.

DataSecOps provides a development environment that is

>> **Agile:** Developed in a rapid, almost ad hoc, manner by related teams.

>> **Democratized:** Data is touched by a large number of people throughout the organization, each with a say in how it's used. They all should have security in mind.

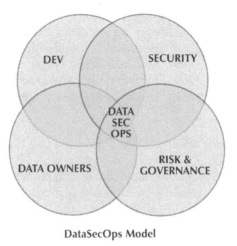

FIGURE 4-4:
DataSecOps is
the collaborative
method of
data analytics
development.

DataSecOps Model

Security considerations are part of the data analytics development cycle. Automated testing is an important part of this cycle, and that is a perfect place in the cycle to review security concerns.

As with DevOps, your teams should make a list of security concerns when the project is first conceived and then revisit these during each release cycle. For example, if data is sensitive or is governed by regulations, these should be reviewed to make certain that they're taken into consideration. This process makes security an integrated part of the analytics development rather than something cobbled on later.

Make security an integrated part of your DataOps development cycle.

REMEMBER

Considering data security

Perhaps the most obvious data security consideration is establishing who has access to the data being used for analytics. Ask questions like these:

>> Have you restricted access to only those people who have legitimate authority to view the data?

>> Has the data been modified in such a manner that private data is either obscured or not included in the dataset being examined?

>> Will my analytics reveal confidential information to the wrong people?

Guessing isn't the way forward. Knowing about your data beforehand can save you a considerable amount of time and headaches.

As with many IT challenges, the answer is automation. Testing is an example of a laborious and mundane task that needs to be automated. Once your data has been tested to eliminate as many future problems as possible, it's then a great idea to include automated monitoring to catch issues before the user does. These systems check the quality of your production data, analytics processes, and new code releases.

TIP

Catch data errors in testing before the customer or end user finds them.

You can automate traceability and issue tracking with continuous code releases. Automating the day-to-day tasks of testing and monitoring increases the efficiency and agility of the entire data analytics process.

In addition to freeing your team from mind-numbing tasks, automation has a direct impact on the TCO — total cost of ownership — which includes the ongoing cost of maintaining your code.

Ending data siloes

Data that ends up in a data warehouse is generally subjected to some level of security that sometimes makes it difficult or impossible for users in the same organization to integrate data between datasets. Business units protecting access to their data often create new privacy silos. This is particularly true of data stored across multiple cloud storage environments. It's common for departments to create their own cloud resources and then store their data there, away from both the prying eyes of others as well as the company data analytics teams. This causes a frustrating duplication of data and effort, as well as increasing the security risks involved exponentially. One way around this quandary is the development of a data store — a shop of sorts, not a storage location. A data store is a database of all your data, where it lives, a description of the data, and in some cases, data analytics that have already been performed. In some cases, it is important to query and analyze data that is located in multiple applications and locations.

TIP

You may consider using a product such as the Starburst Analytics Engine (www. starburst.io) to simplify querying data that is distributed throughout many applications and storage locations. It makes access to distributed data fast and easy and works well within a DataOps environment.

Developing your data store

A data store is a company-wide marketplace for data. It can take on many forms, but in essence it's simply a shopping list of datasets. This is far from a silly idea. The shopping list (or a menu, if you like that analogy better) describes the dataset using metadata. This datastore is how you overcome data siloes where only a small group of people have access to specific data. Now, anyone in the company with the proper access can gain new insights by viewing data published by other departments or groups within the company.

Part of the metadata that describes the data also specifies the security level of the people who can access the data. To make the data available to the greatest number of people, the data is often scrubbed or modified to obscure the sensitive data while continuing to offer important elements useful in data analytics. For example (and, yes, this is a silly example, but it can give you a broad idea), the HR department releases a dataset describing all the company employees but with personal information obscured. The people responsible for facility parking can use the data to do capacity planning by viewing how many people drive cars to work, or perhaps even what kinds of cars so that they can figure out how many electric charging stations will be needed to accommodate employee needs. Without access to employee personal information, financial data, or salary data, the facilities team still has a useful dataset they didn't have to create for themselves by sending out a company-wide email asking people for their auto information, duplicating data that may already exist and creating a siloed dataset.

Another example, along the same lines, is an analytics assignment to figure out how far people commute to work each day. This can include employee addresses, which may be accessible only to people with specific authorization to view that level of sensitive data. A security review of the data, as part of the DataSecOps development cycle, considers that the data be further anonymized by eliminating employee names or street numbers while still providing fairly accurate distance information.

A more real-world example is a hospital looking at the types of gallbladder operations performed each year. To get this information, hospital reps need to have access to patient records governed by HIPAA regulations. Security analysts working with the data analytics team can continuously review this analytics project to make sure that all HIPAA guidelines are being followed during the development of this project. The data could provide invaluable insight while protecting patient privacy.

ELEMENTS OF A GOOD DATA STORE

A good data store clearly describes the dataset. Part of that description should specify whether it's a static dataset that was created in the past and contains no live data. It should include the date the set was created, by whom, and who maintains responsibility for the dataset.

The data store should clearly specify the security access levels required for access to the data. If this is done in a clearly coded manner, access can be granted in an automated fashion, speeding up access to the data. This also makes it clear to data scientists what level of confidentiality their users must have in order to review the analytics they create. For instance, their analytics might review competitive business analysis that would harm the company if released to the wrong people.

Where the data is stored is another element a good data store must have in its description of a dataset. It should tell potential users of the data whether it's stored locally or in the cloud. When describing the data storage, the type of DBMS should also be mentioned to make querying the data simpler. This is also important if you're integrating data from multiple datasets that might be stored on multiple clouds and data storage types.

Meeting the Challenges of DataSecOps

Securing application development keeps hackers from breaking into your application to steal data. Securing data analytics is a bit more direct because it means not handing data directly to the hackers.

Securing applications is a bit more straightforward because network operations can monitor who has access to an application and can shut down access to unauthorized users. Data is a bit more static, and therefore monitoring access to the data is more challenging. It can easily go undetected. The FBI recently announced that foreign interests have had access to confidential government data stores for years. A group known as Advanced Persistent Threat 16 (APT16) has been stealing data since at least 2011. At the same time, foreign interests had access to the Office of Personnel Management, stealing highly sensitive data of millions of government workers, even including records of CIA agents working secretly in the field. There is no clear evidence that this group and others are not still camped out on servers full of sensitive data.

REMEMBER

Data breaches can go undetected for years.

A challenge for security teams in general, whether protecting data storage, applications, or any other type of security, is that the bad guys tend to outspend the good guys. The value of stolen information is so great that the resources applied to obtain it are extraordinary. This isn't a call to throw up your hands and give up. It's more of a call to create better data security measures.

Increased data security can have a dampening effect on the use of data. No one wants to use data that is difficult or impossible to access because of the security measures placed on it. People want fast-and-secure access to data that provides important insights. This might be the single greatest challenge of the teams involved in DataSecOps.

Selecting the appropriate privacy-enhancing technology is one of the more technical challenges within DataSecOps. Overprotecting data — making it difficult to access, or so anonymized or obscured that the end result is meaningless — is always a danger. The trick is finding a balance between overprotecting and under-protecting your data. This is definitely one of those collaborative discussions your team will need to have when building your data store.

DataSecOps borrows the underlying principles of all the Ops methodologies. Good DataSecOps are

>> **Agile:** This term means continuous delivery and continuous security.

>> **Collaborative:** All stakeholders, security professionals, developers, and data scientists need to be involved.

>> **Security-embedded:** Security isn't tacked on at the end but rather is an integral part of development and tested at each release cycle.

>> **Staged:** Separation of development into stages, similar to what's done in a software development project, needs to be encouraged. This keeps testing from being done on production environments where faulty software can wreak havoc.

REMEMBER

When developing a DataSecOps strategy, it's important to focus on your most sensitive data. Chapter 1 talks about creating a risk assessment to understand where the greatest risks lie within your data, whether stored locally or in the cloud. That's great advice to follow.

When developing your data store, include a clear picture of who created/owns the dataset, when it was created, and perhaps why it was created, and then, if you don't think you'll ever need it again, get rid of it. Old, stale data can become a huge security risk. Don't be a data hoarder.

Establish clear policies about who has access to specific data or types of data. You can do this in a role-based policy matrix to make determining who has access to what data, at which levels (for example, read-only), and under what conditions. Conditions might include annual tax filings or an HR audit. This is specific to your business and the types of data it collects and uses. The goal is to be crystal-clear so that you can avoid lengthy approval processes that slow access to critical data.

REMEMBER

You must include freelancers and contractors when checking for data access restrictions. Don't forget about them!

A successful DataSecOps environment provides for rapid access to data without sacrificing quality or security. Clarity and collaboration can take you a long way toward that goal.

TIP

If you're ready to make your move into DataSecOps, it helps to use a ready-made platform. This is still a new methodology, so not many players are in the market. Here are a couple to start with:

>> **Satori:** https://satoricyber.com

>> **Exate:** www.exate.com

DataSecOps is sure to mature quickly, which means lots of additional products becoming available. The need for security in development and in DataOps only becomes more critical with time.

Understanding That No Cloud Is Perfect

When you depend on software written by someone else, you increase your risk factor. The number of applications in use in a typical cloud environment is multitudinous. (Yeah, that's a word.) This chapter covers what it takes to write secure software. This is what happens when things go wrong in someone else's development.

While I wrote this chapter on cloud security, Microsoft warned thousands of cloud customers about exposed databases. Security researchers were able to discover keys that allowed access to Microsoft's Cosmos DB databases. To change the keys, the customers had to modify their own keys. This was merely a hassle in this case and disaster was averted.

It was reported that there was no evidence the flaw had been exploited, but the potential for a monstrous data leak was there for thousands of companies using their cloud database service. The team that found the exploit called it ChaosDB, because it certainly had the potential to have inflicted chaos. Many companies have abandoned local databases for the benefits of using a cloud-based DBMS.

The discovered flaw was not in the database software itself, but rather through a visualization tool called Jupyter Notebook, which ended up being enabled in Cosmos by default. The flaw gave enough access to the database to allow for a complete database wipe or changing individual records. This points out that the sheer complexity of the software used for analysis, and the applications that make use of cloud databases have the potential for great harm when security flaws are exploitable.

The company that discovered the security flaw, Wiz (`www.wiz.io/#`), has its own cloud security software that identifies high-risk attack vectors without the use of agents. It can track security across several of the top cloud services by scanning all your virtual machine layers and containers, either active or offline, and looking for possible exploits.

Chapter **5**

Restricting Access

Restricting access to data is one of the important (and perhaps stunningly obvious) parts of cloud security. This chapter delves into that topic, but also introduces the basics of compliance because, though not limited to access restrictions, most of the compliance requirements deal heavily with who has access to which types of data.

Protecting data with user access restriction has been around since the first days of computers, when users had to log in to a mainframe over a hardwired dumb terminal. There isn't much new to the idea of user validation, but how it's done in the 21st century is quite different. This next section goes into detail in determining the types of access restrictions you should set for your data and corresponding applications.

Determining the Level of Access Required

Properly configuring your resources so that only authorized people have access can be a complicated matter. The reason it isn't as straightforward as it seems is that there may be no clear idea of how sensitive data might be and what kinds of people should have access.

Some basic principles can help you along, but much of what you need to determine is subjective — until it involves compliance regulations, which I cover in some detail later in this chapter. You should begin by knowing who is capable of legitimately accessing your data. Sadly, it's often difficult to know when people are accessing your data without authorization and, what's even worse, this kind of a breach can go on for *long* periods. Someone masquerading as a legitimate user may be able to fly under the radar and gain full access to your data.

Artificial intelligence is improving at recognizing patterns of use. This is one way it's possible to figure out when someone's user credentials have been stolen and are being used by hackers. For example, knowing what times someone normally logs in and out helps AI tracking logins to spot outliers. Someone logging in during the middle of the night may be an unauthorized user, and a good AI system throws up flags alerting network administrators that a hack may be in progress.

Catching flies with honey

One possible way to know when your account has been hacked is by way of a *honeypot*, when you put fake and recognizable data online for a hacker to steal, which may allow you to spot a breach when someone starts accessing the fake resource. Honeypots are most often used to catch someone who has gained unauthorized access to your data by using someone's credentials, which is why it's being mentioned as a tool in the section on user authentication.

A honeypot can be a database table, an entire database, or even an entire virtual server. Honeypots are categorized by the types of "bait" you offer:

>> **High interaction:** Uses virtual machines with a full set of services to keep your actual data as isolated as possible

>> **Low interaction:** Uses a virtual machine with a limited set of services, such as a DBMS

>> **Canary:** A cloud-based honeypot

A pure honeypot involves setting up a physical server, but this is costly and a more dangerous type of lure because, once someone has accessed a physical server, they likely have access to your network and other servers.

The cloud honeypot has some distinct advantages over more traditional hardware and VM honeypots. They can be easily placed geographically in high-risk areas to lure hackers. The geographical location is easily moved. Also, the cost of setting up a cloud honeypot is low, for a couple of reasons: First, no physical hardware is involved and new instances can be spun up in seconds. Second, cloud resources generally cost very little when not being used, and, hopefully, your honeypot isn't getting slammed with usage.

REMEMBER

Honeypots are one of the oldest tricks in the book. However, luring hackers into your network, whether local or part of your cloud setup, is a dangerous game. Hackers have become more sophisticated and, once on your network, have powerful tools to discover vulnerabilities in your system. Honeypots are still used today because they are cheap, easy to set up and sometimes catch the less skillful hacker.

Honeypots can also include fake data, fake documents and fake accounts that throw up red flags when accessed.

Determining roles

Stepping away from catching the bad guys for a minute, it's important to figure out how to grant access to the people who need it. One of the first steps you should take is to create a list of roles. You can think of roles as job titles, something one or more people might carry.

Rather than grant access to individuals, you grant access to a role. Figure 5-1 shows a typical role-based security system.

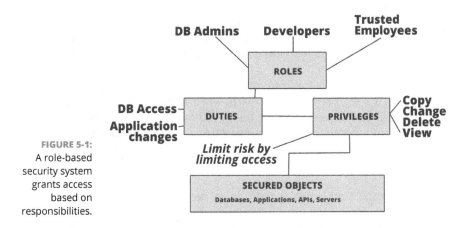

FIGURE 5-1:
A role-based security system grants access based on responsibilities.

Auditing user requirements

Tracking user requirements is one of those things that should be done regularly, as requirements change over time. Identity access management (IAM) is a set of policies and technologies that manage user identities and control access to all your cloud resources. In addition to 3rd party providers, major cloud service providers employ an IAM. It has been said that this is the system that protects a company's crown jewels. Because access management is no simple matter, you need to find the system that works best for you and balances expense, agility, and flexibility.

TIP

One thing you might consider is employing your configuration management database (CMDB) to help you track and audit the requirements users have for access. A good CMDB system not only tracks devices, data, and applications but can also track users and their interactions with the other components.

REMEMBER

Careful planning and preparation can simplify the task of identity auditing. Carefully tag user roles. Once tagged, make sure that you have clear and auditable policies for why a role should have access, when, and where. Most importantly, a person can have multiple roles, and roles can change over time. You need systems like those in a CMDB to help you track users and the roles they have.

Understanding Least Privilege Policy

Least privilege policy essentially states that you should grant no unneeded privileges. It's kind of a bare minimum policy that restricts anyone from gaining access beyond their absolute need.

TIP

When restricting access to your data and applications, consider more than people. Also take into account things acting like people, such as programs and processes.

Databases are notorious for granting access to people and programs far beyond their need. It's so common, particularly when building websites, to grant "the kitchen sink" to everyone and everything. You can grant users permission to do a lot of stuff to a database, including the right to create new databases, delete old ones, or modify, add, and delete records. When a particular user needs only read access to a database, that's the level of privilege that should be granted.

The idea behind least privilege policy is to limit the number of roles that have unfettered access to data and applications. Greater care can be focused on users within sensitive roles and less on accounts that don't require that level of sensitivity. This eases the burden on the security administrator. If someone does compromise one of these lower-level accounts, they aren't granted access to sensitive data or given the ability to do any harm.

REMEMBER

It's not always a human hacker directly attempting to access one of your systems. Malware can be devious and unrelenting at attempts to worm its way in.

When looking at the sensitivity of your data, you might be tempted to think, "Who cares about how many socks I keep in inventory?" Perhaps no one really cares but you. If you no longer had access to your inventory information, though, how would it impact your business? Would you be able to continue selling socks? Would it slow you down or require you to take a physical inventory? Many exploits care little about the information and care more about its value to the owners. That's why ransomware attacks work so well: Hackers encrypt your data and ask for payment to decrypt it. It's best to limit the possibility of attacks in the first place.

Granting just-in-time privileges

Granting access to your systems doesn't have to be a one-and-done kind of deal. You can grant access on an as-needed basis. For instance, if someone needs root access to a server to perform an administrative task, you can grant root permission for as long as it takes to perform the task and then restrict privileges, once again, to only what is needed.

You can limit the ability to perform actions based on date and time. This way, no one can perform these actions except during a particular window of time. For instance, AWS allows the ability to restrict actions to specific periods by setting these values in its identity and access management (IAM) policies.

The need-to-know strategy

The idea of least privilege may seem to be straightforward on the surface. In fact, it's a simple idea: If someone doesn't need to know something, or access something, don't allow it. But it gets far more complicated than that.

An example of a complicated scenario is a DevOps team that releases code in a continuous development environment. The team regularly changes databases, updates applications, and pokes around in general in some sensitive areas. Figuring out who needs what access and when can be a complicated task.

TIP

Avoid creating roles with unlimited privileges (*God roles*). Though it's tempting to just grant access to everything all at once, this is the most dangerous type of role, and if exploited, it can be devastating.

Granting access to trusted employees

When building your identity management system to manage the principles of least privilege, start with your employees. Consider the roles each of them plays within your organization. Don't get sucked into the idea that just because someone's pay grade is higher, they need more access. It just makes them a bigger target for hackers. For example, you might want to give the CEO every one of the privileges, but in fact the CEO may need zero privileges. Other people/roles are responsible for supplying decision information, and therefore the CEO has zero need to have privileges that grant access to your data.

In large enterprises, consider segmenting your identity privileges. Because someone has rights over one database doesn't mean they should have the same rights over another department's database, or even someone else's database within the same department. Creating a more fine-grained set of privileges limits risk should access be exploited.

With many companies relying more on remote work environments, employee access must be managed even more carefully. The trend to remote work has been a boon to hackers. It has also created a larger access landscape. More tools and applications are being used to get the job done remotely where they were once used directly on a desktop with local network access to resources and data.

Restricting access to contractors

When you're faced with a scenario where you've just hired a contractor on UpWork or one of the other freelancing sites and they've given you a list of privileges they require to get the job done, take a step back before blindly handing over those privileges. You don't know these people — and though they may be trustworthy beyond belief, you have no idea what types of security measures they have in place to protect access. If *they* are hacked, *you* are hacked.

Chances are good that there are trusted employees that manage contractors and freelancers. Consider giving them the privileges for tasks like the release of source code. Let freelance developers write code and release it into a sandbox until it's time to release the code. (See Figure 5-2.) Then grant the employee the privilege in the source code control system to release code into production. This extra step can save you a lot of grief.

The same idea is true for changes to databases. In Chapter 4 I introduce the idea of creating copies of data for development using DataOps. The GIT source code control system has this ability to quickly and easily create copies of data so that you aren't risking direct access to your production data. You might also consider working with sample data. This is particularly true when your data contains sensitive data, or when access to the data is restricted by governance policies.

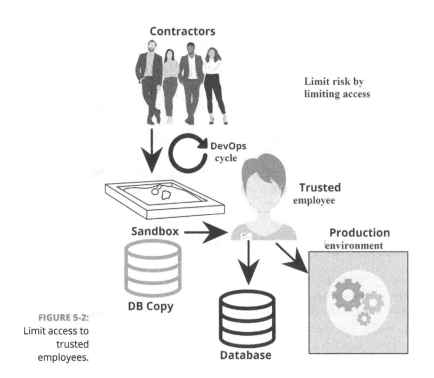

Contractors

Limit risk by
limiting access

DevOps
cycle

Trusted
employee

Sandbox →

Production
environment

DB Copy

Database

FIGURE 5-2:
Limit access to
trusted
employees.

Implementing Authentication

Authentication is, if not the heart of cloud security, certainly at least one of the chambers of the heart. Controlling who has access to your systems is the most direct and basic form of security. The days of simple user ID and password authentication are no longer sufficient, and so authentication has become a more complex task, beginning with multifactor authentication.

Multifactor authentication (Or, who's calling me now?)

Multifactor authentication is covered in greater detail later in this book, but, as an introduction, this term means asking for a third or even fourth form of authentication beyond simply knowing a user ID and password. In some cases, systems send an email or text message with a code to validate that you have access to a trusted system, such as a known device like a cellphone or access to the email account. This system isn't perfect, of course, because if your account has been hacked, it's possible that the hacker has access to these systems as well.

Another method of authentication is knowing something private, such as the questions often asked when setting up accounts, like your first pet's name or your father's middle name. The struggle with this method is that social media phishing has made it almost useless because so many people answer all those stupid Facebook questions. (Sorry if I offended you, but they really are stupid.)

Fingerprints, iris scans, and other biometrics are harder to fool, but not impossible. Even Face ID, common on many phones now, is not perfect. But such strategies are a step in the right direction. Simplifying multifactor authentication will aid in its further adoption. There may never be a perfect method of authentication that can't be fooled, but things are headed in the right direction.

Authenticating with API keys

Application programming interfaces (APIs) use authentication keys in order to authenticate application access — normally, to a third-party resource. Programmers often use APIs to gain access to information not normally held by the application provider. For example, you might use an API to look up a zip code. Sending an API request to a third party then returns information about a zip code, such as a place name or even surrounding zip codes. These are important resources, but if your API keys are discovered, hackers can gain access to these resources — or to the resources you might provide. A good key management system helps manage your API keys.

Using Firebase authentication

Software developers need the ability to include authentication in the applications they build. One such system, known as Firebase, provides a software development kit (SDK) that you can use to authenticate users to your apps.

Firebase supports authentication by using these methods:

>> Email and passwords

>> Phone numbers

>> Federated ID providers such as Google, Facebook, and Twitter. (A federated ID links a person's identity across different identity management systems in a form of single sign-on technology.)

Firebase integrates with industry standard authentication methods such as OpenID Connect and OAuth. (More on OAuth in the next section.)

WARNING

OpenID was an idea to allow people to use the same ID to sign in to different sites. The problem is that, after a hacker knows your credentials, they can then log into multiple sites. This idea has now come and gone. A newer version of OpenID was developed as a part of OAuth.

Employing OAuth

OAuth, or Open Authorization, isn't exactly an authentication system — it's really an authorization framework that provides a system where, once you've logged in to an application that knows who you are, you can then grant authorization to another application and never have to give the "other" application your user ID and password. OAuth uses access tokens sent to third-party services without ever revealing a user's credentials.

The advantage of using OAuth is that it limits how many people know your user access credentials. Once you've logged into one place, you can authorize other places using an OAuth access token either temporarily, or in some cases, for recurring access. Additionally, applications using OAuth tokens don't need to maintain a user account database, increasing security.

Google and Facebook authentication methods

Google has a smartphone app known as Authenticator, which provides two-factor authentication by displaying a code that resets regularly. The benefit of using Authenticator is that it needs no network connectivity to create the code; a two-factor system that sends an SMS message does. Authenticator works by creating a code on both your phone and the server at the same time using a hacker-proof algorithm authenticating you as a valid user.

Facebook, rather than use the Google method, has an authentication system built directly into its cellphone app. When you try to log in to Facebook from a desktop that isn't recognized, you may be asked to access your mobile account and use the Facebook app to send an authorization message. This method does require network connectivity to work.

Introducing the Alphabet Soup of Compliance

Companies that collect sensitive information — whether it's financial, credit, or health information — must comply with regulations. This statement is even more true when dealing with international restrictions such as the European Union (EU) privacy regulations.

Global compliance

Cloud computing has made it cost effective to do business online, anywhere in the world. Of course, some physical limitations still exist, such as product fulfillment, but a larger hurdle for many businesses is meeting the demands of global compliance.

The International Standards Organization (ISO) defines compliance this way:

"The state where an organization is meeting all its obligations and commitments."

There are compliance standards when it comes to cybersecurity — many of them, in fact. This list describes some of the best known:

- >> **PCI DSS:** One of the best-known compliance regulations for most businesses, the Payment Card Industry Data Security Standard regulates how credit card and credit cardholder information is kept private.

- >> **GDPR:** Failing to meet the requirements of this regulation, the EU's General Data Protection Regulation, can come with some heavy fines.

- >> **HIPAA:** The Health Insurance and Portability and Accountability Act of 1996 protects the privacy of your health records.

- >> **POPI:** The Protection of Personal Information Act is South Africa's own, personal set of information protection regulations.

- >> **FERPA:** The Family Education and Rights Privacy Act is the set of compliance regulations that pertain to protecting the private information of students.

WARNING

Don't think that you can comply and forget it later, like a bad date. Security compliance is an ongoing process that will involve your constant attention (as long you both shall live).

CYBERSPACE

Curious where the term *cybersecurity* came from? Essentially, it means to protect *cyberspace,* which is a word that was used to describe the Internet in its very early days. The term *cyberspace* was first used by the science fiction author William Gibson, in 1982, in his short story "Burning Chrome" and then again in his novel *Neuromancer.*

Complying with PCI

One of the common compliance regulations relates to protecting credit card information. Commerce today is done primarily by credit card, whether personal or corporate. The health of our very economy now depends on the security of credit card information. Because of this, PCI compliance is one of the most stringent sets of regulations.

Complying with PCI is a complex task. PCI compliance that has as its goal the protection of credit card details generally requires meeting these 12 requirements:

>> Build and maintain a firewall to protect cardholder data.

>> Use passwords and security parameters that exceed vendor default values.

>> Protect stored cardholder data.

>> Encrypt credit card transaction data as it passes over public networks. *Hint:* The Internet is a public network.

>> Employ antimalware software.

>> Be certain that applications you build are secure. (See Chapter 4.)

>> Limit access to cardholder data.

>> Assign a unique identity to anyone with computer access.

>> Restrict physical access to cardholder data. (Try that with your teenager!)

>> Monitor and track all access to network and cardholder data.

>> Test security systems and processes regularly.

>> Establish a security policy for employees and contractors.

Each one of these 12 requirements has many detailed subrequirements. Meeting the PCI requirement is no simple task, and many companies have chosen to have companies that specialize in credit card data manage their transactions rather than bear the cost and risk. Even those companies are much stricter now about how clients communicate with them. Using a third-party vendor to process credit card transactions saves a great deal of overhead and hassle. Rather than try to store your customer's credit card information and set yourself up for a terrible data breach, it can make sense to make this process someone else's problem for the small percentage they charge for the service.

One of the largest-ever credit card detail breaches happened in 2017 when Equifax was hacked, which led to the release of the private information of 143 million people along with credit card details of just over 200,000 individuals. More recently, Capital One was breached in 2019, revealing the credit card details of more than 100,000 of its customers. Capital One is the fifth largest credit card issuer. ("What's in your wallet?") Over the years, hundreds of millions of credit card details have been revealed by way of hacks. Many of those details are then sold over the dark web, an off-the-beaten path area of the Internet not accessible using standard web browsers.

Complying with GDPR

Businesses doing business within or with EU companies are required to comply with the GDPR (https://gdpr.eu/). Failing to do so can result in some stiff fines.

The goal of the GDPR is to protect the privacy rights of its citizens, residents, and even its visitors. This requirement is placed on businesses within, and operating outside, the EU and is enforced via treaties.

The GDPR goes beyond financial transactions. If you're offering any goods or services to people in the EU, then the GDPR requires that you comply. You can get started doing this by first gaining permission to use someone's private information. Permission is part of the way there.

TIP

Maintaining an EU-happy privacy policy on your website helps you comply with the GDPR.

As with many security issues, always do an impact assessment. Figure out what happens if the data you're using is released into the wild during a breach. If your answer is "It's bad," it behooves you to take extra steps to protect the data. This begins with encryption.

Encryption isn't the great fix-all that everyone wants it to be, but it keeps out the wannabe hackers. Always make sure your communications have end-to-end encryption. Use a TLS (formerly SSL) certificate with your website, and this happens automagically. These certificates ensure that users are communicating with the right website and not some random hacker. The encrypted form of web communications protocol HTTPS takes over from them and sets up end-to-end encryption.

Though the buck stops with you, it's your responsibility to make sure that any of your contractors or vendors who have access to your private customer data also comply with the requirements of the GDPR. This includes the cloud provider you've selected. If you use cloud-based services, such as an email provider, that service also has to comply with the GDPR when doing business with EU customers.

One of the more unusual hoops you need to jump through to comply with the GDPR is to appoint a representative in the EU. This doesn't apply if you're just occasionally processing the personal data of EU folks. As long as you're not processing tons of information, you might be able to skip this step. The question to ask yourself is whether the release of the information will impact the rights and freedoms of people in the EU.

You need to know what to do if there's ever a data breach involving the private information of EU residents. (Moving to Russia is not an option). If you're using strong encryption for your communications, this goes a long way in mitigating any fines for negligent handling of data, and in some cases avoiding some of the reporting requirements.

Using your best efforts to comply with the spirit of these requirements should keep you from being scrutinized by EU regulators.

HIPAA compliance

If you've been to the doctor's office or hospital lately, you've likely had to sign a document informing you that the doctor or hospital must comply with HIPAA regulations. If your organization is health-related and must comply with HIPAA, you should take this regulation seriously because fines for failures to comply can be serious. In fact, even if you didn't know of a breach or, using reasonable diligence, should have known of a breach, you can still be fined for each occurrence. One breach can lead to multiple violations, one for each record that was released. For example, if a laptop is lost or stolen containing private data that has a thousand records stored on it and that data is released, you could get fined for a thousand violations. Serious stuff. Paying attention matters, though, because, if you can show you've taken reasonable measures, you might be forgiven and slip by without fines.

Here are some steps you need to follow to comply with HIPAA:

- >> **Put someone in charge of your HIPAA security.** At least a single point of contact is required. You can give them a cool title, like HIPAA security officer.

- >> **Know the rules.** Basically, you can't release private information covered under HIPAA without permission of the person whose information you're storing. There are exceptions but getting permission is the easiest way to be safe.

- >> **Know what rights people have.** HIPAA grants rights to people regarding their personal information. Essentially, a person can control what information is released or specify who receives that information (an insurance company or a specialist medical provider.) Rather than stand at the nurse's station for everyone to hear, individuals can request privacy.

- >> **Put it in writing.** It's *vital* to put your HIPAA policies in writing. Failure to do this constitutes willful neglect, and that's bad. You need to have policies regarding privacy or notification of a breach, for instance — thus, the paper you sign at the doctor's office.

- >> **Make some forms.** Part of putting it in writing means you've created forms that meet the HIPAA guidelines. All these are available from HIPAA websites. It's nothing you have to create from scratch. Don't feel you can simply have a piece of paper that says, "Mum's the word. Sign here." A sample can be found here: `www.southernute-nsn.gov/wp-content/uploads/sites/15/2020/06/AAOS-HIPAA-Notice-of-Privacy-Practices-2013.pdf`.

- >> **Execute associate agreements.** This is one aspect where cloud security definitely plays a role. When you store private data in the cloud, you must have a signed agreement with the cloud provider. This also pertains to their subcontractors. A cloud storage provider that handles HIPAA-compliant data will most likely have those in place.

- >> **Complete a risk assessment of your hardware.** A solid assessment of the security risks involving all your hardware has been and always will be an essential first step in implementing your cloud security policy. Your risk assessment should be done regularly and be well-documented. Be diligent. In today's mobile world, it's easy to overlook hardware that may allow access to your HIPAA-controlled data.

- >> **Put in administrative, technical, and physical safeguards.** No system is perfect, and there may be occasional unintentional disclosures. But you can get off the hook without a fine if you can show that you've done a reasonable job of putting the right safeguards in place. Following the cloud security guidelines in this book will help!

- » **Implement training.** Who doesn't like a day off from work to eat doughnuts and watch PowerPoint slides? New employees must receive training within a reasonable amount of time from their hire date or else you risk the wrath of the HIPAA compliance folks if one of your employees suddenly decides to post private medical data on Facebook. If they were trained, it's not so bad for you, because you did your part. (In training sites Krispy Kreme doughnuts are usually appreciated.)

- » **Respond quickly to breaches and violations.** This requirement should be true of all your security measures.

- » **Report breaches within 60 days.** You must let people know if you've unintentionally disclosed their private data.

TIP

Each state maintains their own requirements for breach notification. For a spread-sheet of the requirements by state, check out `https://iapp.org/resources/article/state-data-breach-notification-chart/`.

Complying with HIPAA can seem tough, but if you take reasonable precautions to protect private data and document all your efforts carefully, you should be able to avoid fines and hassles and maybe even disclosures.

Government compliance

When your company works with the US federal government, you must meet compliance standards as well, depending on the level of confidentiality or secrecy of the data. It's way beyond the scope of this book, however, to cover all those guidelines. It's good to meet at least the most basic compliance guideline pub-lished by the National Institute of Standards and Technology (NIST) known as NIST 800-171 (`https://csrc.nist.gov/publications/detail/sp/800-171/rev-2/final`). This covers unclassified but controlled data.

You'll be happy to know that complying with NIST 800-171 requires no outside audit of your organization. You can self-report compliance. These are the three basic compliance requirements:

- » **Create a security plan.** The plan should cover a description of your overall IT environment, including all cloud resources you use. You can easily overlook these when creating documentation of your physical plant. Make sure your plan describes all interconnections your system has with the outside world. You also need to specify which measures you'll take in case of a secu-rity breach.

- » **Document exceptions.** You need to document any reasons that your company might fail to meet reasonable security measures to protect private data. Along with your list of exceptions, you need a plan for how you'll make those failures right. You can't just say, "We've got problems, and we'll fix them." Also, document what you actually did to remediate the exceptions.

>> **Give yourself a score.** NIST 800-171 has an assessment methodology you need to follow when giving yourself a score, and then that score is stored in a federal database, allowing you to show compliance so that you can get certain government contracts.

Compliance in general

Draw seven letters from your favorite word game and chances are high that you can spell one or more acronyms of compliance requirements. There are international, federal, state, and local compliance regulations and guidelines. In a nutshell, put someone in charge, give them a fancy title, give them a filing cabinet large enough to hold all the paperwork, make a security plan, document everything, store it in the filing cabinet (locked, of course), and train everyone.

TIP

Your cloud security measures must comply with the requirements of all the various information security and privacy guidelines. Your cloud provider can most likely guide you in documenting your cloud security compliance.

Maintaining Compliance and CSPM

As with all security measures, it's not enough to simply make all the efforts once and then sit on your laurels and say, "Job well done." All security measures must be revisited regularly, from minute by minute for complex network infrastructure to weekly or monthly for smaller organizations working with data that may not be as sensitive.

When your organization handles private data that is covered by one or more compliance regulations, you will likely submit to a regular audit of your security. In a smaller organization, you may be able to squeak by with making a list of the processes, infrastructure and security measures that are regularly audited and then check them regularly to verify that they're still in compliance. Larger companies need to use tools to help validate compliance, which makes verification and reporting easier.

TIP

Cloudcheckr (https://cloudcheckr.com) is an enterprise-level tool that can handle the heavy lifting of compliance. This tool works across the various cloud infrastructure designs covered in greater detail in Chapter 9. In addition to assisting you with compliance, the Cloudcheckr CMX platform performs tasks such as asset management and resource utilization.

CSPM, or cloud security posture management, automates the task of locating and fixing security problems across cloud infrastructures. The risk identification handles IaaS (Infrastructure as a Service), SaaS (Software as a Service), and PaaS (Platform as a Service) cloud services.

The complexity of cloud services means that, for a medium- to large-size business, the cloud services you connect with and disconnect from can number in the thousands each day. This type of complexity is what makes clouds extremely useful but also makes them even more difficult to make secure.

The reason clouds are particularly difficult to secure is that they have no perimeter, such as a local- or wide-area network might have. In those cases, you can simply throw up firewalls to keep out the unwanted. With clouds, you don't have that delimited barrier to protect.

With the complexity of cloud connections and services, there is just no way you could ever hope to protect your cloud services manually, even with a network operations center working 24 hours a day. It's simply impossible, or at the very least unfeasible.

REMEMBER

You can't protect what you can't see.

Visibility is the key to good cybersecurity. Working across many clouds of various types and brands makes visibility *difficult.* In fact, it makes trying to protect your cloud infrastructure a bit like groping in the dark. Another thing that makes visibility difficult when working with clouds is that the cloud is merely the platform on which innumerable technologies operate and new ones are popping up every day. Keeping abreast of the new services and how you might protect them is an onerous task.

Visibility is also more than just an overview of the programs running on cloud platforms. Trying to oversee an environment with thousands of users connecting and disconnecting from multiple devices and platforms is worse than air traffic control at Dallas/Fort Worth International Airport. Each one of those users is a security risk.

A CSPM application automatically discovers entities as they connect and disconnect. This includes applications as well as users. As the entities are discovered, the system can see when they are operating within their security guidelines and when they are outliers in the system. That information then gets passed on to network operators.

Discovering and remediating threats with CSPM applications

Threats are a bit like a rat infestation: Once you're infested with rats, it's difficult to find them even though they seem everywhere. Cloud security threats are like rat infestations for a number of reasons. First, we tend to invite them in. A high percentage of threats occur because we've misconfigured something. Human error is responsible for most of the weaknesses we bake into our cybersystems.

Another reason that cloud security threats are like a rat infestation is that they gnaw away at the good infrastructure until catastrophic failures occur. It doesn't take the entire system to be overcome, only the weak spots. Once they're in, rats or hackers, it's game over. It's then hard to get rid of them and the damage is done.

In larger enterprises, infrastructure management has been automated in code, a process known as IaC (Infrastructure as Code). That means instructions on managing infrastructure are written as code instructions, which can be the source of many errors and security holes. CSPM systems are designed to find and correct the misconfigurations that plague complex systems.

A good cloud security and posture management application monitors and helps prevent disaster by using these methods:

>> Prevention

>> Detection

>> Response

>> Prediction

Prevention involves setting up safeguards against both intentional and unintentional breaches. Intentional breaches are what you might think they are — hackers trying to break into your systems, looking for those vulnerabilities they usually find with enough determination. This is the focus of most cloud security applications.

When preventing breaches, you should also be looking toward the unintentional breach — when human error reveals private information in places that are easily accessed, even by people not trying to hack your systems. The history of cybersecurity is full of examples where, on one fateful day, a company somehow manages to accidentally start displaying all its customer information on the web for everyone to view.

CSPM systems work to avoid intentional as well as unintentional breaches by providing clear and simple visibility over even the most complex cloud infrastructures. Detecting security problems from alerts is what a good CSPM system does well. When security holes are easily detected, they are easily fixed. Part of the benefit of using a unified system to manage the cloud security posture is avoiding *alert fatigue*, which happens when security alerts start popping up from multiple systems and become overwhelming, kind of like crickets. One cricket is kind of fun to hear at night — tens of thousands becomes an overwhelming drone. The same thing happens with security alerts. This causes many important alerts to be overlooked.

CSPM systems generally employ AI to sort through alerts. This enables alerts to be combined from multiple sources into a single alert. AI-enabled CSPM systems can then either recommend responses to specific threats or be automated to handle them on their own through prewritten automation scripts set up to solve issues as they happen.

The AI then becomes predictive, letting you know when the systems are ripe for a breach, spotting all the small risks that later turn into big risks.

TIP

Using AI to predict security failures allows them to be corrected before they actually occur. You're then being proactive instead of reactive, and though you might lose hero status for solving problems, you'll be known for not allowing them to occur in the first place.

Automating Compliance

Earlier in this chapter, you can see how complying with regulations that work to protect private information can be difficult to manage. A good CSPM system goes a long way in managing your compliance across complicated cloud environments.

Because many of the corrective actions to security problems can be automated within your CSPM application, you can self-correct when compliance begins to wander from the guidelines. Being able to do this in an automated fashion reduces the manpower required to oversee a large cloud-first system. Automated threat detection works tirelessly around the clock with reduced risk of operator failure.

Integrating with DevOps

Your developers use DevSecOps to secure applications before they're released. The CSPM system provides monitoring after an application has been released and reports security issues with released applications back to the DevOps team for correction. In a perfect world, security risks are caught during the continuous testing that happens before each release. Coding errors do happen, however, and catching them quickly and efficiently is important when it comes to establishing trust in the software. You don't want the end user catching the problem or, worse, having this be the cause of a security breach.

WARNING

When CSPM systems detect misconfigurations, they are corrected in the runtime environment and not in the IaC instructions. That means that configuration changes to the virtual environment are not saved when the runtime ceases to exist. The IaC (Infrastructure as Code) instructions are not changed. To make sure that the same misconfigurations don't occur each time an application is launched, they must be corrected within the IaC. This strategy maintains the instructions in the IaC as the single source of truth.

Companies like Sysdig (https://sysdig.com) have added CSPM modules into their DevOps applications. This module lets you write rules for accessing cloud infrastructure. One nice feature is that this module monitors cloud utilization that turns off cloud resources when they aren't being used. Running only the services you need reduces the overall security risk. This Sysdig module works together with the Sysdig open-source Falco security platform for Kubernetes (https://falco.org) and the threat detection system donated to the Cloud Native Computing Foundation (www.cncf.io).

Controlling Access to the Cloud

Controlling access to cloud resources is perhaps the single most important facet of cloud security. Misconfigurations of cloud access control have been responsible for some of the largest data breaches in history. Cloud service providers generally offer an access control system that allows individuals access to cloud resources in a controlled manner. (For more on role-based permissions, see Chapter 4.)

TIP

Use logging tools to discover when cloud access permissions have been misconfigured. Many logging tools will report errors alerting network administrators that a problem exists. Error logs are often the first indication that something's gone wrong.

You may choose to go beyond the capabilities of the cloud access system of your cloud provider for greater flexibility as well as uniformity across multiple cloud environments. This is done with a Cloud Access Security Broker. More on that option in the next section.

Using a cloud access security broker (CASB)

Cloud access security brokers (CASBs) enable companies to develop policies beyond those set by the cloud provider. You can do this to make sure that your cloud environment security policies fall in line with your on-premises (local) security policies. It also allows you to catch security problems that may have fallen through the cracks with traditional or in-house security systems. You can see where the CASB system fits into your IT infrastructure as a whole by checking out Figure 5-3.

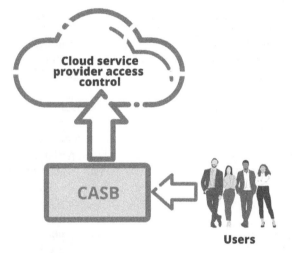

FIGURE 5-3:
The CASB system sits between your users and your cloud access control system.

Using a CASB can be revealing. When it comes to visibility, you might be shocked at what a CASB can reveal. You might believe that your corporate cloud usage is at one level, only to find that it's ten times or even a hundred times the usage level you'd imagined. One of the original uses for the CASB was to eliminate or at least greatly reduce shadow IT systems (computing environments operating outside the purview of the IT department), the bane of all cybersecurity officers. The use of a CASB has become essential to enterprises operating complex cloud environments.

CASB products have various offerings, but most of them offer a range of basic services, such as

>> Data loss prevention

>> Sharing and collaboration controls

>> Configuration audits

>> Virus and malware detection

>> SSO (single sign-on) and IAM (identity access management) integration

>> Governance risk assessment

Risk assessment of cloud apps is an important feature of a CASB. Monitoring access to cloud applications provides the kind of visibility into your cloud app usage that enables intelligent decisions about when to throttle or stop app usage due to risk. This kind of decision is usually done manually by a security team, but they need the information provided by the CASB to make intelligent decisions.

A CASB system can provide guidance in complying with regulations, either the ones mentioned in this chapter or any of the other government and industry compliance regulations you may face. The CASB identifies areas of high risk that will help you focus your security efforts more effectively.

In addition to visibility, a CASB solution provides data security measures such as collaboration control, encryption, data tokenization, and digital rights management. Most importantly, CASB can create, using AI pattern recognition and entity behavior analytics, an idea of what normal usage patterns look like and report anomalous behavior patterns or even block user access because of outlier patterns. It's a little like when the bank blocks your ATM card because of an unusually large purchase or one outside your normal geographic location.

The CASB system works by first developing a list of all your services. There are two ways this list is compiled. One is agent-based, where a software agent constantly searches for connected resources. This is the more difficult type of discovery system to employ. The second is agentless, which doesn't rely on a hardware or software device constantly scanning; instead, the system registers users and devices when a user attempts a login to the device or application. It's a type of on-demand service that makes use of the machine's (or virtual machine's) native services.

TIP

Agentless CASB systems may be easier to employ in the cloud because of their increased ability to operate in high-density virtual server environments.

Bitglass (www.bitglass.com) is a multimode CASB that allows protection of data at rest as well as data being accessed. Most security systems only offer to protect data at rest. Bitglass uses a reverse proxy to provide agentless CASB services.

Middleware protection systems

CASB systems are one part of the overall cloud security software plan. Other *middleware* applications (those that sit between applications and system software) provide additional security services. For full security coverage, you should consider using a secure web gateway and a data loss prevention system.

Employing a secure web gateway (SWG)

The web has grown over the years as the foundation of application development. Web development has outstripped traditional desktop application development because there is no need to distribute it. Changes made to web applications impact everyone immediately, without the need for downloads. Built-in encryption also secures applications end-to-end. A secure web gateway protects users and applications from external and internal threats.

The Fortinet SWG (`www.fortinet.com`) provides services like these:

>> URL filtering

>> Data loss prevention

>> Malware protection

An SWG sits between users and your web server and acts as a security filtering device. It directs connection requests based on your company security policy. Checking certificate validity and deep SSL/TLS inspection can keep web communications safe from people trying to redirect web traffic or spoof a website. It also blocks malware from entering your network when users initiate web traffic.

Come up with use policies that allow you to restrict access to inappropriate websites, enforce security policies, and protect against unauthorized data transfers. Secure web gateways are often used alongside VPNs when employees are accessing applications while working remotely.

Data loss prevention (DLP) systems

Data loss prevention (DLP) systems inspect network traffic, leaving your systems looking for sensitive data, such as social security numbers, credit card information, medical information, or intellectual property. Traffic that is carrying unauthorized data is then terminated to protect from data loss.

TIP

DLP systems can run as stand-alone software applications or are often embedded in commercial secure web gateway applications.

Using a Firewall as a Service (FWaaS)

Firewalls have been protecting networks from the early days of the Internet. Once, the Internet was the wild, wild west of development — until hackers saw the opportunities and simple vulnerabilities afforded by Internet access through network ports. Almost overnight that came to a halt, when almost all Internet traffic was forced to use Port 80, the World Wide Web port. This was the dawn of the web-based Internet application, as nearly every other application was shut down except for email and FTP and a few others.

Now that networks incorporate one or more clouds, protecting networks has become more difficult, and it created the need for a firewall that can protect cloud resources. With a shared responsibility for security between your company and the cloud provider, it's up to you to add the additional security not provided by the cloud.

An FWaaS runs in the cloud and performs all the same basic services you might expect from a traditional hardware or software firewall running on your local network such as packet filtering, IPSec VPN, SSL/TLS support, and IP mapping.

Additionally, FWaaS services can

>> Aggregate the network traffic from both cloud and onsite networks

>> Enforce uniform security policies across a diverse network

>> Give you more visibility and control over your network

>> Identify malware

When the firewall inspects the header of each data packet trying to enter your network, it does an intelligent discovery of the source of the packet using deep packet inspection (DPI) and alerts network operators to seemingly innocuous but dangerous traffic. Some FWaaS systems incorporate AI learning systems that have the capability to spot never-before-seen malware.

Because of the agile nature of today's network and cloud infrastructure, installing traditional firewalls no longer makes sense. Employing cloud-based firewall systems makes good security and financial sense.

Secure Access Service Edge (SASE)

Secure Access Service Edge (SASE) is a model for networking and network security that is the combination of wide-area networking, CASB, FWaaS, and the implementation of Zero Trust policies that delivers services based on these factors:

>> Identity of the entity

>> Real-time context

>> Your company's security policies

>> Compliance restrictions

>> Risk assessment

According to Gartner, a leading technology research and consulting company, SASE provides unprecedented integration. This integration includes a number of different entities, including users, groups of users, departments, divisions, applications, toasters and refrigerators, and other IoT devices, no matter where they are located — locally or out on the edge of the cloud where you deliver services. SASE identifies users and devices and then applies zero-trust and policy-based security to traffic between applications and users.

Many solutions exist for implementing SASE. Lookout (www.lookout.com) has an application designed for remote workers that provides end-to-end security between remote workers and the cloud. It provides some of the following features:

>> Dynamic access control

>> Visibility into endpoints, users, cloud apps, and data

>> Protects data at rest or in motion

>> Policy control, threat identification, and investigation

Using an SASE solution such as this creates an environment like one that has a perimeter, such as a local- or wide-area network, except that this includes diverse cloud infrastructure and mobile workers from a large array of devices. This is known as a *software-defined wide-area network* (SDWAN).

You might also take a look at Netskope www.netskope.com/, one of the market leaders in the CASB marketplace.

Identifying user behavior

One way that risk is mitigated in a SASE solution is by using AI to understand user behavior and identifying possible risk at every endpoint. This is different from traditional cybersecurity, which tends to provide security through deep scans comparing results against malware profiles. Because malware changes by the minute, the databases of malware information are quickly outdated, making them nearly useless. With AI, it's like having a grade school teacher at the head of the class with their back turned. The teacher hears talking and immediately knows who is speaking, based on previous behavior. There's no need for the ubiquitous question of "Who's talking?"

Combine anomalous user behavior with app, device, and network threat detection, and you have a powerful security barrier. Having it all combined into a single solution means that you avoid the risk of overlooking security policies between multiple security software applications. A single and consistent solution operates seamlessly over many different cloud types and networks.

Carrying out forensic investigations

After an attack, network security operations need telemetry data, logs, and running audits to find the source of the attack and harden the network against future attacks.

Hackers almost always leave footprints, and progress toward eliminating attacks is possible only when you have the right information from all your network-connected devices.

REMEMBER

When you consider the amount of money companies spend on network security, hackers funded by criminals spend considerably more to defeat it.

Using a managed service provider

You may be using some or all the technologies that make up the SASE framework. An option to doing it all yourself is to outsource this complicated task to a managed service provider. AT&T (www.att.com) offers a SASE-managed service provider plan. Using this plan allows you to

>> Reach your security goals faster

>> Enable scaling

>> Outsource expensive and manpower-intensive 24/7 monitoring

>> Take advantage of the security solutions and expertise of a large company

You can choose to have a managed service provider like AT&T fully manage or co-manage your SDWAN.

Getting Certified

It doesn't do much good to spend time, money, and effort on developing rock-solid network security if the people you do business with have not taken a similar path. But how do you know? One way is by achieving a network security certification. When you have such a certification, other businesses will know that you've jumped through all the hoops and dotted all the i's. It also makes it easier, particularly if your company must comply with security regulations, to know exactly what level of security your vendors or partner companies might have.

ISO 27001 Compliance

ISO/IEC 27001 is an international standard of managing information security. You can voluntarily choose to have your organization certified as compliant with this recognized standard. As with most certifications, publishing your compliance means that other organizations trust your security efforts in protecting not only your own data but theirs as well. See Figure 5-4.

When your business is larger than a few desks by the window, you can limit which parts of your organization carry an ISO 27001 certification. It's not necessary that every part of the business comply with the standard. It can be limited to a single business unit.

Businesses that carry ISO 27001 certification make themselves better suited to be trusted business partners.

Business A carries ISO 27001.

Business B trusts Business A with private data.

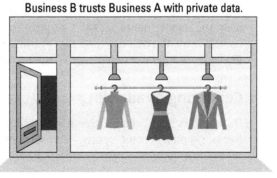

FIGURE 5-4: Certification leads to better B2B information security trust.

SOC 2 compliance

The SOC 2 certification (short for System and Organization Controls 2 certification, as opposed to the System and Organization Controls 1 certification) was created by the American Institute of CPAs (AICPA). Figure 5-5 shows the five pillars of SOC 2 certification. Each auditing company provides its own certification logo upon successful certification that your company can then proudly display.

FIGURE 5-5:
The five pillars of
SOC 2
certification.

Certifying security

SOC 2 audits make certain your business complies with reasonable levels of access security. Auditors check for

>> Protection against system abuse

>> Protection against data theft or unauthorized deletion

>> Software security

>> Methods to protect against unauthorized information disclosure

Implementing the tools of an SASE-compliant network enables your company to meet the requirements of SOC 2 security compliance. The tools auditors look for include intrusion detection, access controls, and firewalls — traditional as well as Firewalls as a Service when your company employs complex cloud environments.

Certifying availability

Data centers have been certifying availability for many years. You often see promises of 99.999 percent uptime. The services your company provides need to be able to guarantee uptime (availability) by having in place all the right service level agreements — contracts that guarantee availability and the infrastructure necessary to make all that happen. The infrastructure can include disaster recovery, failover plans, and security incident response teams.

Availability simply means you can get to the programs you need; it doesn't mean the applications run well or run bug-free. That is handled by the next SOC 2 pillar.

Certifying processing integrity

Do your applications deliver as promised? You need to show that they operate accurately and securely, and that data handling meets expected standards. If your development team uses a good DevOps and DataOps model, chances are high that your applications will meet the standards required for SOC 2 certification.

REMEMBER

Being able to show that your applications are operating securely via monitoring is important for both compliance and certification.

Certifying confidentiality

When access to data is restricted to a person or group of people, it's considered confidential. The levels of confidentiality you need depend completely on the nature of the data. Governments maintain standards of confidentiality for government data, the same as you will be expected to maintain standards of confidentiality. Chapter 1 goes into more detail about applying risk assessments to data release.

Not all confidential data can be found in a database. Your company maintains all sorts of confidential information from internally protected business plans, intellectual property, and accounting data. Certification checks to see how this type of information is being protected.

Certifying privacy

Personal information and its collection, distribution, and use should be carefully controlled within your company. Some government compliance regulations, such as those in the EU, demand careful control over private data. At the very least, your public-facing website should have a privacy policy, and your company should be careful to honor it.

Certification will likely involve the Generally Accepted Privacy Principles, or GAPP. You can download a document describing those guidelines here:

www.michigan.gov/documents/dmb/GAPP_2009_327570_7.pdf

PCI certification

PCI certification audits your use and protection of credit card data. When your company stores credit card data, auditors ensure that you're using best practices for security and dissemination. This includes firewalls, encryption, and antimalware at its most basic levels.

Your monitoring system must ensure that only authorized people have access to credit card information. Even customers who make use of credit card processing systems must ensure a level of PCI compliance. (For more on PCI compliance, see "Complying with PCI" earlier in this chapter.)

There are four levels of PCI compliance:

>> Level 1: Greater than 6 million credit card transactions a year

>> Level 2: Between 1 million and 6 million credit card transactions a year

>> Level 3: 20,000 to 1 million transactions a year

>> Level 4: Greater than 20,000 transactions a year

The highest levels of PCI compliance require annual security audits and quarterly scans by an approved scanning vendor (ASV). Lower levels must submit to an annual assessment and quarterly scans.

This chapter covers compliance and certification when dealing with complex cloud systems securely. Following the guidelines of compliance, whether your company is required to comply with regulations or not, goes a long way toward ensuring that your company is well protected against data theft and loss. Chapter 6 goes into greater detail in managing your cloud resources. Knowing which resources your company uses and where they are helps you gain visibility into your network.

2

Acceptance

Chapter **6**

Managing Cloud Resources

Y ou probably adhere to best practices when it comes to the security of your network and devices that attach to your network. Making the move to include cloud resources into the mix will require that you make a paradigm shift in your thinking. You must wrap your mind around a great deal more. Incorporating the cloud into your IT world means you've done away with the protected border you've been managing. A new, virtual border must now be envisioned for you to adequately protect your cloud resources. More importantly, because cloud resources are interconnected with your local network, your safely guarded perimeter is no longer safe. Figure 6-1 shows how you may have safely guarded your local network but many of the resources your company uses are out in the cloud somewhere and you are responsible for security because these resources reach inside your network.

Managing cloud resources will give you visibility over the applications and tools you use in the cloud and how they integrate with services you use in your local data center or within company departments. For small companies, this is a fairly straightforward task, but for larger enterprises, this job can be overwhelming. This chapter gives you some suggestions on how to best manage a complex cloud environment and how managing cloud resources allows you to create a more secure environment.

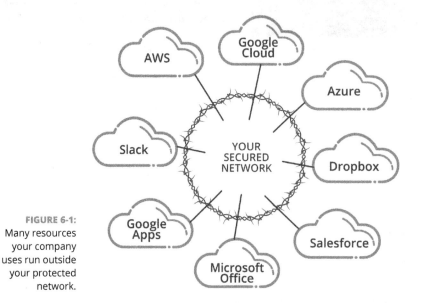

FIGURE 6-1:
Many resources
your company
uses run outside
your protected
network.

Defending Your Cloud Resources from Attack

Before you can start protecting cloud resources, you have to know what they are. In Chapter 2, I talk about some of the various types of cloud services on the market — that alphabet soup of "things as a service," including SaaS, PaaS, IaaS, and several others. In addition to this, clouds are often used to run applications that are either not offered as a service to others or are generally not web applications, where web browsers serve as the front-ends. For example, you may run an accounting system application that runs on a cloud-based server that only specific people within your company can access.

Another commonly used cloud resource is data storage. This might be in the form of file storage, like Dropbox, MediaFire, Google Drive, or any one of a number of commercial file storage services. You may use a different type of data storage that involves storage of database files. This generally also involves using a cloud DBMS or a DBMS that can be configured to access data in the cloud, such as ORACLE.

REMEMBER

One well-known cloud storage solution is Amazon Web Service's Simple Storage Service, known as AWS S3. You may have heard of an S3 bucket. AWS refers to its storage containers as *buckets*. Unlike real-world buckets, the AWS versions are elastic; they stretch and shrink to meet demand.

Buckets have built-in access control to limit who can gain access to objects stored in the bucket. But security isn't limited to the default access control. You can add these items:

>> AWS Identity and Access Management (IAM), an access control system that also manages user permissions

>> Object-level access control lists

>> Security policy management at the bucket level

>> Audit logs for researching access after the fact

>> Amazon Macie (Amazon's own data security and data privacy service), which can detect when sensitive data is being transferred

TECHNICAL STUFF

Data stored in buckets can be accessed using a REST API. This makes connecting it to applications that use it simple, but using an API comes with its own security concerns. A REST API has user credentials that are authenticated whenever a request is sent from the client to the server. These credentials must be carefully managed.

WARNING

When using a REST API to access data, credentials are sent with each request.

Living in a Virtual World

Most cloud resources today are *virtual,* meaning that, compared to the past — where setting up new resources meant installing new hardware, an operating system to run on it, and applications to fill out the needs — most of that work you had to do is now somebody else's job, and it's a job they take care of by using technology you don't need to concern yourself with. For example, in the bad old days, a company wanting to set up a new database server would need to complete all the tasks I just listed and then would have to install a DBMS. This device would then require monitoring and physical space in a data center (or closet, depending on the size of the company).

When the need for additional DBMS resources would grow, perhaps during a holiday sales cycle, more hardware would need to be added. Conversely, when the need was no longer there, the machine would then be shut down, or worse, left operational and just not used — posing a huge security threat.

REMEMBER

The greater the landscape, the more chances a hacker will penetrate your security.

Moving to virtualization

Virtualization, simply put, means running applications and full servers in software rather than installed on dedicated hardware. Virtualized resources are installed on hardware, but many emulated resources (for example, servers) can be installed on a single piece of hardware. Each resource can run its own operating system, or enough services to run applications. When these environments are created by an emulation software application known as a *hypervisor*, they're known as *virtual machines (VM)*. Hypervisors can run multiple virtual machines.

When a hypervisor application creates a new virtual machine, a new operating environment is created, or *spun up*. One of the many advantages of virtual machines is that when they're no longer needed, they are simply erased and no longer exist. From a cloud security perspective, this is ideal.

TIP

Virtual machines can also be run on desktop computers. This is a great way to run different operating systems on your desktop computer. (See Figure 6-2.) This is commonly done so that applications can be run in various operating systems for testing purposes by developers.

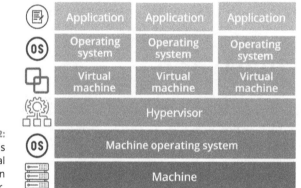

FIGURE 6-2:
Applications running on virtual machines within a hypervisor.

Addressing VM security concerns

Virtual machines run on hardware that has its own operating system. Vulnerabilities that allow remote access to that physical machine may allow someone to access the hypervisor and your virtual machine.

In a cloud environment, virtual machines are running on physical hardware that is generally shared by other customers — usually, running their own virtual machines. It's possible that a security breach in one virtual machine can allow access to the underlying hardware and to the virtual machines belonging to other customers, although cloud service providers promise to do their best to ensure that this doesn't happen. To fully protect yourself from any potential breach involving the underlying hardware and operating system functioning in the cloud or elsewhere, you need to protect your VM and any software defined networks (SDN) you may be using.

The top 3 things you can do to protect your VMs and SDNs are to:

>> Implement good malware software.

>> Limit access to these resources using the principle of least privilege.

>> Implement a CSPM Cloud security posture management system.

Using containers

A *container* is a block of code designed to run a single application without the need for virtualizing an entire operating system. Each time a virtual machine is launched, an entire operating system is placed into the memory of the host computer. Get a few of those running at the same time and you can quickly see the limits of memory becoming a constraint. The more memory efficient container is an executable block of code that contains everything it needs to run an application, including these items:

>> Runtime libraries

>> System tools

>> System libraries

>> System settings

You can think of containers as virtual boxes cleverly packaged with all the necessary files to run. Package containers have the application and its configuration as well as all necessary application dependencies, which means you can avoid the hassle of setting up applications with different libraries, dependencies, and configurations. They are, however, constrained to running on the operating system they were designed for. If they were designed to run on Linux, they can only run in a Linux environment. The same is true for Windows and iOS containers.

REMEMBER

Containers have the advantage of being extremely lightweight, and they run in a plug-and-play manner, whereas a VM — which needs an operating system, libraries, applications, and other dependencies in order to function — can become huge compared to a slimmer container. That makes containers a much better fit than virtual machines when running scalable applications.

Docker containers (www.docker.com), which are the most popular brand of containers, run in both the Linux and Windows server environments. A Docker client is used to run and manage Docker containers. After it's constructed, you can store your container in Docker Hub, a repository service provided by Docker that allows you to easily find and share container images with members of your team. Learn more at https://docs.docker.com/docker-hub.

TIP

You can always implement your containers inside a virtual machine, but many cloud service providers offer a PaaS application for running containerized applications without the need for running a virtual machine.

Securing Cloud Resources with Patch Management

One of the top ways cloud resources are hacked is by running applications where a required security patch has not been applied. Hundreds of applications are commonly used daily and are running in every type of device. Many of these applications connect with servers running in the cloud, which is particularly true of mobile apps. Almost all mobile apps rely on cloud servers to process and store data. Keeping applications patched can be an onerous job and, with the number of applications increasing daily, nearly impossible to keep up with manually.

As with most things in the rapidly changing IT world, responding to change using automation saves considerable time, money, and the unwanted headaches of dealing with situations caused by overlooked tasks, like patch management.

Manage Engine's Desktop Central (www.manageengine.com/products/desktop-central) is an automated patch management application that handles the overwhelming task of ensuring that all your company devices, laptops, desktops and virtual machines are running applications with the most current patches.

Zoho's Patch Management Plus (www.zoho.com/patchmanagerplus) is a cloud-based solution for patch management that includes important applications that get used every day, such as Java, Adobe, and WinRar.

REMEMBER

Some companies have opted to use SaaS applications running in the cloud whenever possible to avoid the hassle of licensing and patch management. In this case, applications are patched by the SaaS vendor taking the burden from you.

Patching VMs and containers

One of your security tasks when running virtual machines and containers is keeping them patched and updated. This is no different from keeping the operating systems of your local computers and networks patched against bugs and possible security holes.

Because VMs come and go, and it's likely you're running more than one, you will want to use the hypervisor software to patch your VMs. This way, they all get patched at the same time and any future VMs you launch will contain all the latest patches.

TIP

Don't overlook the hypervisor — it often needs upgrades and patches.

Implementing patch management

As with VMs and containers, you' need to make certain that your cloud infrastructure is patched, to avoid malware intrusions and hack attempts. Patches are provided by the individual OS developers. You can scan your cloud environment for required patches. For example, when using AWS, you can scan your EC2 instance, AWS's elastic computing resource, for any required patches.

To begin implementing patch management of your cloud technology, you need an inventory of all applications running in your cloud environment that may need to be updated or patched. This should include operating systems.

TIP

When possible, try to standardize the kinds of cloud applications you use across multiple clouds to make the process of patching them simpler, because they use the same applications. They should all be running the same versions of the software to make patch management standard across several application installations.

When patching operating systems, the cloud service provider you use is sure to have an application that simplifies the patch management process. For example, Google Cloud uses the OS patch management system and AWS employs the AWS Systems Manager Patch Manager. For a company that loves to use acronyms for a name, that's a *long* application name.

REMEMBER

Test your patches in a sandbox before releasing them into production environments. This ensures that changes instituted in the patch don't crash your applications.

Plan your patch updates for a time when your cloud is least used. This can be challenging for enterprises that span the globe. In that case, you might consider planning a rolling patch management schedule. Choose a regular schedule for patch implementation — possibly, monthly. This regular schedule helps ensure that patch management isn't overlooked.

Keeping Your Cloud Assets Straight in Your Mind

Cloud assets are like children: If you have more than one, they need a name to distinguish one from another. They also tend to misbehave, need constant supervision, and, when treated right, provide years of services like washing the dishes and mowing the lawn. Now that you know this information, saying that tags are metadata assigned to resources might make you realize that giving kids a name is like assigning metadata to them.

Tagging, a term that should now be used to refer to naming your children, is an important step in managing cloud resources. Tagging resources allows your IT team to

>> Quickly locate and identify cloud resources

>> Promote cloud resources among enterprise departments by name

>> Create better visibility for resource management and security

Looking more closely at tags, you can see how useful they are. You often see tags used to describe products online. You may have seen tags accompanied by a hashtag (#). Tags are useful for searching large amounts of data and retrieving information based on a specific tag. If you were looking through products and wanted only blue-colored products, you might search on *#blue.* If you're looking for garden products, you might search on *#garden* or combine them to search for blue garden supplies. This same idea works for identifying cloud resources.

A tag for a cloud resource might identify it as a database engine (dbms), or as a marketing application with the tag marketing. Each tag is applied to give more meaning and understanding to what an asset is, what it does, who owns it, and what its security risk might be, and, of course, to give it a name so that it's easily identified.

TIP

When tagging cloud resources, the hashtag generally isn't used.

A resource usually has more than a single tag. Yes, these additional tags are like middle names but far more meaningful. For example, data resources can be tagged, letting you know the security level and how the data is disseminated. Here are some sample tags:

» **Public:** Used when sharing data with the public unrestricted.

» **General:** Used normally for business data that is not sensitive but also not generally shared to the public.

» **Confidential:** Business data kept close to the vest, and generally not shared outside the business or with "just anyone" in the business.

» **Taboo:** Maybe a little silly and better tagged as secret or highly confidential. Polynesians had a law of tabu and if you broke the law, you probably didn't live to make the same mistake. Great tag. Use it!

Tags can be applied to many different cloud resources. Virtual machines can be tagged. After giving them a name, think about tags that describe their function. This might mean tagging as accounting a virtual machine containing an accounting system. Virtual machines can also have a security tag like the ones just described. This allows you to quickly see when a VM might contain sensitive data and need extra protection.

Tags can be name/value pairs. This is when you have a tag name such as Tier followed by a value Web. This is normally written as Tier = Web. Using name value pairs allows you to create powerful and creative tags. One tag you might consider using is an ownership tag, as in owner = marketing. Of course, you can use name/value pairs to clearly call out any security concerns:

» Impact = high

» Impact = moderate

» Impact = light

This is an example of the same name with different values being used as a tag. It's easy to see how powerful tagging becomes in identifying cloud resources with tags, particularly using name/value pairs.

REMEMBER

Many cloud environments that support tags are case-sensitive. It's a good idea to make your tags all lowercase so that they're simpler to use.

Figure 6-3 shows a contrived sample of what an AWS tagging resource looks like. The selected highlighted resource has the name/value (or, in this case, the key/value pair values) on the right with the corresponding tag on the left.

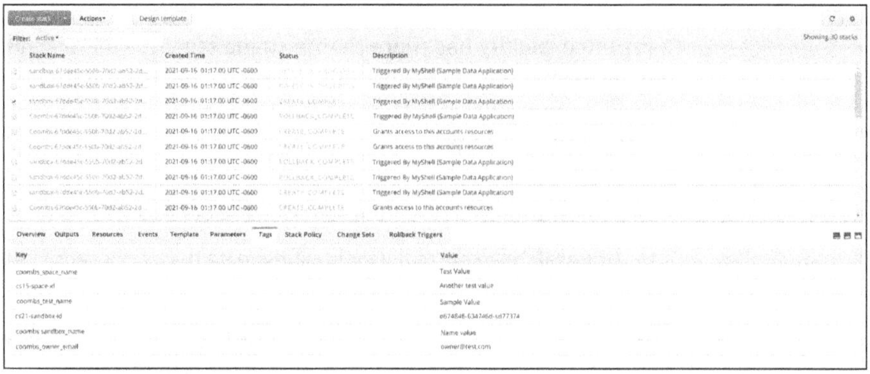

FIGURE 6-3:
Sample of an
AWS tagging
resource.

Tags are stored using many different forms but for simplicity you can use some of the industry favorites, such as JSON or XML. Here is how a tag might appear in this format:

$tags = @{"owner"= "marketing"; "security"= "moderate", "use"= "sales"}

In this example, `owner`, `security`, and `use` are names, and `marketing`, `moderate`, and `sales` are the associated values.

Keeping Tabs with Logs

Logs are often overlooked gems full of important information on the status of your services and applications. Keeping logs literally lets your services and applications communicate their health and safety status to you. Like many software resources, cloud resources generally maintain logs of their activity. These log files are important tools in discovering when and how someone may have breached your network and accessed one or more of the cloud services.

Though the topic of logs and audit files seems less than exciting, you may soon learn how important these concepts are when you start using some of the newer AI tools that alert you to potential breaches — or even send you alerts about problems before they become breaches. These tools can tell you not only which applications are affected but also which customers are being impacted.

Using Google Cloud Management software

Cloud Logging (https://cloud.google.com/logging) is a managed service that lets you manage application logs hosted in Google Cloud. Not only does this Google

Cloud management software let you read through the logs of your standard applications, but you can also read log data from custom applications. This is a powerful resource because many applications that are run today are written for in-house use, or for business-specific requirements. Google Cloud Logging allows you to

>> **Read log data in real time.** This action is important if you're monitoring applications that may be throwing up flags alerting you to potential breaches.

>> **Handle extremely large log files.** Many heavily used applications can create log files in the exabyte size. That's a billion gigabytes. It will ingest a terabyte per second.

Yet another Google log application, Logs Explorer in the Google Cloud Console, gives you fine-grained access to your logs, allowing you to manually view your log data in a powerful web dashboard. This feature of the cloud console lets you search and analyze your log data using built-in analytics tools such as the Query-builder. You can access this same data from other custom or third-party applications through the Logging API. The Logging API gives you access to these same features in your custom applications through this application programming interface. You can also build custom applications using the Cloud SDK (Software Development Kit).

Using AWS log management

AWS also has a power logging application known as Elasticsearch `https://aws.amazon.com/log-analytics/`. This AWS service allows you to collect log data, index it, and unify log data from logs across your entire AWS environment.

Elasticsearch has built-in integration with some of the other AW'S applications such as Kineses Data Firehose, Kafka, KMS, Cognito, IAM and CloudWatch.

Amazon CloudWatch lets you monitor logs from all your AWS servers and applications. You can view your logs, search them for keywords and error codes, or search by specific fields. CloudWatch archives your logs so that they can be searched later when you need to do analysis to identify the source of a malware incident. It saves your log data indefinitely, or you can specify a period between one day and ten years after which the log data is erased.

Log data from AWS CloudTrail includes calls made to the AWS Management Console, the command line interface (CLI) and many of the other AW'S services. These logs are then sent to an S3 bucket of your choice. More importantly, you can log calls into the Identity and Access Management (IAM) system.

Log all data from your social media streams, application logs, market data feeds, and others through the AWS Kinesis Data Streams application, which allows you to collect and process large data streams in real time, or at least have them available in less than a second. From this data collection service, you can build custom applications to process your data or use one of the third-party services I cover later in this chapter. If you choose to build your own applications, you might consider using the AWS Lambda Service.

TECHNICAL STUFF

The AWS Lambda web service allows you to build functions that process real-time data in a highly scalable and self-managed system that doesn't require you to run a separate server to run your code. With these functions, you can build triggers that alert you whenever your log data contains specific information.

You can also use the AWS Centralized Logging dashboard application (https://aws.amazon.com/solutions/implementations/centralized-logging/). This application lets you organize and analyze log data collected in the CloudTrail log system. You can gather log data from several AWS accounts into this application, giving you more visibility into the entire landscape of your AWS cloud environment. Use the open-source OpenSearch service (https://opensearch.org), which includes a set of visualization and analytics tools, to view and analyze your AWS log data. Figure 6-4 is an Amazon suggested layout for your logging system.

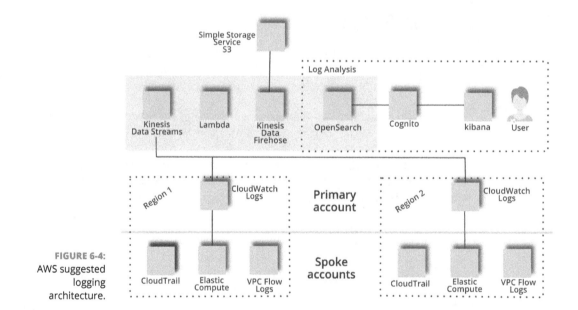

FIGURE 6-4: AWS suggested logging architecture.

Using Azure log management

Azure, Microsoft's cloud service, also has its own log management system. Azure Monitor Logs is part of the Azure Monitor application, which manages your log and system performance data from the following sources:

>> **Resource logs:** Manages logs from the many built-in Azure resources. A list of the Azure services can be found here: `https://azure.microsoft.com/en-us/services`.

>> **Activity logs:** Provides log data from all your Azure subscription services

>> **Azure Active Directory logs:** Sign-in activity made using the Azure Active Directory service

Using the Log Analytics in the Azure portal, you can create queries that search your log data. Critical to rapid response, an alert can notify network operations when something has gone wrong and starts sending error messages to the log. Additionally, you can program in automated remediation routines that are triggered by log alerts. This powerful ability can save your team considerable time when managing your cloud application security. For example, if an application is complaining about disk space, you can automate the process of adding additional disk space, one of the nice features of using a cloud.

WARNING

The Microsoft Azure cloud system has a vulnerability called OMIGOD. (Yes, that's its name; it's not a joke.) Opting into Azure distributed logging installs a service in your virtual machine known as Open Management Interface, or OMI. This server-like service listens on a network port, and normally requires authentication. Bugs in the service allowed unauthenticated users to act as the root user and issue commands.

Working with third-party log management software

Many businesses provide log management across one or many different cloud environments. When your company has focused on a specific cloud service, you can choose to use the built-in services provided by the cloud service provider or select a third-party service that provides an automated way to alert you whenever things are operating outside the norm.

Using a third-party log management service has the added benefit of being cloud neutral, accepting log data from several or many different cloud services.

ManageEngine (www.manageengine.com) has an application called Cloud Security Plus, which manages log data from AWS, Azure, and Google Cloud platforms as well as uses activity from Salesforce. The application has a dashboard that allows you to view critical event information and alerts, as well as predefined reports that include information such as user activity or changes to network security groups, virtual networks, application gateways, DNS zones databases, and storage accounts. With all its features, Cloud Security Plus is able to simplify even the most complex logging environments, such as AWS.

One of the best ways to manage your AWS logs is to use the information that Cloud Security Plus collects from Amazon EC2 logs, S3 server access logs, and AWS CloudTrail logs to detect attempts by malware to breach your cloud services. These logs include actions such as

>> User logins

>> Application events

>> Web application firewalls

>> Relational database services

>> Security token services

>> AWS elastic block store

>> AWS virtual private cloud (more on private clouds in Chapter 9)

>> AWS elastic load balancer

>> AWS Simple Storage Service (S3)

When events occur that are out of the ordinary, this service sends you an email message alerting you to a possible breach or security threat.

Logging containers

In the world of cloud virtual computing, many applications run in virtual containers, the most popular of which is a Kubernetes container. A Kubernetes container contains no logging storage solutions of its own. Application messages are simply sent to stdout and stderr outputs, making them nearly useless.

TECHNICAL STUFF

Stdout and stderror are the machine destinations for messages being sent from within an application. In some cases, this could mean, "send these messages straight to the computer monitor. These messages need to be captured and sent to a log file for storage."

Kubernetes, a container-orchestration system, manages its applications as pods — a group of containerized components. Because of the ephemeral nature of these pods, if they are deleted or they crash, all data that was part of that pod is gone forever. For this reason, you want to build a cluster-level logging system or some type of centralized log management solution. This system needs to collect log data from many different pods running on many different machines.

For a more powerful logging capability, you might consider using one of the many third-party logging solutions that work with Kubernetes containers. One of these applications is called Sematext (`https://sematext.com`), which uses an agent to collect log data from several containers and send it to a central location for storage. It then provides a powerful dashboard for log analysis.

TIP

Institute cluster-level logging that sends your log data to an external storage location for further processing. If a container crashes and eliminates your ability to view your applications, you can still view the log data the applications generated.

Building Your Own Defenses

Occasionally, the kinds of defenses you need you can't get out-of-the-box and you need to build them yourself. This type of development should be undertaken only when absolutely necessary. Security development is costly and can be filled with its own security concerns. Some of the concerns you face include the types of people you will want on your development team and whether to start from scratch or begin your development using an open-source software application as a starting point.

Creating your development team

Building the right development team can be a complex venture before you even get started with actual development. Your team needs skills and knowledge in areas such as these:

>> Security software development

>> Encryption

>> Compliance regulations related to your business

>> Cloud security and local perimeter security

>> Development in a continuous delivery/continuous integration environment

Consider using a trusted in-house team to do your development. This strategy lowers the risk of your security being compromised later. If you choose to use a contractor, however, be sure to do a little background investigation on the contractor before handing them the keys to your security. Though some of the greatest developers live in other countries, it isn't always wise to hand over encryption keys or access to private data when you can't guarantee the security of their systems or know their intentions. Contractual agreements such as NDAs have little possibility of enforcement across borders. There can be a huge trust factor that may even be governed by regulations.

You can build a hybrid team of both in-house and contract developers if you feel more comfortable sharing the development load and security concerns. You can always set up permissions so that less trusted development staff have no access to your most sensitive information.

TIP

Use the zero trust strategy when building your teams, giving access to private data only when necessary.

In some cases — for example, dealing with PCI governed financial data — developers are required to be PCI certified. Some compliance regulations don't require this level of certification (HIPAA, for example.) In these cases, you need to use your best efforts at protecting this private data, even from your own development team. It's possible to develop using obscured data.

Using open-source security

Though many cybersecurity defense applications are on the market, sometimes you may want to implement some of your own applications to protect your cloud resources. You don't have to start from scratch. There are many open-source projects you can install and modify for your own needs.

TIP

Get started with open-source security development by using NSA-released open-source projects found at https://code.nsa.gov. You can also find open-source projects by the hundreds on GitHub. For example, you can find a handy antivirus project for AWS buckets at https://github.com/widdix/aws-s3-virusscan. (If you go to this particular project's home page at https://bucketav.com, you can find pricing for the commercial version of this project. You can choose either one, depending on your constraints.

REMEMBER

Many companies still have constraints against using open-source software because it generally doesn't have a lot of support. When using open-source applications, whether complete applications or blocks of code within your own codebase, keep track of where it's used. This is sometimes required during security audits.

Protecting your containers

Protecting the applications that run in your containers is vital. You can find a number of open-source applications that will scan and monitor your containers. You can make use of these applications as they exist or choose to extend them using your own development team. I recommend checking out these products:

» **Anchore Engine:** When you want to scan your Docker containers for vulnerabilities, consider using Anchore Engine (`https://github.com/anchore/anchore-engine`), itself a Docker container image. It has additional plug-ins you can add after it's installed, or you can build your own.

» **Dagda:** Dagda (`https://github.com/eliasgranderubio/dagda`) performs analyses of malware, Trojans, and other vulnerabilities targeting Docker containers. It monitors the Docker daemon, looking for suspicious behavior. This is installed as part of the Sysdig Falco security system, a Kubernetes threat detection system. Sysdig (`https://sysdig.com`) has a number of open-source applications for secure cloud operations.

» **Falco:** Falco (`https://github.com/falcosecurity/falco`) is a cloud-native runtime security tool. This open-source project has the important ability to scan inside containers, looking for vulnerabilities and sending alerts if suspicious activity is detected.

» **Clair:** Clair, a RedHat (`www.redhat.com`) open-source project, scans containers for vulnerabilities based on the Common Vulnerabilities and Exposures database (CVE). When new vulnerabilities are added to the database, the Clair application already knows when your containers are vulnerable, without doing an additional scan.

» **OpenSCAP:** OpenSCAP (`https://github.com/OpenSCAP/container-compliance`) scans containers for compliance with the NIST SCAP Security Content Automation Protocol, a set of community-derived specifications. Learn more about this specification at `https://csrc.nist.gov/projects/security-content-automation-protocol`.

Protecting your codebase

Many distributed development teams, particularly those that participate in open-source projects, make use of GitHub (`https://github.com`) to store their source code in a repository that allows for distributed check-in and check-out of code. Because these projects are often used by many others, hackers scan these projects, looking for potentially insecure information such as API credentials that they can exploit to gain access to systems.

GitHub, however, isn't the only Git in town. There's also Gitrob (`https://github.com/michenriksen/gitrob`), which clones your repository and scans it for potentially insecure information such as credentials or other sensitive information left inadvertently in your code made public. Finally, there is Git-secrets (`https://github.com/awslabs/git-secrets`), another scanning tool you can use to catch potentially sensitive information before it's even uploaded into your Git repository, catching it during *commits* — that step when changes made by your developers are uploaded and saved to a source code repository like Git.

Chapter **7**

The Role of AIOps in Cloud Security

One of the blessings (and curses) of cloud computing is that it's decentralized. It's a blessing because it allows for edge computing, bringing your applications and processing closer to the customer wherever they happen to be in the world. It's a curse because decentralization makes securing cloud infrastructure more difficult and more complex.

With the complexity of cloud resources, the IT world has also needed to cope with the challenge of managing the security of Internet of Things (IoT) devices, monitoring mobile devices of all sorts and flavors, and now meeting the challenge of security of people working from home (which has become a real thing). Figure 7-1 doesn't even begin to show the complexity faced by an IT operations team in managing its resources.

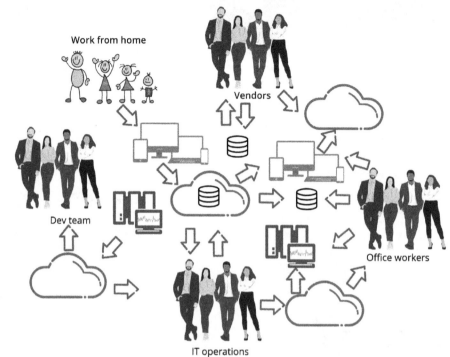

Taking the AIOps Route

The level of complexity Figure 7-1 hints at didn't just happen overnight. It took *decades* of technology enhancements to create this mess. The one thing that was supposed to make everyone's lives simpler (technology) has made it increasingly complicated. Just ask any 85-year-old person whether they'd rather have a smartphone or an old push button phone.

What is needed is a tool that sits above all that mess and can help manage the growing complexity using artificial intelligence to make sense of it all. AIOps, or artificial intelligence for IT operations, is just such a tool. It

- ❯❯ Collects data from devices and applications
- ❯❯ Uses big data technologies to find patterns in the collected data
- ❯❯ Collates the data from logs, alerts, and response data from monitoring tools
- ❯❯ Assists IT operations in quickly identifying root causes of problems
- ❯❯ Finds potential problems before they become problems and alerts operations teams or fixes problems on its own using automation

IT departments are typically overwhelmed with the day-to-day help desk response. They are responding to issues as they arrive on their desk rather than being able to truly manage all that's going on within their enterprises. The larger the business, the larger the chaos. This puts a highly skilled team of people in the position of doing things that suck the life out of them rather than use years of knowledge to create better systems and innovate — like people in departments other than IT. Giving them a tool that simplifies their job and frees them to be creative again adds an incredible resource to your business.

REMEMBER

AIOps doesn't replace tools you may already use — instead, it's a process that orchestrates the data coming from many tools and data sources to create a more comprehensive view of your environment.

The *AI* in AIOps is short for *artificial intelligence*, which is a huge and multifaceted field. The branch of AI most used by AIOps is machine learning, which is the ability to analyze massive sets of data (big data) and answer questions about what has been digested, and constantly improving its answers from user feedback or its own ability to improve based on its ability to achieve goals.

Two types of learning are employed by machine learning:

>> **Supervised:** Uses structured data and has the ability to check its answer. It then autocorrects, giving a better answer each time.

>> **Unsupervised:** There is no expected outcome to check against. An example might be examining data in a log file to look for common occurrences and reporting when applications or devices are operating out of the ordinary. It can also find associations or links between problems and outcomes.

Machine learning in AIOps can speed normally complicated and time-consuming tasks such as correlating alerts that might occur during a cloud breach. When things go wrong, alerts might come at you from many sources and, at first glance, they may not appear to be coming from the same problem. AIOps correlates these alerts and shows dependencies. (I talk more about dependencies later in this chapter.)

One of the most time-consuming tasks for operations professionals is finding the root cause of a problem. AIOps can normally locate the root cause and even offer suggestions on how to fix the problem based on which of your efforts succeeded in the past. Some advanced versions of AIOps can use another form of AI that can read journal articles, gaining insights on how you might correct your problem. Figure 7-2 shows the process used in various stages of AIOps incident resolution.

FIGURE 7-2:
AIOps will
detect, prioritize,
assign, diagnose,
resolve, and
self-improve,
getting smarter
all the time.

Efficient IT operations require communication between the stakeholders of an organization. AIOps becomes the shared workspace that leads to a shared understanding of the issue at hand and where people and resources can be brought to bear to fix a problem. This type of cooperation between people in different disciplines can bring about greater efficiency within your company.

Before getting into the nitty-gritty of problem-solving with AIOps, it helps to understand that one of the major features generally included within enterprise AIOps systems are communications systems that allow for sharing messages and key diagnostic information between stakeholders. This system is also how the AIOps platform will communicate with the team and automatically assigns tasks.

Detecting the problem

The old Commodore 64 game *Pirates* would continually announce, "Your island is under attack." This is the kind of anomaly detection you want. AIOps has pattern detection tools that detect system behaviors outside the norm. Watching CPU rates and comparing them to historical data is one example of how machine learning algorithms can detect anomalies. This type of automated detection reduces the workload of manual observation. Also, with automated threshold adjustments, there is no longer a need to program hard-coded rules.

REMEMBER

When everything changes in an IT environment second by second, it's impossible to manually set thresholds. Allowing AIOps to dynamically set thresholds by examining change and demand means that you get fewer false positives. Thresholds can also be set to change based on seasonal or temporal demand. If you're providing services that have specific peaks and valleys, there is no reason that your thresholds should not change accordingly.

Using the pattern recognition capability of AI, your system can detect anomalous behavior that can indicate machine failure or hacking attempts. The AIOps dashboard can provide you with an intelligent analysis of how a problem first started and show you how it has progressed over time, even showing you what systems are being impacted by the anomalous behavior. An example of this type of pattern recognition is when a security patch is applied by the DevOps team and performance alerts start showing up in many systems impacted by the change that was made. Receiving a fully correlated alert that links all the alerts helps the operator spot the most likely root cause that initiated the alerts. DevOps might then need to repatch or roll back the previous patch.

Using dynamic thresholds

When you have a dynamic business that changes with certain business cycles such as seasonal holidays, your expected IT thresholds also change with the season. AIOps gives you the ability to set dynamic thresholds that can change from hour to hour or seasonally to create a smarter system that isn't sending alerts when a normally expected increase in load or usage occurs.

TIP

False alerts aren't the only factor that can add to an operator's workload: Dynamic thresholds can save you from looking through many false alerts. Responding to alerts coming from many systems over a single failure can be overwhelming.

Another way thresholds are determined in some AIOps systems is by maintaining Big Data systems full of anonymized data from companies like yours. Matching the thresholds your systems use to report errors with those of like businesses makes setting the threshold (an onerous task) much easier. The learning algorithms can continually improve and learn how to make your systems run better, and the feedback can also help others improve their systems.

Catching attacks early in the Cyber Kill chain

The Cyber Kill chain refers to the phases of a cyber attack. Most intrusions don't end with the intruder simply gaining entry into your network. There is usually a next step — finding data to steal, for example. Early in the chain of events, you need to determine where the attacks come from, or how they got into your network in the first place. Not all attacks are *external*, meaning that attackers, though physically elsewhere, might already have control of systems within your network. A great deal of cybersecurity effort is spent keeping the wrong people out of your network, but when — not if — attackers make their way in, you want to be able to recognize the attack and respond as quickly as possible.

Deep learning can be trained to recognize failure patterns and mitigate them. This AI can

>> **Detect patterns in the malicious traffic:** The AI learns, even when under attack, to better recognize attacks in the future.

>> **Update block lists:** Updating blocklists helps defend your systems and others against similar future attacks from the same IP addresses.

Prioritizing incidents

Not everything is critical! It's important to get a handle on which incidents need your immediate attention and which can wait for remediation. Being able to prioritize means that you know the impact of an incident. Who is it affecting, and what kinds of damage is it doing to systems or your reputation?

REMEMBER

AIOps, with its 50,000-foot view of the problem, gives you the best view of which systems are being affected by any particular incident and the levels of risk involved. The section "Managing Resources, CMDB-Style," later in this chapter, explains how this tool can be used to note the dependencies, relationships, and potential impacts of an incident. Armed with this information, you can easily prioritize problem resolution.

Assigning tasks

When your organization is moving at digital speeds, routine task creation is essential. This frees your staff to focus on high-value tasks. Let the IT staff oversee the AI and improve its ability to do the job. The machine learning can also be applied to learning the history of how tasks have been assigned, allowing it to automatically make intelligent task assignments.

TIP

People are resources, too. When creating your list of resources, make sure you include the people who play a role in each stage of problem discovery and resolution.

One huge benefit provided by AIOps is its ability to categorize an alert and assign it to the right team, group, or person. This doesn't replace the problem manager and the problem management process — it *assists* them.

Machine learning builds patterns of behavior using historical data. With this historical understanding, AI can help with categorizing tasks based on how tasks were handled in the past.

TIP

The challenge of finding the right assignment group is reduced by making the task more specific. This strategy also reduces the sheer number of tasks being assigned.

This automated task assignment frees the problem manager from being responsible for problem categorization and assignment and gives them the freedom to spend their time training and refining the machine learning algorithm based on their personal experience.

Diagnosing the root problem

One of the best things AI does is find patterns, and it is precisely this capability that is used to find patterns in your alert data using a machine learning algorithm. AIOps correlates these patterns with other data, such as change data and system performance data, and what you end up with is a *powerful* triage system. When alerts do appear, they appear as a single, primary alert rather than as a series of disconnected alerts. From this primary alert, you can drill down into more detail regarding all related alerts.

REMEMBER

You can't fix a problem when you don't know what's causing it.

Getting to the root cause of incidents is what it's all about. The root causes may cross several IT disciplines like security, storage, networking, and databases. AIOps correlates data from each of these systems to give you the best possible chance at quickly solving the problem.

Reducing time to MTTR

Somehow the Mean Time To Resolution (MTTR) is appropriate because what really matters (MaTTeRs) is how quickly you can solve problems that arise. You don't want your operations team spending long hours, days, or weeks trying to resolve issues that can damage your company's reputation and suck the soul out of your operations team. AIOps, with all its insights and abilities, can drastically reduce the time it takes to resolve problems.

REMEMBER

Problem resolutions involving cloud security can impact many of your company departments that might be relying on applications or data in the cloud. Rapid resolution times are critical.

Spotting transitory problems

When your IT environment is changing at digital speeds, it's tough to find problems that may appear transitory at first but later prove to be symptoms of larger problems. For example, a hard drive might be experiencing intermittent glitches that progress over time.

Sometimes alerts are spread out over a long period and a human operator may not notice the steady trend toward potential failure or system degradation. Temporal alert patterns are readily seen and responded to by AIOps.

Digging into the past

AIOps can provide data from past incidents as well as historical metrics and insights into alert notifications. This guides the operator in understanding the conditions underlying the root cause. AIOps have the ability to gather data from tools that cross a number of disciplines.

One of the most significant advances in artificial intelligence in the past few years has been that natural language processing has finally become useful. Natural language processing (or NLP, not to be confused with neurolinguistic programming) allows humans and computers to interact using natural language, whether written or spoken. Not only can we humans now have conversations with an AI, but AI can also read text and draw inferences. In other words, after reading something, the AI application has a pretty good idea of what was said and what it means.

Natural language processing gives AIOps the ability to correlate additional forms of data only found in text in order to uncover insights into problems and their remediation. For example, trouble tickets describe a problem. Their resolutions describe what was done to fix them. Read enough of these tickets and you have a pretty good idea of how similar problems were fixed in the past. This is a powerful feature of AIOps that "shortcuts" a great deal of research and trains the AI to suggest solutions based on past resolutions.

In addition to dealing with trouble tickets, you can use AI to read any number of journal articles, blog posts, security announcements, and any other type of published articles and then correlate the information into useful suggestions — even when your organization has never faced a particular problem in the past. The great thing about this strategy is that the second anything gets published, the AI app has already read it and incorporated the information into its ability to offer assistance.

Knowledge base articles are an important part of the problem management process because they document how problems get solved. They can be used by staff to help troubleshoot and solve problems, thus closing alerts.

Though knowledge base articles are important, they can be time consuming to read, and working your way through them can sometimes make it even more difficult to come up with a solution to the problem. AI can read them instead, using NLP, and derive insight well enough to propose solutions. The proposed solution may involve manual steps you should take, or an automated action recommended within the article.

Solving the problem

Routine problems are best handled by instantaneous and automated routines. Though companies generally build libraries of automated routines, allowing the AI to provide the solution means it's no longer necessary to program the automated response. Canned responses are for canned problems, and environments now change too fast to keep up with the number of problem resolutions that can and should be automated. The AI can handle events itself or adjust workflows and configurations.

AIOps can examine business processes and propose steps in these processes that can be optimized, or possibly suggest a change in organizational structure. Organizational structures change because the underlying responsibilities have shifted. When AI is automating most of the mundane tasks and continually learning how to do it better, the people responsible for those tasks can be moved to more productive positions. A good example of managing the mundane tasks is software license management. Let AIOps manage these issues for you, freeing up the people who now manage software licenses.

Cloud software licenses are generally an issue with PaaS and IaaS systems. When using SaaS applications, licensing generally isn't involved. PaaS and IaaS systems mean that you're responsible for the licenses of applications running on those platforms. Licensing can be challenging because of the way different software companies choose to charge for licenses. For example, licenses can be based on

>> Number of users

>> Number of processors using the software

>> Usage itself (a method that's popular in the world of cloud computing)

Achieving resolution

When given the insights provided by AIOps, operations departments can quickly see the root cause of a problem and, in most cases, receive suggestions on how to repair the problem. These suggestions can come from how your teams have solved the same or similar problems in the past or from how another business has solved the problem and published the solution.

The ability of AIOps to see how problems impact different systems comes from the ability to correlate how resources interact — a topic I cover in greater detail in the section "Managing Resources, CMDB-Style," later in this chapter.

Automating security responses

Security responses can be so sophisticated that automated responses aren't always possible, but in many cases attacks (such as distributed denial of service [DDoS] attacks) can be spotted by an AIOps system monitoring the traffic on your website, which can then respond by performing automated tasks to counter the attack. The AI can spot traffic patterns outside the norm or see a pattern that has already been reported to security response servers.

For example, in a DDoS attack, automated response can

- **>> Detect attacks instantly:** The AIOps system knows the thresholds your website operates within, and when traffic suddenly spikes for no apparent reason, it assumes that the site is under attack.

- **>> Instantly redirect traffic:** Once a DDoS attack has been identified, the offending traffic is redirected away from the web server.

REMEMBER

Machine learning can search past events and learn which tasks were automated previously. This way, it can assist in recommending new tasks for automation based on what it has learned.

Machine learning can also learn from the automated corrective actions that have been applied previously and begin providing insights to operators on what automated actions should be applied to an alert. Most larger companies build libraries of automated responses. This kind of discipline will serve you well.

Because not everything can be automated, humans are still required to handle a great deal of the IT management workload. AIOps can provide operational insights to speed up and improve the response times of human operators. Further reducing their workload by automating mundane event management increases the team's efficiency.

Continually improving

One goal of IT Service Management (ITSM) is continual improvement. ITSM builds customer experience and service quality by way of several software tools. The data collected by these applications is important in managing IT operations and customer support. The goals for continued improvement should include these factors:

>> **A better user experience:** This will make you a hero with the end users.

>> **Issue prevention:** You don't want to solve the same problem more than once, if at all possible.

>> **Improve key performance indicators (KPIs):** ITSM does that by measuring the impact of improvements.

AIOps can examine business processes and either propose steps in these processes that can be optimized or possibly suggest a change in organizational structure. Organizational structures change because the underlying responsibilities have shifted. When AI is automating most of the mundane tasks and continually learning how to do it better, the people responsible for those tasks can be moved to more productive positions.

Making Things Visible

Being able to intelligently manage increasingly complex IT systems with local data centers and cloud resources all begins with visibility. Imagine a dashboard that gives you an intelligent view of every portion of your operation and its status. AIOps doesn't quite have that capability on its own — it gains visibility by ingesting data from many different sources.

Implementing resource discovery

One theme echoed throughout this book is knowing what you need to manage. Doing the work on the front end of the project and using as many team members as possible, you'll want to search your organization to find all the hidden data stores, departmental cloud operations, machines, applications, mobile devices, and even Internet of Things-connected devices. Each of these needs to be managed for optimal cybersecurity, for storage limitations, and for efficiency.

TIP

Overcoming siloed data, particularly when it's stored in the cloud, helps you create a more secure and efficient IT environment. One goal in adopting AIOps is silo-busting: Using a single solution that consolidates your IT tools into a single data model allows you to gain visibility and automate your workflows, and it provides a better experience that improves your team's productivity.

Service maps have long been the method for tracking things such as servers, databases and software applications, network connections, and more. Service maps are difficult to maintain, even more difficult to visualize, and almost never up to date and accurate.

Additionally, your service map may track incidents and events as well as the operation of your network and application efficiency. Managing this level of data is manpower intensive. Historically, all you could do was find the next monitoring application, throw money at the problem, and then add more skilled employees.

REMEMBER

Service maps show how all your applications and resources are interconnected. They also show the health and operational state of the entire system. Service maps commonly show the flow between elements of an IT system such as databases, applications, dependencies, interconnections, services, hosts, and out-of-process services. Good service maps are critical to the successful implementation of AIOps.

Automating discovery

Service maps were once created manually. One benefit of automating discovery is that you can better detect and track configuration changes to infrastructure. It's not something you want to do manually — connected devices, both physical and virtual, change much too quickly to keep track of them, particularly in a cloud environment, where virtual machines and containers are being created and destroyed all the time.

The AWS Cloud Map (`https://aws.amazon.com/cloud-map`) is one way to automate discovery in an AWS environment. Using this application, you can track all your dynamic resources and even create custom names for your applications to make them more meaningful.

Cloud Map tracks not only application resources but also all other resources on which they're dependent, such as databases, object stores, queues, and microservices. Once resources are discovered by Cloud Map, they're checked regularly to determine their health.

When using cloud services other than, or in addition to, AWS, you might consider using a product such as Matilda Cloud (`https://matildacloud.com`) for automated discovery. This app works with AWS, Azure, Oracle Cloud, and Google Cloud.

TIP

In the service map application available for Azure users, see this documentation for more information: `https://docs.microsoft.com/en-us/azure/azure-monitor/vm/service-map`. This application builds a dependency map across all your services, displaying both inbound and outbound connections. It can even identify problems such as the failed network connections your applications are attempting to make.

REMEMBER

Operational efficiency can be improved when processes, such as discovery of new resources, are automated.

ServiceNow (`www.servicenow.com`) offers many applications that support the AIOps environment. The ServiceNow Discovery application automates the discovery of Google Cloud platform components. To take advantage of it, you need to install the Discovery and Service Mapping Patterns app from ServiceNow.

Managing Resources, CMDB-Style

As with most security measures, knowing *what* you're protecting is one of the key steps. There is a technology for doing that, which, though technically not an AIOps solution, is nevertheless an important resource for AIOps to function effectively.

A *configuration management database* (CMDB, for short) is a specialized database used by AIOps in tracking resources. In a system where visibility is everything, a CMDB is crucial to its ability to identify resources and learn more about them. Where are they located? Whom do they belong to? What is their patch status? What kinds of data do they contain? A CMDB not only lists resources but also shows you relationships and dependencies. For example, think of a server running containers that have databases running in them. If the server goes down, these databases also disappear. The CMDB has this information and can show the impact of a failure. Perhaps the databases were the back end of an app the company runs. Loss of these databases would then impact all users of the app.

REMEMBER

A CMDB stores resource information and relationships between resources.

Seeing potential impacts

It's possible to see potential impacts of things that aren't even a full-blown problem yet. For example, a power management device, controlling the power to the server in the previous example, has also been reporting its status. It begins reporting that temperatures are above average and, when the threshold is exceeded, begins sending alerts to the operations staff. When the server fails, an alert is also sent. Customers begin contacting Support and complaining that the app isn't working. The AIOps system can filter the alerts and show the dependencies and quickly point to the root problem of why the app has stopped working: It's a power controller failure. It's even possible to program the AIOps application to switch power controllers and restore the server. Better yet, when a threshold shows a potential problem, the AIOps system can switch power controllers before the server fails and the app never goes down and customers never complain, at least not about the app. All this is possible because the resources were in a CMDB and the relationships between resources were stored there as well.

Adding configuration items

A CMDB contains information about a configuration item (CI) stored in metadata. This includes information such as a unique identifier (see Chapter 6 on the importance of naming things), a long name, tags, the description of the CI, its risk level, and the relationship between CIs. For example, it could specify that Application M, a marketing database, contains a Database XYZ.

When listing CIs in your CMDB, they should include

- » Hardware devices

- » Software applications

- » Networks and communication devices

- » A physical location

- » Detailed information about the CI

- » The names of the people responsible for the CI and their contact information

REMEMBER

Keeping a CMDB up to date should be automated. Old information is useless. Automated inventory discovery is the key to a successful CMDB.

Employing CSDM

The Common Service Data Model (CSDM, for short) is a ServiceNow (www. servicenow.com) framework and set of guidelines for building out your CMDB. This framework employs a specific set of database tables necessary for a powerful CMDB. Learn more about the latest CSDM framework at

    https://community.servicenow.com/community?id=community_
    article&sys_id=b96b84e7db5fd85011762183ca9619c9

Using AIOps

AIOps uses are nearly endless because of its ability to incorporate new tools that provide improved functionality. With the way cloud resources change, this is a particularly important feature of AIOps when protecting an IT network that includes cloud resources. The added complexity of using various cloud resources makes using AIOps a no-brainer.

Gaining insights

One great thing about computers in general, and AI specifically, is that it's always there and always on top of the latest information. New insights are drawn from real-time analysis of event data, remediation solutions, and changes that are being tracked by your integrated change management database.

You want to strive to improve at managing your cloud environment by finding ways to optimize either how you're collecting information, what metrics you're gathering, or what you're automating.

You need to have a goal and you need to know how you're tracking toward that goal. For the tracking part, metrics such as Mean Time To Acknowledgment (MTTA, the time it takes your team to respond to an alert), Mean Time to Repair (MTTR, how long it takes to fix the problem), incident assignment, and SLA attainment can be helpful. When you have AIOps helping you, it gives you the most relevant assistance in attaining your goals by offering continuous insights.

One difficult thing in IT operations using old methods comes from having to draw insights by integrating otherwise siloed information. Your service management (ITSM) applications are great sources of insight. Machine generated data on everything from application response times to storage levels are also important for staying ahead of the game in a proactive manner rather than responding when things hit their limits. Of course, change management is the key, and tying this all together in a machine learning system like AIOps provides powerful and continuous insights.

Examining a wireless networking use case

A good use case for AIOps is wireless networking in commercial settings. These can be complicated scenarios involving radio equipment, routers, firewalls, and, of course, users of all types — mobile, desktop, and unattended IoT devices.

Network routers and gateways report many kinds of data. This includes every time someone tries to log on to the network and the signal strength of the connection. Now imagine devices scattered throughout a football stadium and you're receiving logon-attempt data from hundreds of wireless routers with tens of thousands of people carrying cellphones connecting to these devices, and you can quickly see that this is a big data issue. The AI watches all this data and may spot problems such as a failing router or discover traffic patterns where a single device is overloaded and would work better with more routers added within a location.

A real-world example of how AI can discover networking problems and fix them is when a retail business has wireless routers that receive logon attempts from cellphone users walking past the location. (See Figure 7-3.) AI can help discover that the signal strength from people walking by is lower than those within the facility. The operations team can then adjust the threshold for allowing logon attempts to ignore those with lower signal strength and thus free the network for use by people inside the building.

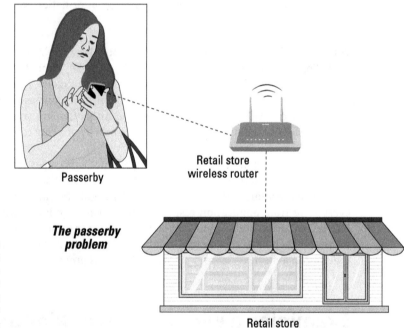

Passerby

Retail store wireless router

The passerby problem

FIGURE 7-3: AIOps can help solve the passerby problem experienced by retail locations.

Retail store

TIP

Don't get in over your head. The best way to bring about a successful AIOps implementation is by focusing on one data source at a time. That way, you can better train the machine learning system, and operators can see the impact of adding a data source and provide feedback that better teaches the AI. One important thing is measurability. Implementing AIOps can be overwhelming. If you can measure your success, you'll see progress and so will the rest of the company.

Using Splunk to Manage Clouds

If you're just getting started with cloud management, Splunk Cloud Observability (`www.splunk.com/en_us/observability.html`) is a great way to get started. Splunk has a more powerful AIOps implementation, with features such as simple-to-use search processing language, apps for creating custom implementations tailored to your AIOps needs, and it is completely scalable. Because it is so customizable and scalable it works in a broad range of IT scenarios and has the ability to change as your company needs change.

Observability

The Splunk platform allows you visibility into any cloud from any vendor. This means you can monitor applications and resources using a web dashboard. Using the Splunk Observability Cloud, you can see a minute-by-minute view of your systems, applications, and other business metrics. Begin by selecting which data source to connect to, as shown in Figure 7-4.

FIGURE 7-4: Select your data sources from the Splunk site.

When selecting a data source, you're notified that you must be an administrator in both your data source and in Splunk Observability Cloud.

TIP

You associate a service account with your cloud service that impersonates the service, becoming the service's default identity. You need the key associated with this service account for Splunk to connect.

Figure 7-5 shows the Splunk Observability platform tracking the number of transactions per second in a demo application.

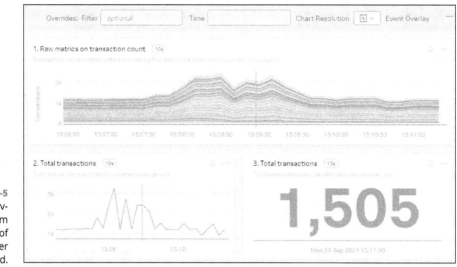

FIGURE 7-5
Splunk Observ-
ability platform
chart of
transactions per
second.

Alerts

Use the Splunk Alert system to set up alerts. When thresholds you've set are reached, you' receive a notification that the threshold has been reached. To use the alert system, you first define a detector, which contains the conditions for the alert. For example, you can set this up to give you an alert for AWS network traffic parameters.

Setting the alert condition includes these factors:

» Static threshold

» Heartbeat check lets you know your resources are still active.

» Resource running out

» Outlier detection

» Sudden change

» Historical anomaly

» Custom threshold

For example, in a heartbeat check, the alert setting might be to send an alert when the resource hasn't reported for 15 minutes. You can even set the severity of the alert — critical, major, minor, warning, and info, for example.

TIP

Use Splunk to assign a list of recipients for a specific alert condition. This way, only the right people are being informed when an alert occurs. Simply activate your defined alert and Splunk is working for you.

Splunk and AIOps

Splunk IT Service Intelligence (ITSI), the IT operations, and the AIOps application serve your AIOps needs by allowing you to monitor your services, apps, and infrastructure and — when things go wrong — help you troubleshoot the problem by telling you what's going wrong.

TIP

When using AWS, you can use Splunk Security Analytics for AWS. Check out the following site for more information:

www.splunk.com/en_us/pdfs/resources/product-brief/Splunk-Splunk-Security-Analytics-for-AWS-PB-106-web.pdf

Predictive analytics

Splunk's ITSI predictive analytics module uses machine learning to create a predicted health score for your resources using KPI data collected in the past and other stored performance data. It may not be able to see the weather next month, but it's pretty good at letting you know what it believes the health of your resources will be about 30 minutes in the future. This is beyond the capability of human operators.

REMEMBER

AIOps isn't designed to replace human operations staff — only to make them more efficient.

Adaptive thresholding

Earlier in this chapter, I talk about how dynamic thresholding can improve a company's ability to adapt to changes that occur, usually due to peak business hours, or seasons. Splunk takes that idea and runs with it, incorporating adaptive thresholding as part of its toolset in order to give you this powerful AIOps capability.

Thresholds — expected limits of operational performance such as demand, bandwidth, CPU usage — can all change based on everything from the time of day when customers shop in your online store or when employees begin adjusting the settings in your nuclear reactor or seasonally, like when Black Friday shopping puts extra loads on your ecommerce systems. Being able to adjust expected threshold limits eliminates false positive alerts and makes your system far more adaptable.

Views of everything

Visibility is everything. The Splunk Executive Dashboard gives you a simple graphical representation of the health of your resources. Digital Channels gives you a deeper look into the performance in real time. The Operational Status page shows you exactly what its name implies — the operational status of your resources.

The Splunk Service Analyzer is another view into your system's health. You can see how each resource is operating compared to key resource indicators. When systems are having issues, they are moved to the head of the line — an apt illustration of the squeaky wheel idea. Also, a tree view, a display of how one service (a branch) is connected to another (a trunk), enables you to see the services within their operating context and quickly see dependencies

Deep Dive in Splunk

Dashboard overviews are useful for showing you quickly how everything is operating. At times, however, you should look deeper into how things are operating. The Deep Dive shows you graphically how all performance metrics are operating in real time. Each of the entities is a configuration item (CI) in your CMDB. The data is then displayed in *swim lanes* — those fancy charts that show the comparison of one type of data to another by placing their charts one atop another — allows you to see performance trends. Deep Dive lets you spot which KPI is impacting the service. You can then add additional services to see how one is impacting the other.

Event Analytics in Splunk

Events are the alarms — the sharp nudge in the ribs — that let you know when things are amiss and need attention. Becoming overwhelmed by a massive number of alerts is counterproductive. When one thing goes wrong, it can impact so many other things, all which begin complaining (sending alerts.)

The Event Analytics module cleans up the noise, reducing the number of alerts that come to your attention by as much as 95 percent, by grouping them into something Splunk calls *episodes*. That's like having your app say, "I'm having an episode" rather than saying, "The following 37 things just started happening." This is known as an *event storm.* Another way to say this is that episodes are created using a *notable event aggregation policy.*

You can look at historical data to try to determine the root cause of the problem, or you can send it off to Phantom, part of Splunk Domain App, which makes it easy to automate your responses. (Phantom's actually much more than that — it's Splunk's adaptive orchestration app, and I talk more about it in a sec.)

Splunk On-Call

Once you've used ITSI to gather the data relevant to an incident or episode, that data is integrated with Splunk On-Call. (Your Splunk implementation may still say *VictorOps* on the button used to engage it, but it's been rebranded as Splunk On-Call.)

Once an incident is sent to On-Call, you can automate a couple of tasks:

>> **Escalation policies:** You know immediately who is on call from the different teams that have been set up to respond to the issue at hand.

>> **Team Scheduling:** You don't want to be updating schedules all the time.

Escalation automation means that if someone is contacted to handle an alert and doesn't respond, On-Call simply contacts the next person on the list of people who are designated to handle that type of problem. Automating this process prevents you from having someone on the phone "smiling and dialing." You want to get the right people quickly involved and solving the issue.

On-Call users get the contextual information that was forwarded from the ITSI application, allowing them to see where they need to go next to fix actionable alerts. This may even mean adding responders to the problem — a task that can be done from inside On-Call. Selecting which teams need to respond — the database team, for example — will set On-Call busy paging people on these added teams.

Once the teams are involved, they can chat with each other or do things like create ServiceNow tickets, see the Deep Dive information, view the ITSI event dashboard, or interact with other applications. (See Figure 7-6.) The links are added by a rules engine, so you can customize which of your applications you want listed.

Once the application has been resolved, On-Call creates a resolution history *(post-mortem review)* showing who was involved, who was paged, chats, and what was done to resolve the issue. This feature saves time spent trying to create after-event reports manually by trying to gather information from a variety of communications systems and people. If you have tied together your Splunk and ServiceNow applications, resolving the ticket in ServiceNow updates the resolution status in Splunk.

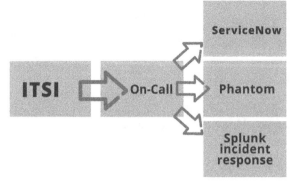

FIGURE 7-6:
Data moves from the ITSI into On-Call, where it can be redirected to an automation system or to ticketing or to another application.

TIP

When enterprises use applications such as ServiceNow, some of the functionality in On-Call is duplicated in ServiceNow, creating a choice of where to direct your data from ITSI — to On-Call or directly to ServiceNow to have teams alerted. On-Call is action-oriented, whereas ServiceNow tends to be more ticket oriented.

Splunk is great at things like log monitoring and general visibility. Integrate Splunk with all your other tools to superpower it.

REMEMBER

Downtime is inevitable. Having the right tools in place to make it as short as possible is important. Downtime kills customer satisfaction, impacts your workforce, and has a negative impact on revenue.

Phantom

Once you've figured out what is causing your episode (that bad thing that's happening), you can pass this alert information on to a system that allows for better resolution orchestration and the automation of responses.

Splunk Phantom is an excellent tool that provides

>> Security orchestration

>> Task automation

>> Response to the alert through automation

This combination of capabilities — security orchestration, automation, and response — is known as SOAR. Resolving problems can be complicated and involve people from many disciplines. The Splunk Phantom application orchestrates the infrastructure and also has playbook automation and case management capabilities. These help integrate your team, your processes, and all the tools you use to orchestrate workflows and automate the mundane tasks that often overwhelm your team. It also makes it possible for you to respond quickly to security events as they happen.

Putting ServiceNow Through Its Paces

When it comes to serious AIOps, ServiceNow (www.servicenow.com) is one of the leaders in the industry. One of this application's primary advantages is that all operational analytics are done in the cloud. You can think of clouds as being far above you, and in this case, positioning analytics in the cloud allows you to reach even remote installations within your organization. Also, companies are choosing to move operational data into the cloud, where APIs make it easier to connect up your resources. API's also make your application more scalable as new resources can be added by tapping 3rd party services.

AIOps require an overhead view

IT operations staff need visibility into every facet of what's happening digitally in a company. The operations team needs more than just a snapshot understanding of what's happening; it needs to be able to view your resources as they are actually performing. ServiceNow makes that happen. It mirrors in many ways the Splunk ITSI application but does the work with a slightly different philosophy. The ServiceNow application can be thought of as a pipeline. Applications are monitored, and resulting data is fed into analytics, including a powerful deep learning AI that gives incident response metrics and recommended solutions.

REMEMBER

AIOps requires visibility into every service and all its supporting infrastructure. Accurately mapping relationships between infrastructure and services is critical to this visibility. Also, this mapping needs to be accurate and timely.

Continuing along the ServiceNow pipeline, when services and infrastructure are mapped, AIOps connects the outputs of monitoring tools that will be sending events and metrics.

React to problems

Monitoring tools can put out massive amounts of data. This Big Data trove provides the needed information for the machine learning engine to begin recognizing and learning patterns that allow the AI to know when it has detected problems.

ServiceNow provides a holistic approach to AIOps and resolving incidents by combining the capabilities from its Enterprise IT Operations Management (ITOM) and IT Service Management (ITSM) applications. These are tightly integrated into a single solution.

Visibility starts with discovery. Though cloud services do offer their own discovery applications and there are numerous third-party discovery apps, ServiceNow Discovery can scan networks to discover IT resources and applications and then automatically store the configuration item data into a ServiceNow brand CMDB.

ServiceNow Discovery uses a top-down approach to create topology maps that relate services to its underlying infrastructure; it then creates service maps, which are stored in the CMDB. Such service maps are updated through a regular discovery process, keeping the CMDB up to date as it keeps track of the changes it finds. Problems that occur because of changes are more common than those that occur because someone has decided to hack your network. So, keeping track of the changes allows your AI to spot where problems may have been introduced.

Gauge system health

ServiceNow Event Management gathers event data from monitoring tools, processes them to create alerts whenever they fall outside of predefined thresholds, and then applies machine learning to group, or correlate, alerts. This is similar to the Splunk ITSI system, which prevents event storms by grouping related events. The AI allows these groups to be created without the need for manually defined rules. (There are so many perturbations that manually defining such rules would be a nearly impossible task.) These grouped alerts are then treated as a single action item. Groups can create easy visibility for the IT operations team, who can then take actions on the group — by opening an incident report, for example. When they're used with service maps stored in the CMDB, you can rapidly discover the root cause of the problem, or at least quickly see what systems have been impacted.

Bad behavior sounds like the name of a movie, but it's what ServiceNow's Operational Intelligence is designed to detect. Anything that falls outside of normal parameters or isn't captured by raw events coming from monitoring tools is caught by this application. It analyzes performance data originating from your local environment as well as from the cloud. The AI analysis results in models that identify operational thresholds, even adjusting for seasonal changes in your business. It's no longer practical to manually adjust thresholds for hundreds or thousands of metrics.

To improve the AI's ability to create working thresholds, the settings are checked against normal or projected thresholds, the results are scored, and learning occurs. (Yes, even AI needs to pass tests.) When a qualified anomaly is caught by the AI, it generates an alert, which is then displayed on the ServiceNow alert console and Event Management dashboard. It then provides the underlying intelligence that helps in finding the root cause of the alert.

With software monitoring a huge number of events, it's possible to see the overall health of your environment. But the ServiceNow software goes beyond looking at the real-time data — it also compares the real-time data against historical data, human feedback to previous alerts, and the service context to create a holistic view of your environment. This machine intelligence has led to a significant decrease in outages and serious operational events.

REMEMBER

Monitoring system health using machine intelligence frees your operational team to do more creative things, decreases burnout from being burdened with mundane tasks, and keeps you from missing things in a degrading environment that may be degrading so slowly it's just not possible for a human operator to catch.

Automation makes it all happen

An AIOps environment would be a huge bonus as a tool to support your operations team, speeding them toward rapid incident resolution. Add automation into the mix and you've superpowered your system. A system that promotes the automated collection and processing of your system data, where problems are fixed as they happen or even before they occur, without the need for operator involvement, lets you compete in the highly competitive marketplace. Automation even extends to building the supporting data around an alert that, when it hasn't already fixed the problem, directs operators to past fixes, industry background on the problem, or suggestions as simple as, "This is broken — fix it."

Automation is used extensively by the ServiceNow ITOM and ITSM applications. You have already seen how Discovery and Service Mapping provide automated updates to the CMDB. The Event Management application can open an incident, update an active incident and, when the problem has been corrected, close the incident. Event Management can also run corrective tasks on local systems as well as those running in the cloud.

Getting the Job Done with IT Service Management

IT service management, or ITSM, is the job of designing, building, delivering, and operating those IT services offered to customers. It's a huge job that has grown in complexity over time.

When you combine IT Service Management with IT Operations Management (ITOM) as the ServiceNow AIOps environment does, you make your life far easier. The ITOM feeds incident response data, change data, or other problem documentation to the ITSM system.

How ITSM is different

IT service management is different from more traditional approaches such as network management or IT systems management. ITSM is more of a process approach that has a customer-oriented focus. Rather than just see machines and software that needs to be managed, the idea here is to set goals and create performance indicators, all with the desire to improve the customer experience. This improved experience comes from the quality of the services you deliver.

REMEMBER

Cloud security plays a large part in your ability to offer quality services.

ITSM takes a workflow approach to IT management. Things move in a fairly linear and predictable path toward goal accomplishment, whether it's achieving better security or dealing with the problems of corrective actions due to system failure. Taking this type of workflow approach to your processes allows for the perfect integration of cloud security. In other words, cloud security seems overwhelming until you take a process approach to it.

Performance analytics

Managing IT services, particularly when they include cloud services, is a bit like walking a tightrope: It's one giant balancing act. You must always balance factors such as security risk (use a cloud or stay local?) against cost, ease of use, functionality, or, in the case of cloud computing, the ability to do edge computing. This management challenge can feel like managing a house of cards in a wind tunnel.

All the applications and hardware within your IT realm generate vast amounts of data — some of it useful only in the short term. When you combine operational

ITOM data with your service management ITSM data and then pair that with your CMDB, you're then able to

- >> Spot trends
- >> Continually learn and improve
- >> Solve problems proactively instead of reactively

TIP

Measure the results of your actions against goals you've set. This allows you to continually improve and report to those who fund your operation that you're actually making progress.

ServiceNow has a Performance Analytics application that provides business intelligence that will enable your company to best align with its objectives, make intelligent data-driven decisions, manage change intelligently, spot trends, and deliver operational insights.

A simple-to-use dashboard displays real-time measurements of KPIs. This allows your business teams to focus on the tasks that will have the greatest value to your company — including being able to focus on creating the highest level of cloud security for your organization.

Changing Your Team

By implementing AIOps, you're sure to change how things get done in your company. Just as the operating model changed when technology began moving to the cloud, similar changes will happen in how you build teams — as well as how they get things done. Things you once did will disappear or be reduced in focus because they are just no longer relevant, meaning that traditional roles and responsibilities will also change.

With AIOps creating automated routines on its own, the people responsible for developing automated routines will most likely shift to roles where they are supervising the AI and improving its ability to create dynamic routines. This frees the humans on your team to use their intelligence to best guide the machine at doing what it does best — recognizing patterns and learning.

TIP

Cloud security is more than a one-person job. It takes a team of stakeholders across a broad set of disciplines to bring about better security. You may find yourself rethinking the makeup of your cloud security team.

An example of how a cloud security team might differ in focus is that, whereas understanding traditional border security is important, the problem has also become a big data problem. Data analytics now plays a big role in understanding the larger issue. Cloud security is embedded in so many different disciplines, from development to networks to physical security.

A (Not So Final) Word

Cloud security is not a stand-alone challenge. How you choose to manage all your systems impacts how well you manage security. When you take a process approach like ITSM and move processes along a workflow such as those within AIOps systems like Splunk or ServiceNow, you soon find that what once seemed unmanageable is now simply a part of the bigger picture.

Don't manage systems in a silo. If your cloud security team isn't operating alongside other management teams, you're missing the big picture.

Visibility is the key to great security management, not just cloud security. Data discovery and storage of CIs in CMDB systems builds an intelligence system that a learning engine can then use to find root causes of problems — including attempts to hack your cloud services. Complexity can be managed and scaled using AI and automation.

Chapter **8**

Implementing Zero Trust

More than any other framework or technology, the zero trust framework embodies all that is important in defending your network from people trying to break in. For example, DataOps is a good way to build security into your development, and AIOps is an intelligent way to monitor your network from unusual activity, from either attempted security breaches or hardware failures. But *zero trust* is a more fundamental approach than either of those because it has at its core the idea that people should never be given more security privileges than they need. That means managing access to applications, devices, virtual machines, networks, and data in such a way that everyone must first be

» Authenticated

» Validated

» Continually checked for validation

Managing access is critically important in protecting your resources, no matter where they exist.

REMEMBER

Making the Shift from Perimeter Security

Perimeter security, which is the idea that you can protect your digital assets behind a firewall, no longer applies. It's the difference between trying to protect a herd of corralled horses compared to a flock of birds. Zero trust protection is like making the switch from the ancient ways of protecting cities by throwing up a high wall with guards to putting everyone in body armor: Every resource becomes "personally" responsible for its own security. That isn't to say that the security necessarily needs to be built-in; it only means that you have to make certain that anyone trying to access has full trust and permission. By default, no one is trusted. So imagine the old city walls and the people at the gate shouting downward, "Who goes there?"

The old-time perimeter that was protected was usually the company network (or networks). Great pains were taken, and at great expense, to make sure it was difficult to get into the network if you didn't belong there. Once you were in, it was carte blanche. This was like standing in line at a night club and waiting for the bouncer to decide whether you were allowed to enter. Once you were in, you were golden and it was party time.

John Kindervag, a cybersecurity guru, came up with the idea of the zero trust framework, built on the much older idea that you should start by trusting no one and grant allowance from that point.

For about 70 years, applications were either unprotected or merely required a user ID and password, so most IT technology today uses that scheme of authentication. The oldest applications didn't even need passwords — if you could get into the network via a terminal of some sort with a user ID and password, then the applications you found there were available for use.

Enter cloud technology. Now the perimeter no longer surrounded all your digital assets. They were off in some nebulous place where they may or may not be protected by the cloud service provider. In your shared trust model, some of the responsibility for security was yours and some belonged to the cloud service provider. On top of that, every cloud had its own policies, applications, and procedures — making a unified approach difficult. Yes, user IDs and passwords were required in order to gain access to the cloud, creating several or several hundred little perimeters, depending on the size of your company (okay, maybe thousands), that had to be protected. The need for a unified security policy was born out of that chaos.

Examining the Foundations of Zero Trust Philosophy

The primary idea or philosophy behind zero trust is that cybersecurity protections should move from perimeter security (like firewalls) to the resources themselves. To implement this kind of security, you have to ensure, at minimum, that you have five features in place. In the next few sections, I take a look at each feature individually.

Two-way authentication

Communication between users and resources requires that you have policy based authentication with each connection. To do this, both parties need a way to authenticate each other. (In other words, you have to know who's on the other end of the line.)

WARNING

Applications that use third-party single sign-on providers to provide authentication tokens don't meet the standards of the zero trust philosophy.

Using more than a single means to authenticate someone — traditionally, a user ID and password — increases the likelihood that the person on the other end is who they say they are. Yet user IDs and passwords are stolen every day around the world, making them next to useless for serious authentication. Using more than one method of authentication is known as *multifactor authentication*. That term isn't as commonly used as the more specific terms that detail how many forms of authentication are required, such as two-factor authentication or three-factor authentication. Here are some types of authentication:

>> User ID and password

>> Biometrics, such as fingerprints or retinal scans

>> Other biometrics, such as facial recognition and voice ID

>> One-time keys from physical fobs or RFID chips, also known as *token authentication.*

>> One-time keys *(tokens)* from software applications like Authenticator

>> Telephony, such as SMS text message or a phone call

Implementing multifactor authentication requires that you use at least any two of these authentication methods, as shown in Figure 8-1. There are other weird authentication methods, such as your typing style. (Yes, some apps actually claim that they can recognize you from how you type on a keyboard.) Some claim to know you merely by seeing your ear.

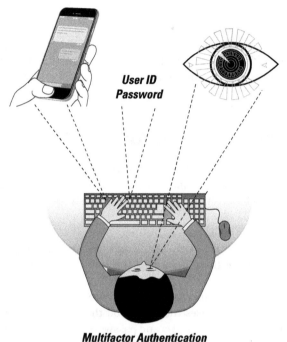

User ID
Password

Multifactor Authentication

FIGURE 8-1:
Using more than one type of authentication increases security.

Many web applications now require that you enter a user ID and password, use a login method from a third party that has OAuth (an access delegation standard) for authentication, and additionally require that you receive a text message with a code that you then enter into a web form.

Multifactor authentication can increase security and provide more options for authentication in different situations. However, authentication must take place between the two communicating entities.

Endpoint device management

People are involved in communication, but the actual communication channel is between two devices, as shown in Figure 8-2. It's up to the hardware devices to establish secure communications, including authentication. This sets up a pattern of trust that doesn't end with the authenticated folks trying to communicate; you also need to know that the hardware you're using to communicate has not been compromised.

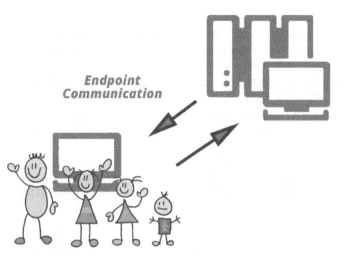

FIGURE 8-2:
Even though
people are
involved
communication
exists between
endpoints.

Endpoint device management relies on a verifiable hardware root of trust in each device. Following the zero trust principle that security is at the endpoint and not in the network or out on the periphery, each device continually checks its health status by uploading log files to a central monitoring system, such as an AIOps AI monitoring system (See Chapter 7). In this case, the monitoring system becomes the source of trust for each endpoint.

End-to-end encryption

End-to-end encryption is a method of communication where the information is encoded in such a way that only the users on each side of the communication can decipher it. This keeps snoopers from reading the communications you send.

Using the web, which has been the de facto operating environment of the Internet since the 1990s, in combination with firewalls (first introduced to reduce the number of ports on which software could communicate), encryption has also become the way most information is processed before being sent out onto the net. Most modern web browsers now warn you when you're communicating with a server and not using encryption.

Public key/private key encryption

There is a point of truth where you know that a connection can be trusted when using encryption across the Internet: Web servers need an SSL/TLS certificate issued by a certificate authority (CA). These are purchased from the same registrars where you purchase domain names and are installed on your server. The certificate authority verifies websites so that you know who you're communicating with — hopefully, preventing a type of attack known as *spoofing*, where nefarious actors pretend to be something they are not. This is a key part of the type of encryption commonly used on the web, called *public key cryptography*. Using pairs of keys, public and private, information that's encrypted with a public key can only be decrypted using the associated private key. They are mathematically paired. (See Figure 8-3 for the story of public key/private key cryptography. Tissues not included.) This is a huge topic, but this resource can quickly bring you up to speed: www.dtos-mu.com/understanding-the-basics-of-public-key-cryptography.

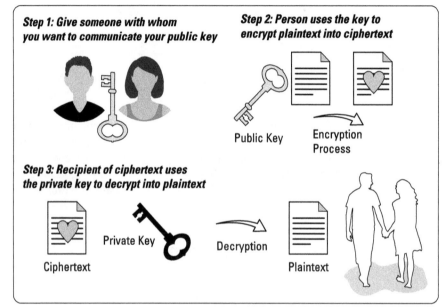

Step 1: Give someone with whom you want to communicate your public key

Step 2: Person uses the key to encrypt plaintext into ciphertext

Public Key   Encryption Process

Step 3: Recipient of ciphertext uses the private key to decrypt into plaintext

Ciphertext   Private Key   Decryption   Plaintext

FIGURE 8-3: The happy story of public key/ private key cryptography.

A scary bit about email

By default, email communications aren't encrypted. As your email travels across the network as open text, hackers using sniffing tools can read it — unless, as is the case with Gmail, the communication path between your device and your email server is encrypted using end-to-end encryption. Here are some facts you should know about who has access to your email:

>> Did you give your kids access to your phone so that they can play games? Adding that game could have added spyware, keyloggers, or other malware on your device — potentially granting malicious individuals access to your email.

>> Your network administrator may be able to read email as it's being sent or read it in your inbox.

>> Your Internet service provider (ISP) can read any data you send and receive traveling unencrypted.

>> Your email service provider can read your email.

This is really only half the list because the same is true for the recipient of your email. Anyone who has access to their machine can read the email you sent and so on.

Policy based access

Writing a policy is exactly how it sounds: You create rules that become policy in the same way your business creates rules about everything from parking to break time. These rules become policy. When it comes to making rules about who can and can't access your cloud resources, policy based access is considered the most flexible access control system. It has these characteristics — it is

>> **Flexible:** Yes, I already mentioned this one, but it pays to say it twice. When policies are built of multiple rules, you can modify them, making access flexible.

>> **Scalable:** You can add new rules to your policies as needed (to include new resources, for example).

>> **Compliance friendly:** Regulatory agencies love to be able to see exactly who and how you've decided to let people access your systems.

>> **Makes your distributed workforce happy:** The new work-from-home trend has created some new security challenges. In a policy based system, you can design access rules that take working from home into account.

A brief look at the strategies that came before policy based access should convince you that, in situations where you need fine-grained access control, policy based access is the way to go.

>> **RBAC:** Role based access control (RBAC) looks at roles rather than policies when assigning privileges. The challenge of role based access is that of *role explosion,* where security managers are handling thousands of roles for hundreds of users. It becomes a bit of a management nightmare.

>> **ABAC:** Attribute based access control (ABAC) allows for Boolean logic to create logical combinations such as "if an accountant" and "if has payroll privileges" and not "risk level high." These attribute rules can become quite fine-grained, such as traffic must come from a specific IP address and only during certain hours of the day. These rules can be assigned to users, actions, resources, or environments. As with the complexity of role based access, managing the attributes and rules can also become extremely complicated.

Another problem with ABAC access is that IT security folks need to know how to write rules using an older and more difficult XACML language. This can increase the queue time for allowing someone access to a critical system.

>> **PBAC:** Policy based access control (PBAC) is generic to the application using it — it's written in natural language. A policy might say, "Accountants can access the accounting system." The accounting system will have a server back-end and a web based user interface. The theory behind using natural language is that it frees you from using a programmer to create access policies. Business managers can define their own access policies in real time, down to the document level.

TIP

Access policies can be ephemeral and apply only during specific periods.

Involving people with an average skill level in the process broadens the responsibility for security and fits with the mindset of making stakeholders more responsible for the day-to-day workings of their systems and data.

>> Because policies can be fine-grained, they can include the broadest range of users: employees, suppliers, freelancers, collaborators — whomever. Because each of these groups of people can be assigned roles as well as risk levels or any number of attributes, what you have is a scalable and flexible access control system. (If only refrigerators had that kind of access control, you could assign roles, such as cook and snacker. Then you could grant access based on weight or cholesterol numbers or connect to the Fitbit and allow access only after so many steps — and then only to the fruit drawer.)

REMEMBER

Just because PBAC can be excessively fine-grained doesn't mean that it has to be. It completely depends on how coarse you want to make the rules.

A PBAC system creates policies for Segregation of Duties (SOD, also referred to as separation of duties). SOD is a basic building block of risk management. The idea is that the responsibility for a resource is shared among more than one role. The example often given is one of responsibility for nuclear weapons, where the launch keys and launch codes are shared among several people to avoid the dangers of personal vendetta, coercion, blackmail, and human error. A good example of this strategy is the fairly recent announcement in Hawaii of an inbound missile attack sent over the public alert system. Many people were scared. It turns out that this one was sent because of human error.

To find out more about how you can implement PBAC, check out the plainID website at www.plainid.com. You'll find that the Policy Manager application allows for visibility into access privileges at both the user and resource levels.

Accountability

When bad things happen — and they will — the basic premise of zero trust means that when said bad things happen, someone is to blame or will be held accountable. Devices as well as people must be trusted, and therefore can also be held accountable. Accountability is determined by monitoring applications that perhaps didn't catch the security breach before it happened, but you can be certain that it's gathering after-the-fact information about who-did-what-to-whom.

Logs are a first layer of accountability. Once considered a nuisance because they would just grow until the hard drive was full and then need to be deleted, logs are now considered big data and are archived in cloud storage for use by AI as a way to predict the next problem.

TIP

Accountability systems go a long way toward satisfying some of the most stringent compliancy requirements.

Guarding against external threats with SIEM

SIEM is a combination of security information management (SIM) and security event management (SEM) that provides tracking of security information and event tracking for the purpose of auditing and compliance. I include this discussion of SIEM in the chapter on zero trust because two of its hallmarks are accountability and security. Zero trust implementations require both.

In addition to providing accountability, this AI-based solution (similar to AIOps) uses machine learning to recognize anomalies in user behavior, detect threats, and provide incident response. It can also automate many of the more mundane security tasks.

One way SIEM falls short is that it tends to be rule-based and good only for spotting real-time threats. Many modern threats have become far more sophisticated and require a more nuanced approach, using machine learning to spot attacks previously unknown.

Protecting against internal threats with UEBA

Similar to SIEM, user and entity behavior analytics systems (UEBA) can spot anomalies in both user and device behaviors using machine learning, statistics, and algorithms. UEBA focuses on insider threats, designed to focus on user analytics rather than on external security threats.

Behavioral analytics could almost be called a biometric security system. Though it's possible to snag a person's login credentials, it's almost impossible to perfectly mimic their behavioral patterns after they're logged in. For example, a person may always first download the company's daily newsletter and then read

Scott Adams' *Dilbert* page before reading their email. This is the same way credit card companies spot fraud. If you use your card only to grocery shop and suddenly you're buying chocolates in Belgium, a red flag goes up. UEBA can spot nuanced attacks that can take months or years to implement using a risk scoring system.

TIP

Implementing both SIEM and UEBA into your zero-trust-based systems can provide the maximum amount of threat intelligence while also serving as an advanced accountability application.

Least privilege

The principle of least privilege is the foundation of zero trust. (It's known by other names, such as the principle of least authority or the principle of minimal privilege.) In a nutshell, it means that you grant privileges only when someone absolutely needs them in order to accomplish some task and has also earned the privilege based on having a risk profile that matches the data or resource to which you're granting access.

Least privilege applies to more than just people: It also applies to applications, processes, files, and systems. For example, an application that needs access to sensitive data may not always need that access. Granting access to sensitive data all the time puts the application at a higher security risk because, if an unauthorized person gains control of that application, it has access to sensitive data all the time. Restricting when the application is able to access sensitive data means you have reduced the amount of time during which the application poses a security risk. You can even make plans to increase security around the application during times it accesses the sensitive or private data. To increase the security of the application temporarily, you can reduce the privileges of others to access the application for a specified period, as shown in Figure 8-4.

Network access control and beyond

Network Access Control (NAC), sometimes called Network Admission Control, is a set of protocols that, as its name suggests, controls the access to a network by implementing policies that limit where a user can connect and, once connected, what they can connect with.

A computer attempting to connect must first satisfy policies such as these:

>> Level of antivirus protection

>> Software update and version levels

>> Configuration settings

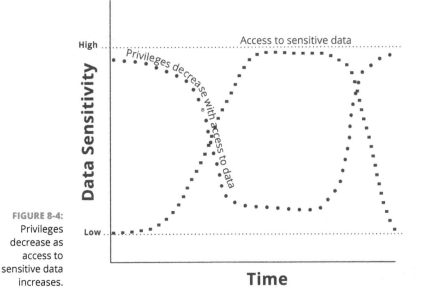

FIGURE 8-4:
Privileges
decrease as
access to
sensitive data
increases.

The graph shows "Access to sensitive data" and "Privileges decrease with access to data" with axes labeled "Data Sensitivity" (High to Low) and "Time."

NAC can be either agent based or agentless. In an agent based solution, the software agent, installed locally, checks to see whether the computer meets the required policies. If the computer doesn't stack up, the agent allows the computer to connect to resources that help it meet the requirements. For example, the computer might be directed to a software update or to new antivirus databases. Once the policy is met, the agent then allows the computer to connect to the network or to resources within the network, depending on the type of NAC system that has been implemented. An agentless NAC system does primarily the same thing except, rather than rely on a preinstalled agent to report on whether the endpoint meets the policy, the system relies on other scanning and network information software to gather the information.

There are two basic types of NAC systems: pre-admission and post-admission. Pre-admission agents check adherence to policies — antivirus levels, for example — before allowing someone on the network. Post-admission policies check for user behavior after connecting to the network.

Here's the bad news: NAC is a perimeter safeguard strategy and isn't designed to protect cloud resources. I include NAC in my discussion here in order to point to companies that are already using this older strategy in a slightly different direction while employing the same ideas.

This new approach uses a *cloud access security broker (CASB)*, a system that can be implemented as a cloud-hosted solution, installed locally as software or as a hardware device. It's designed to protect SaaS, PaaS, and IaaS cloud environments. A CASB, like NAC, is based on policies. If you're already using NAC or another policy based system, you can extend those policies to the cloud using a CASB system. You can see in Figure 8-5 that, although the NAC is set to control local resources using policies, similar policies can be used to protect access to cloud resources using the CASB.

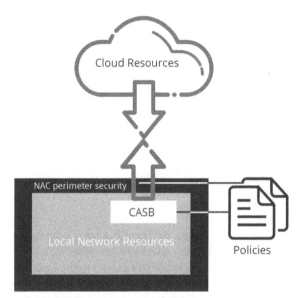

FIGURE 8-5:
The NAC and CASB systems can have the same policies when it comes to controlling access.

Many implementations of cloud access security systems are based on policy control. Not all of them are known as CASB systems — here are some examples:

>> **McAfee's MVISION Cloud:** www.mcafee.com/enterprise/en-us/products/mvision-cloud.html

>> **Aruba ClearPass:** www.arubanetworks.com/products/security/network-access-control/secure-access

You' need to think beyond perimeter security to make sure your cloud resources are protected.

REMEMBER

CSPM risk automation

Cloud security posture management (CSPM) is an automated system for identifying and handling cloud-based security threats. The goal of CSPM is to prevent breaches, detect security flaws, respond to any of these occurrences, and, most of all, figure out where such occurrences may occur next. CSPM handles threats in all the major cloud environments, including SaaS, PaaS, and IaaS. CSPM provides services such as these:

>> Incident response

>> Compliance monitoring

>> DevOps integration

Chapter 9 discusses multicloud environments in detail, but you should know that CSPM excels at providing incident response across many cloud configurations, right down to the container level.

REMEMBER

Both intentional and unintentional risks are out there, with unintentional risks responsible for as much as 90 percent of all breaches.

Unintentional risk — accidentally leaving the barn door open, in other words — is responsible for the greatest number of security incidents, far greater than those caused by hackers attempting to break through your security. That isn't to say that determined people aren't out there looking for your mistakes to exploit them.

It's possible to monitor misconfigurations, often caused by malformed Infrastructure as Code (IaC) configuration files, for potential configuration errors. CSPM is capable of monitoring these and other configurations across multiple cloud environments simultaneously and provides visibility in a single console.

Dealing with Zero Trust Challenges

Zero trust is a challenging goal. It's likely to be a multiyear endeavor unless your business is just getting started and you have no legacy systems to design around. In that case, implementing zero trust is a bit more straightforward — you simply choose resources that are designed with zero trust in mind. But things are rarely that simple.

REMEMBER

Engage the greatest percentage of employees and educate them on the principles of zero trust and why it's important. You need their support in implementing the strategies that bring about a zero trust environment.

Zero trust is a bit like taking away the little jar next to the snacks where you expect employees to pay their fair share. Zero trust is more like the vending machine that requires you to pay first, receive snacks after. Though it may not seem like the friendliest approach, it's the safest in a world where people are trying to steal more than your breakroom snacks. The following sections offer several ideas to help implement zero trust in a going concern.

Choose a roadmap

Many roads lead to Rome, and many different paths lead to implementing the zero trust framework. For example, the Cybersecurity and Infrastructure Security Agency (CISA, at www.cisa.gov) has been developing a plan known as the zero trust maturity model. (These are the people responsible for securing resources in the .gov domain.) Though their model offers guidance, a lot of the heavy lifting is still up to you. Even the introduction to the maturity-model documentation states, "This document is not meant to be a robust set of guidance toward zero trust."

Another set of documentation, this time from the National Institute of Standards and Technology (NIST), sets forth the essentials of building a zero trust architecture (ZTA) and then warns that implementing zero trust will take years. It defines zero trust this way:

> Zero trust provides a collection of concepts and ideas designed to minimize uncertainty in enforcing accurate, least privilege per-request access decisions in information systems and services in the face of a network viewed as compromised. ZTA is an enterprise's cybersecurity plan that uses zero trust concepts and encompasses component relationships, workflow planning, and access policies. Therefore, a zero trust enterprise is the network infrastructure (physical and virtual) and operational policies that are in place for an enterprise as a product of a ZTA plan.

To read the entire publication, go to https://csrc.nist.gov/publications/detail/sp/800-207/final.

Take a simple, step-by-step approach

Implementing zero trust can be overwhelming. Giving yourself a step-by-step process for implementing it gives you a clear idea of what needs to be done next. Follow these steps so that I can walk you through the process:

1. **Figure out what needs protecting.**

   Refer to the risk assessment you may have created earlier, while reading Part 1 of this book. It gives you a clear picture of what you need to protect, including the items described in this list:

   - *Critical applications:* These are applications that if they went down would cripple your business, even in the short term.

   - *Critical data:* This is data your company relies on or, if released, corrupted, or locked in the case of ransomware, would hurt your business. It also includes data protected by privacy regulations such as credit card or health data.

- *Assets:* This includes critical points of entry into the systems that make your company work — for example, hospital equipment, manufacturing equipment, or critical infrastructure such as dams and power grids.

- *Services:* These are the IT services critical to your business, such as Domain Name System, or DNS (Facebook recently learned how critical this one is), Dynamic Host Control Protocol, or DHCP, which assigns IP addresses, and many other devices critical to your business.

Some of these assets have no way to implement zero trust. In these cases, you need to build your own perimeter around each one of them.

2. **Map the data flow pattern.**

Being able to easily see how applications interact makes it easier to protect them. Create a map that shows how data flows between them. There are templates you can use to make this step easy. See Figure 8-6 for a simple, fairly no-nonsense, data flow map. From this you can form an idea of how to construct a data flow map that is meaningful for you and your team.

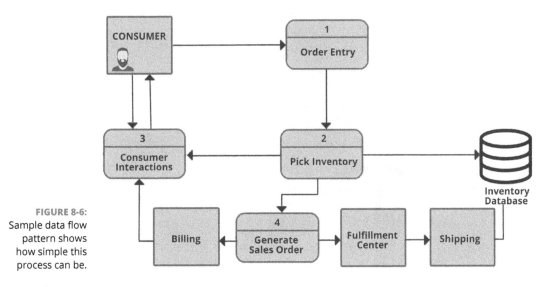

FIGURE 8-6: Sample data flow pattern shows how simple this process can be.

3. **Create a segmented network.**

This next step depends on completion of the first two. You must first know what you're trying to protect. Second, you need to know how the data flows between the various parts of the applications and devices you're trying to protect.

Because so many of the applications in use aren't zero-trust-ready, you need to build a zero trust network that connects them. Of course, this starts with protecting your network with a high-end firewall — one that acts as a gateway and also lets you compartmentalize your network. Compartmentalizing is done by creating subnets (mini networks within a greater network). Zero trust can then be applied to who and how these subnets are accessed. Essentially, you have created wrappers around each of your applications using this approach. This type of segmentation can be set up to protect virtual machines, containers, and bare metal servers.

4. **Architect your access policies.**

This next step involves creating a set of policies based on the Kipling method. Rudyard Kipling was no cybersecurity guru, but he did once write a poem that is believed to be the foundation of the questions What, Why, When, How, Where, and Who. Kipling's poem "I Keep Six Honest Serving Men" was published in the children's storybook *Just So Stories* in 1902 (available on Amazon). It's a poem about curiosity, and that's exactly what you need as a foundation to zero trust. It's important to ask the right questions when creating access policies.

Here's the poem:

Keep Six Honest Serving Men

I keep six honest serving-men

(They taught me all I knew);

Their names are What and Why and When

And How and Where and Who.

I send them over land and sea,

I send them east and west;

But after they have worked for me,

I give them all a rest.

I let them rest from nine till five,

For I am busy then,

As well as breakfast, lunch, and tea,

For they are hungry men.

But different folk have different views;

I know a person small

She keeps ten million serving-men,

Who get no rest at all!

She sends em abroad on her own affairs,

From the second she opens her eyes

One million Hows, Two million Wheres,

And seven million Whys!

—Rudyard Kipling

Creating these policies by asking questions results in a resource access policy list. These policies should answer the following Kiplingesque questions:

- **What** applications access resources within the protected network segment?
- **Why** is the protected resource being accessed?
- **When** is the resource accessed?
- **How** is the resource being accessed?
- **Where** is the data going?
- **Who** needs to access a resource?

Answering these questions results in policies that result in fine-grained control over application communications within your network. Asking yourself these questions when developing zero trust policies and procedures or when implementing new security strategies will put you on a sure path to success.

REMEMBER

Malware breaches occur as a result of policies that allow access. You need to play close attention to who is allowed rather than on who is not allowed.

5. **Monitor and maintain the network.**

This final step includes reviewing all logs (internal and external) from the base physical and data link layers network layers all the way through the network application layer, focusing on the operational aspects of zero trust. Because zero trust is an iterative process, inspecting and logging all traffic provides valuable insights into how to improve the network over time.

Once you have completed the five-step methodology for implementing a zero trust network for your first protect surface, you can expand to iteratively move other data, applications, assets, or services from your legacy network to a zero trust network in a way that's cost-effective and nondisruptive.

Keep in mind some challenges you face in implementing zero trust

Because zero trust is a framework, and a little loosey-goosey at best, there is no single correct way to implement it, and no application lets you just set it and forget it. So, challenges lie ahead. Here are some of them:

>> The inevitability of change

>> Legacy systems integration

>> Full visibility

>> The lack of complete solutions

>> The lack of business collaboration

>> Zero trust agility requirements

>> Multiple zero trust standards

>> The responsibility to build the right team

The next few sections look at each challenge in some detail.

Dealing with change

Everything changes, and you're literally working against people who are working against you. This is a thought that you more than likely would love to put out of your mind, but the truth is that bad people are out there who don't have your best interests at heart. Many of them are well-funded — or even government funded — to build systems and procedures with the goal of breaking into your network and either stealing information or doing dastardly harm, like holding your data for ransom. The number of novel attacks, according to AV Test, is about 450,000 per day (www.av-test.org/en/statistics/malware). These hundreds of thousands of malware applications are divided among many different platforms and operating systems.

Your plan for implementing zero trust must be fluid to meet the continued and changing demands. Basically, at its heart, the concept of trust-no-one probably won't change. This idea was around long before the name zero trust adopted it. You'll want to review the applications you use to implement zero trust and be able to change direction at a moment's notice.

Integrating legacy systems

One of the difficulties in any large IT environment is backward compatibility. This isn't just a software idea, where new releases must work with older ones — it also has to do with hardware, networking, and people. Yes, legacy people exist. Don't become one. Be adaptive.

Older resources relied on the concept of *implicit trust*, which means that you trust without question. Nobody has to prove that they're worthy of trust — you just trust them. It's that "goes without saying" problem that has you looking at zero trust today.

Review your older software systems — there is a chance your larger mainframes still run COBOL applications. Then ask yourself how you'll implement modern zero trust applications into something that may or may not still eat cards. (This isn't just a reference to old-timey business machines. Research organizations still rely on many legacy FORTRAN applications running on older machines held together with duct tape.)

You then must ask yourself a question that's difficult to answer: Is implementing zero trust in a legacy environment — which might mean recoding old applications or replacing old hardware — worth it? It's not likely that the new infrastructure will be zero-trust-capable. For one thing, the huge financial and manpower intensive undertaking must be considered. Second, on the other side, does continuing to run old applications pose too large a security risk? There are no easy answers. You just have to be ready to face these difficult questions.

The solution in part is to make a burrito. Yes, wrap a big tortilla around the whole thing to hide what's inside. Seriously, putting a software wrapper around the entire project to create some semblance of security is about your only option if you need to keep the program running and it's considered high risk.

WARNING

Some legacy systems aren't necessarily old; they just hide potential security flaws. One example is the P2P infrastructure embedded in Windows 10 to implement Windows Update.

Creating full visibility

To implement zero trust, you can't have any chinks in the armor. A *chink* is a hole. To ensure that there are no holes, you have to check everything — shadow IT operations, any cloud environments, mobile devices, and even the card scanner that lets people in the door. Getting to 100 percent visibility, even with some of the most awesome discovery tools on the market, is not a simple task for a moderately large organization.

One challenge of implementing zero trust is deciding when something is good enough. It's similar to data center guarantees: No one guarantees 100 percent uptime. It's always 99.999 percent or something similarly obscure. When Facebook went down for five hours in October of 2021, you have to ask yourself whether it fell into the 99.999 percent guaranteed uptime. Of course, it didn't — it was human error. Or was it?

Building DIY solutions

A challenge in implementing zero trust when using the cloud is that it wasn't truly designed with zero trust in mind. It doesn't lend itself to segmentation by default. In a perfect world, your applications should have zero trust built in. Migrating existing applications that have been protected by perimeter security to the cloud doesn't cut it. Do-it-yourself solutions will have to account for the legacy systems you need to protect using barrier network security in a segmented network environment.

Many companies need to comply with industry or government compliance regulations. To be certain you'll make it through the audit with your DIY zero trust implementation, your environment needs to include these items:

>> **Logs:** These are definitely a key part of accountability, containing as they do the information needed by AI systems looking for unusual activity.

>> **Policy based access control systems:** These are necessary to keep fine-grained control over the access to your resources, both in the cloud and local.

>> **Encryption:** This one is truly a foundational requirement for today's information security. Use public key infrastructure (PKI) with valid digital certificates.

>> **Malware threat updates from third-party security experts:** These feed you threat intelligence and the most current information on malware.

>> **A security information and event management (SIEM) system:** This gathers the data you need for postmortem analysis of security issues. It also aids AI systems in spotting problems before or as they happen.

Zero trust and the cloud: Using a third-party solution

Citrix (www.citrix.com) has an application that helps wrap your cloud environments in a zero trust security layer, allowing your remote workers to access your network without the hassle of using a VPN.

Citrix Secure Private Access gives you zero trust access to your network and applications without connecting user endpoints directly to the network. This system uses adaptive authentication to monitor user activity after they're logged in. It monitors the security based on the role of the user, the security of the device, and the location of the request. This goes beyond simple multifactor authentication. Based on the role of the user, you can control what kind of functions they can perform such as printing or copy-and-paste, further protecting the unauthorized transfer of information.

Enabling business collaboration

Collaboration is the key when implementing zero trust. It goes partly back to the visibility issue. You must collaborate in-house to make sure you have the maximum amount of visibility. This is also true for vendors and collaborators that also log in to your network and applications. Any one of them can become a weak link, and their risk should be evaluated accordingly.

REMEMBER

Making sure your vendors accessing your systems are security certified goes a long way toward reducing risk and supporting compliance.

Making zero trust agile

Most successful zero trust implementations are those that have been zero-trust-happy from the first day they were created. Trying to make them compliant later by shoehorning in legacy systems is difficult at best and impossible in the worst case scenario.

One benefit of agility is that it can change on the fly. Before agile systems became the norm, change was plodding, full of red tape, costly, and interminable, and it often ended in failure. Agile systems may still fail, but they do so in small and easily correctible ways. With continuous development and integration, you can build zero trust principles into your applications as they're being developed and tested.

REMEMBER

Zero trust is more of a goal than a destination. You don't have to achieve zero trust immediately. Just make sure that, in this fast-paced world of change, you evaluate the changes you're making with zero trust principles as a guide.

Building the right team

Following the agile strategy for team-building — including all the right stakeholders and giving them an environment where communication becomes not only simple but also powerful — empowers your team. If you were able to follow that nasty run-on sentence, you can see that what you want to do is make sure that all employees and partners involved in a project are educated in, and onboard with, the principles that guide zero trust. If you find that your team members aren't trusting one another, that's a good thing.

Chapter **9**

Dealing with Hybrid Cloud Environments

Not all clouds are created equal. You're probably already using a public cloud of some sort. You may be using one of the larger commercial clouds such as Amazon AWS or Google Cloud, for example, or perhaps you back up your photos from your iPhone on iCloud. Data is processed and stored in the cloud more often than you can imagine. Most large Internet applications reside in the cloud, partly for their storage ability and partly so that the services will be geographically close to you. As the need for cloud computing has grown to be an almost ubiquitous part of any computing strategy, so also has the need for flexibility in how cloud computing is used. This chapter covers some of the components that make up a hybrid cloud as well as some of the advantages and challenges that come along with setting up a hybrid cloud. Then you're on your way as you start migrating your current data environment to the challenging but amazingly flexible hybrid cloud.

There is only one kind of cloud, but whether that cloud is available to the public or is privately secured makes a difference. Using a combination of public and onsite private clouds (and often with traditional onsite data processing thrown into the mix), you end up with what is known as a *hybrid cloud,* as shown in Figure 9-1. It isn't just a mishmash of clouds and local computing. Generally, the key feature that makes it a hybrid cloud is that it has a centralized control system — a dashboard of some kind that oversees the entire system of cloud and local resources. In this chapter, I walk you through the basics of the differences between public and private clouds as well as the differences between a cloud environment and a basic local data center. The mashup of these three environments, as shown in Figure 9-1, is what makes up a hybrid cloud. There are some major benefits to running a hybrid cloud as well as some challenges in the way of visualization and security. I spend the rest of this chapter looking at both.

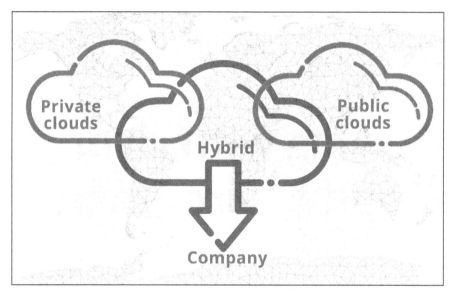

FIGURE 9-1:
Hybrid clouds are made up of public and private clouds connected to your company data center.

Public Clouds Make Pretty Sunsets

Your choice of whether to use public or private clouds can depend on the sensitivity of the data you're trying to protect. Network clouds are similar to clouds in the sky in that they can be beautiful, useful, but still be threatening. Some clouds make you feel safe and secure, and others carry with them more dangers.

Public clouds have become ubiquitous in a cloud-everywhere sort of way. You'll soon see how easy it is to set up a public cloud, the advantages of bringing computing closer to the customer, as well as some of the security concerns you might run into.

Controlling your environment

You're in a far more flexible situation when you can manage where your services or data live — including deciding whether some (or all) of your services and data should live in the cloud.

Some of the advantages of using a public cloud are pretty clear:

>> **Simple and inexpensive setup:** Get going quickly.

>> **Everything available as self-service:** No need for third-party help.

>> **Pay-for-use:** Pay only for what you use when you use it.

>> **Publiccloud service providers provide enhanced security:** You can also add managed cloud services for more protection.

>> **Scalability:** Grow or shrink as your demand requires, without having to add your own expensive hardware.

>> **Global access:** Put your computing close to the customer.

>> **Reliability:** Vendors such as Google, Azure and AWS rarely go down.

You can easily see the appeal of using a public cloud. Though it's true that public cloud companies do their absolute best to provide the best security for your applications and data while they live in their cloud environment, you are responsible for everything leading up to that point. You can have the best application security, but without managing access and authorization, your applications can be sitting ducks for hackers. Also, data doesn't just live in the cloud. It needs to move in and out of the cloud to local devices.

REMEMBER

You need to protect data whether it's at rest or in motion. This is done using encryption.

Optimizing for speed

Public clouds are not necessarily slow, but some latency usually occurs when data must travel in and out of your local network. An IT team will want the flexibility of being able to decide the optimum configuration with a mix of both public and private clouds.

Edge computing, or getting your data closer to the people who use it, is a huge benefit when it comes to using public clouds. You can then weigh any security risks of using public clouds against the advantage of faster access times and lower bandwidth for your customers. Using a public cloud also gives you the advantage of being able to scale up and down as the need arises. Faster interaction makes for happier customers, as shown in Figure 9-2.

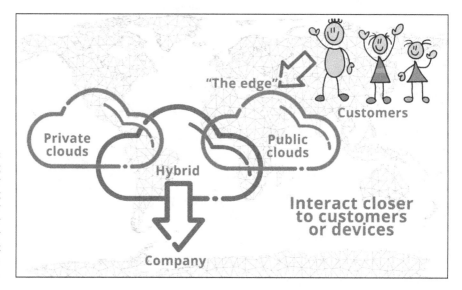

FIGURE 9-2:
Edge computing puts your computing resources closer to your customers or devices that interact with them.

You don't have to sacrifice security when processing on the edge — there are edge security protocols and products.

Managing security

Step one in any security environment, particularly one as potentially complex as an edge computing environment, is to know what's normal. If you have nothing to compare against, you'll never know when something has gone wrong.

Make sure your traffic to and from an edge node is encrypted and signed. It's easy to forget about data in motion. Building firewalls and encrypted data centers and all kinds of barrier security is useless if the data travels over the Internet unencrypted.

Be able to check your edge containers against an official container so that you know whether it has been tampered with. Official Docker containers are stored in a Docker repository. Find out more at https://docs.docker.com/docker-hub/official_images/

TIP

Knowing what's normal can be key to knowing when something is amiss. Without reality checks against known malware-free environments, it can be a long time before you even know you've been hacked. It was years before U.S. government officials realized that the government had been hacked. Many companies go about their daily business without ever knowing that malware is sending out its deep secrets.

Maintain a unified security plan that applies to devices regardless of their size or location. This is often easier said than done, and making it happen could be the biggest cloud security nightmare of all. A good security plan should include things like making sure that all devices receive regular security patches and updates.

Using software to manage all the nodes of your network helps you create that unified security policy and gives you visibility into your entire network. You may need AI to step in if the number of nodes is greater than you or a security team can handle.

TECHNICAL STUFF

Docker (www.docker.com) is a container management service that allows you to develop applications, ship them to containers, and run them anywhere. Docker containers are lightweight and scalable. When web applications need to communicate with each other securely, you should consider using Docker. Each container should run its own Docker network. (For more on working with containers, see Chapter 6 "Using containers.")

Private Clouds for Those Special Needs

Private clouds are the computing resources you keep locally, usually within your own facility. This is where you might share data storage with departments, provide applications throughout your organization, or store the company newsletter that no one reads. As long as your own company's data security is up to snuff, this may be the safest place to store and provide access to the company's most private data, trade secrets, employee information, and that company newsletter that too often leaks important information to the competitors.

WARNING

Running private clouds effectively and securely requires a skilled data center. Trying to replicate public cloud offerings locally can be an overwhelming task.

Private clouds use virtualization just like the public clouds do. Constricted by your own hardware configuration, running a private cloud rather than a traditional data center gives you the advantage of running multiple operating systems, spinning up new servers quickly, and expanding data storage into a system known as *hyperconvergence*.

A system that combines data storage, application programs, and networking into a single system controlled by an application known as a hypervisor greatly simplifies data center complexity. The complexity is reduced because everything ends up being controlled by software. You have software-defined storage, virtualized networking, and virtual machines (VM) that act as servers.

Running a private cloud rather than a traditional data center with purpose-built hardware gives you far more flexibility. The only thing your hardware has to do is run the hypervisor. (Think of the hypervisor as the virtual machine creator.) The VM can then be configured to run any number of different operating systems, storage systems, or virtualized networking applications.

One of the great things about running a public cloud is the control you can maintain over your environment. As long as you can maintain enough hardware to support your needs, it's a secure way to operate and one that is much easier to control from a security perspective.

REMEMBER

When you *need* to lock down your data, the safest place is usually your local data center. Local data centers are more secure because data doesn't have to travel between the cloud and your facility. You may be able to store this data in a location that isn't Internet-facing and therefore is more secure from hacking.

There are definite exceptions to this guideline. If your local data center isn't up to the task of protecting particular data — financial data, for instance — you may want to consider farming out that task to a more secure facility. Both IBM and Microsoft offer public clouds for financial services.

Fun fact: In certain data centers, the servers live in oxygen-free environments. This provides security on several levels — it limits casual access to the server, for example. Someone wearing scuba gear might stick out while trying to break into a server room like that. Oxygen is also an important fuel for things like fire and oxidation. Machines operate better and more safely in these types of environments.

REMEMBER

When storing your important data locally, you need to prepare for your own disaster recovery, backup, and security plans.

Wrapping Your Mind around Hybrid Cloud Options

Hybrid computing environments are made up of more than simply servers and storage devices. They can encompass several types of endpoints:

- » Software application providers, or SaaS

- » Server providers, or IaaS

- » IoT devices

- » Sensors

- » Mobile devices

Communication between the various parts of a hybrid cloud environment is done using several methods. These include local area networks (LAN), wide-area networks (WAN), application programming interfaces (API), and, for more-secure communications, virtual private networks (VPNs).

In the following sections, I describe why a hybrid cloud may be the right option for you. I also help you take a look at the pros and cons of using a hybrid cloud to help you understand what's actually involved.

Hybrid storage solution

Storing data is one of the most obvious uses of the cloud. Using a local cloud to store data and then using a public cloud for backups is a cost-effective solution but may have some security concerns as well as other challenges.

Table 9-1 compares some of the features and advantages of both private and public clouds. The first one is obvious: Data is stored differently between private and public clouds. The cost-controlled versus overall lower costs might be harder to understand if you're simply running a traditional data center. The costs of your data center are normally predictable and known. Public clouds have a pay-as-you-play cost basis. This is true of processing time when running applications or for data storage. This lets you be more flexible during changes such as seasonal peaks. Because this is a book about cloud security, it's important to mention that the security model is different as well. When you run your own data center, all the responsibility for security is on you. When you use a public cloud, the cloud service provider bears some of the responsibility for security.

Hybrid clouds, made up of both private and public clouds, have the advantages of both. For example, in a hybrid cloud you might store your data in the public cloud to take advantage of scalable storage solutions and use your private cloud for application user interfaces because of its inherent low latency. The disadvantage comes with the responsibility of managing both environments.

TABLE 9-1: **Private versus Public Clouds**

Private Cloud Solution	Public Cloud Solution
Data stored locally and privately	Data stored anywhere; good for edge computing
Cost controlled	Cheaper overall costs
Very low latency for local access	Low-latency global access
Local backups	Low-cost disaster recovery
Security locally managed	Shared security

REMEMBER

Hybrid clouds have all these benefits: improved cost control, more control over security, and the flexibility of a public cloud with its ability to have better latency and edge computing.

Tiered data storage

When evaluating your data, security is one concern. How you store your data also depends on how often you intend to retrieve it. Data tiers are organized by how you intend to use your data.

>> **Active data:** This data must be readily accessible and be optimized for read/write operations.

>> **Active Archive:** This data is used infrequently but is available immediately. Examples are disaster recovery data and backups.

>> **Inactive Archive:** This data is stored in archival storage and isn't immediately accessible — for example, tape backups.

Make certain to select the correct tier for your data. Each of the major cloud service providers offers a storage solution that matches one of these tiers. Each will have its own name, price, and performance profile, which takes a bit of planning — it's not one-size-fits-all.

TIP

In case your data storage requirements are not complex, some storage providers offer catch-all storage plans.

WARNING

Be aware that older, tiered storage options can be confusing. When using legacy storage solutions, make sure you store your data in the correct tier.

Gauging the Advantages of the Hybrid Cloud Setup

The advantage of expanding beyond your own corporate resources into the world of AWS, Google Cloud, Microsoft Azure, and others lies in the ability it gives you to expand globally (nearly infinitely) as well as the fact that you can now leverage all those features that public clouds have to offer. (See the "Public Clouds Make Pretty Sunsets" section, earlier in this chapter). Rather than just choose to run applications and store data locally or in a private cloud or abandoning that idea altogether for the public cloud, you can make use of all three scenarios. You gain an unlimited amount of flexibility. Check out the following benefits of using a hybrid cloud.

It's scalable

One of the greatest features of clouds in general are that they can be resized on demand. They grow when needed and shrink when demand shrinks. Most importantly, your data needs are no longer held hostage by the cost and time demands of growing a data center. It's now possible to grow in parts of a second.

The hybrid cloud requires that you maintain a certain fixed set of hardware while connecting to the more scalable public cloud. Private clouds can take advantage of virtualization (thus offering some scalability), but you need to make sure there is adequate hardware to support your cloud's containers or virtual machines.

The costs

Compared to the costs associated with purchasing and managing your own servers, not to mention all the other overhead of traditional data processing, renting space in a cloud environment just makes good sense. Additionally, when using cloud services, you normally pay only when the resource is in use. Costs are a little harder to manage because they aren't fixed, but it has been proven to be a more cost-effective solution because traditional data centers usually have to be overbuilt to handle surges or seasonal business requirements. This is a strong argument for using public clouds. The costs of a hybrid cloud will fall somewhere between the cheaper public cloud and the more expensive private data center.

You maintain control

You get to choose how much control you hand over to a public cloud service provider and how much you choose to keep private and in your local control. You may not have a choice of where to store your data when your company compliance restrictions place limits on the types of storage that can be used. Data storage in a private cloud or local data center is usually the most secure and in some cases be the most cost effective. With today's advanced SSD drives and low-cost, helium-filled drives, data storage devices continue to be more reliable than older HDDs and continue to drop in price making local storage affordable. The disadvantage remains that this solution is less scalable than a public cloud solution where additional drives can be spun up nearly instantaneously.

TIP

Not all applications are meant to run in the cloud. Part of maintaining control includes keeping your mission critical applications local while offloading less critical processing to the public cloud.

The need for speed

Again, flexibility in how you configure and optimize your data processing is at its highest when you can choose which features will give you the fastest processing times. In some cases, keeping processing local reduces network latency (data travel time); in other cases, putting the processing closer to your customers (edge computing) means that the customers get to experience the decreased latency, and that makes you look like a hero.

In certain scenarios, edge computing is a no-brainer. For example, stocks, commodities, and foreign exchange markets need the proximity to the trading computers to be effective. They can't suffer from latency or else they'll lose the trade to other, faster (or closer) systems.

Overcoming data silos

Cloud resources have made it tempting for groups, such as departments or working groups, to come up with their own cloud storage scenarios. These are usually a hybrid of local storage and public cloud storage. Hybrid cloud solutions can lead to a situation where your data is stored in multiple locations, each with the potential of becoming a dreaded data silo. Here are some of the biggest problems associated with data silos:

>> Data is inaccessible to the entire organization.

>> Data security is impossible to manage.

>> Data is unavailable to AI deep learning algorithms, such as those used by AIOps.

>> Data isn't always available to discovery software that maps your resource utilization.

To make matters even more challenging, different administrators may choose different cloud offerings, with one choosing AWS, and another, the Google Cloud Platform. This makes integration more difficult but not impossible. You just don't want to end up with fragmented silos.

There is a huge advantage to creating a managed hybrid cloud used by the entire enterprise: You have visibility over the entire hybrid network, share data across the enterprise in a unified manner, and eliminate siloed data and shadow IT departments. Rather than storing departmental data locally, or in cloud private to the department, sharing it in a public cloud makes it accessible to others throughout the company, and even shareable in a company-wide data store.

Data silos can be annoying for both security as well as application data sharing. When it comes to siloed applications, the dangers appear whenever data can't be shared between applications. What you don't want to end up with is something known as *swivel chair* data entry, when someone has to enter the same data into more than one application or reenter data from one application into another. This is true for end users as well as for those responsible for data security.

Accessing redundant data is simply pointless.

REMEMBER Using APIs and sharing them throughout your organization goes a long way toward visibility. For example, you can create a *data shop* — a listing of the data resources available throughout your organization — and then make it known throughout your organization that the shop's data wares can be accessed via APIs. Such APIs make data use seamless, because the end user will neither know nor care whether the data came from a public or private cloud. Reusing data in this manner is one of the best ways to prevent various departments from going out in search of their own data — data that may already exist in your organization. Figure 9-3 shows how you can access data stored in the cloud through an API. (Make certain your API credentials are secure, because this is yet another area of security that's often overlooked.)

Next, let the IT department manage this data shop. That way, those colleagues maintain an overview of all data usage within the organization, which allows them to manage API security, data security, and data usage. In a perfect world, your company would develop a single and unified dataset. Security, such as authorization and access, could be managed for things like compliance requirements. For example, some datasets can be anonymized, giving wider access to company information without releasing private or identifying information.

Here's an old saying from the early days of the Internet: "On the Internet, no one knows you're a Mac." In the same way, using a unified API system, no one knows whether the data is from a public or private cloud.

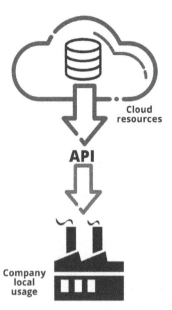

FIGURE 9-3:
Access data
stored in the
cloud by way of
an API.

Cloud
resources

API

Company
local
usage

Make sure your move to the hybrid cloud remains controlled by a central authority, or else the move to a hybrid cloud can lead to more silos.

WARNING

Compliance

Companies that must protect some of their data, such as medical facilities complying with HIPAA, or any of the other many compliance requirements I cover in more detail later in this chapter, need to be able to securely store encrypted data while using less-secure or public cloud offerings to do less-sensitive computing and analysis.

There is a difference between a hybrid cloud and a multicloud: *Hybrid* clouds are made up of a combination of traditional local computing, private clouds, and public clouds; multiclouds, on the other hand, always make use of multiple public clouds. This is slightly different from the Forrester definition of a hybrid cloud that basically just says that a hybrid cloud is one or more public clouds connected to something in my data center.

**TECHNICAL
STUFF**

There are countless products for protecting hybrid clouds. An example of a popular product is Fortinet (www.fortinet.com). This product has the basic features of what you need to effectively manage a hybrid cloud. First, you need a system that lets you see and manage the entire network. Data in motion is protected by using a VPN. It also sends security alerts in a unified way so that you aren't receiving alerts from many different systems. The product also scales security as your cloud needs scaling.

Because clouds are more than places to store data — they also allow SaaS operations — you need to protect your SaaS environments. Fortinet offers its FortiCASB SaaS product, which monitors all your SaaS operations using the SaaS application API. This includes applications your company probably uses, like Salesforce and Microsoft Office 365.

TIP

Another product for protecting hybrid clouds is Hewlett Packard's HPE Cloud Volumes, a suite of enterprise data services that offers a unified data experience and bridges the divide between private data centers and the public cloud (`https://cloudvolumes.hpe.com/welcome`).

Struggling with Hybrid Challenges

Hybrid clouds are complicated. This often keeps companies from using them, despite their benefits. It can be quite a challenge for any IT department tasked with making certain that everything is working as it should and that the entire network complex is safe and secure. In this section, you can see that there are times when using public or hybrid clouds just isn't an option. Also, you can see how organizing is the key to managing a hybrid cloud.

Quite often, before companies transition to using the public cloud for all their needs, they will transition away from using their own data center by setting up private clouds that interoperate with public clouds in a hybrid cloud format. This requires that security is managed for both private and public clouds as well as the data transfer between them.

Handling a larger attack surface

From a security perspective, anytime you increase the size of your network by any number of devices, you increase the attack surface. This isn't unique to hybrid clouds, because some networks become filled with thousands of IoT devices. But the security complexity becomes higher. Is your cloud infrastructure running on the same machine as someone else's? Can you rely on their security if malware takes control of the machine? When using a hybrid cloud, you bring into your own network all these security concerns that are normally unique to using a public cloud.

Data leakage

Because hybrid clouds are connected via the public Internet, you inevitably face the security issues that arise from compromised endpoints, human error (such as leaving passwords taped to your monitor), or more straightforward cyberattacks such as man-in-the-middle or SQL insertion or defeating API security.

WARNING

Ninety-four percent of all malware is delivered by email, according to CSO Online. You can quickly see how humans are the biggest risk in any security environment. Because malware in email is so common, it often leads to weakened security and unintentional data leakage. Many phishing attacks are also delivered via email. Train your employees to recognize phishing attempts.

Human error is difficult to guard against. A data leak can occur simply by sending private company information to the wrong email recipient. To best catch preventable issues that cause data leaks, do the following:

>> Make sure that computer endpoints are correctly configured and patched with the latest security patches.

>> Use network tracking tools that look for keywords in data transmissions, throwing up flags to network operators that private data may be leaking.

>> Encrypt data at rest when possible. Encrypted data is inherently much safer. Even though breaches may be unintentional, the damage they cause can be the same as if a hacker had breached intentionally.

Data transport times

Sometimes, even the best optimized hybrid solution can't manage massive data flow requirements. When computing systems have to handle teraflops of data, hybrid clouds may not be the answer. Most of these teraflop situations are super-computer scenarios such as managing weather data, city-wide traffic control systems, or public utilities needing microsecond control.

Complexity

Managing any type of network is a complex task. Add in the job of managing all the multiple environments, varying security platforms, and interfaces of public clouds and you face quite a challenge. Additionally, because credential management is vital in network protection of any kind, getting a system to work in a distributed manner across both your private and public clouds becomes essential.

Risks to your service level agreements

When you don't control the environment on which your platform runs or your data lives, it's hard to deliver on promises you might have made in the past. Your own service level agreements (SLA) can quickly become a hybrid of many agreements as you sign on with different cloud companies, each with their own SLA. Carefully consider each of the terms of service you're bound by after you sign on the dotted line.

TIP

Read the fine print in your agreements with cloud service providers. These are the nitpicky points you need to provide in your own SLAs to the people who count on your services.

Overcoming Hybrid Challenges

To overcome some of the challenges outlined in the preceding section, you should adopt a strong asset management system.

Asset management

Complexity is one of the overarching challenges to hybrid clouds. The key to most complex matters is organization. After you have things organized, your security issues are also organized and much easier to manage. The factors that make managing hybrid cloud environments difficult are the number and variety of resources. This is overcome with IT Asset Management, or ITAM. Until complexity became the norm in the IT world, ITAM was overlooked. Now it's required. To be able to realize the dream of cloud-everywhere using a hybrid cloud environment, it's critical that you manage your assets.

REMEMBER

You can't manage risks if you don't know what they are. Documenting risk assessment is important to any security plan.

When you manage your IT resources, you create a *single source of truth*. If this sounds a little philosophical, it really isn't. Basically, you're simply documenting your environment, both software and hardware. Of course, it wouldn't be IT-related without an acronym: Software Asset Management is known as SAM, and Hardware Asset Management is called HAM.

An IT Asset Management System lets you not only document what you have and where it may exist but also track requirements such as the ones described in this list:

>> **Cost:** In complex environments such as those relying on hybrid clouds, managing costs is a bit more complex than either running your own data center where costs are known or employing the public cloud where costs are variable but predictable. When managing various assets, you need to document both the fixed and variable costs associated with each asset.

- **Resource consumption:** Planning for and managing a hybrid cloud also means you're somehow staying on top of which of your resources is consuming more than others. In this way, you can effectively move data and applications between your local data center and public cloud resources. For example, some applications may be consuming massive archival data storage. You can do the cost analysis of increasing your own physical storage or using public cloud storage, keeping security and risk in mind.

- **Lifecycle:** Documenting the lifecycle of various assets allows you to scale up and down as assets are needed or have served their purpose. This is one of the huge advantages of virtualized computing — being able to quickly spin up new resources in seconds or sooner.

- **Risks:** Every time you use a cloud, whether to store your data or use a cloud-based application, you're taking a risk. This isn't to scare you, because you take a certain amount of risk even getting out of bed in the morning. The goal then becomes to manage those risks. Before you can manage risk, you need to understand the risk involved with each of your network based assets. You will want to document these risks to get a better handle on what it will take to manage those risks. To coin a phrase, call it *gestalt risk*.

REMEMBER

Your asset management should not become a stale bit of documentation. Like your environment, it should routinely be evaluated and updated. You will want to continually assess the risks associated with each of your assets. So many things can change over time. Malware changes and finds new ways to attack your software and hardware, and this can be one of the key things you track to manage risks.

The number of people who have access and the levels of access they are given are important to continually evaluate. Keep the idea that you want to allow only the minimum amount of access necessary to any resource, to limit risk.

SAM

Software Asset Management (SAM) is of importance for anyone doing application development. In the world of agile software development, most of which is being made cloud-available, keeping track of these software programs and any potential risks they introduce is of utmost importance. DevOps now includes automated security testing as part of the agile release schedule. Additionally, a well secured system will also have ongoing security testing after launch. The results of these tests should become part of your software asset management system.

So much for managing your own internal software development. Just as important is to document what cloud resources offered by others your company uses. (That is one of the cool things about the cloud: You don't always have to build it yourself.) What you need is a good IT governance policy that establishes some guidelines about how cloud resources should be adopted. Without it, you run the risk of having an IT environment outside of your control — the dreaded shadow IT.

Because the real issue at hand in a software environment is the data that is created, processed, and stored, your IT governance policy should include a description of how data is protected as it flows between various software resources and between clouds (data on the move), and how it's protected in storage.

HAM

Hardware asset management (HAM) is a bit more complex than it may seem at first glance. There are the obvious risks of hardware theft. This includes smartphones, IoT devices, laptops, and even desktop computer systems. But aside from this obvious threat is also the risk of attack from having out-of-date firmware or operating systems that lack the latest security patches.

When managing hardware firmware updates, remember to include network devices such as routers and switches.

When using cloud resources, your job gets trickier because underlying those clouds are hardware assets out of your control. In this case, management is done by agreement. You must know and understand how your cloud service provider is protecting its hardware resources, and this understanding should be part of how you document the management of those cloud resources.

IT asset management

Like anything today, there is no need to do any of the previously described processes manually. Consider employing a good IT asset management (ITAM) software package. These generally offer an automated discovery system so that you don't overlook cloud resources you may not even know existed, as well as sophisticated mapping systems to show how all these resources are interrelated.

Using an ITAM software system allows you to fully support an AIOps environment. The machine learning within AIOps relies on automated discovery tools to make certain it has the latest-and-greatest information on which to make decisions. That's another reason now to try the impossible task of trying to manage this environment manually.

Make sure the asset management software you select will integrate with any existing pipeline software or AIOps system you're running.

Latency issues

Network latency, the time it takes data to travel from one point on your network to another, may or may not be part of the SLA you have with your clients, but when it's bad, they complain. Latency can be a challenge in a hybrid cloud setup. It's important to carefully engineer your hybrid cloud to make sure that each of the data interconnections is optimal so that you aren't suddenly stuck with some of the connections clogged with data. Plan your traffic carefully.

To overcome the latency issue (or, even better, making sure it never exists) be sure to use *software-defined interconnections (SD-IX)*: These are software based controllers that communicate instructions using an API with the hardware routers or other underlying hardware that direct network traffic. Implementing controllers in software allows much faster reaction times and increased data flow.

The nature of cloud computing in today's virtualized computing is powerful, agile, and maddeningly difficult to manage — so you need the support of software-defined networking. A workload on any interconnection may change depending on how many virtual machines are spun up or destroyed when they're no longer needed.

For advanced hybrid cloud environments, you may need to go beyond simple software-defined computing to a *hyperconverged infrastructure* — a software-defined system that virtualizes every element of a hardware defined system, including these features:

- **Virtualized computing:** Virtual versions of servers or desktop computers (VMs, in other words)

- **Software-defined storage:** Using software to provision and manage storage separately from hardware

- **Virtualized networking:** Virtual network resources that were once hardware devices. (Virtual machines communicate with each other using virtual networks.)

TIP

When security requirements dictate, you might consider hardwired connections between your hybrid cloud nodes. Some examples of the connections available include the fiber or ethernet cabled connections offered by AWS Direct Connect (https://aws.amazon.com/directconnect/) or Azure's ExpressRoute (https://azure.microsoft.com/en-us/services/expressroute/). Not only do you increase the security of your communications, but direct connections also increase data speeds and lower latency because traffic no longer needs to be routed through multiple network hops.

On the Move: Migrating to a Hybrid Cloud

Figuring out when it's time to make the move to a hybrid cloud isn't always easy. It's a balancing act getting from where you currently are to where you need to be. If you're running your own data center and want to add public cloud services, you can weigh the cost savings against the increase in security responsibility you have to take on. (I don't say the word *risks* because there is no reason to increase the risk. It just requires careful security management.)

If you're already using a public cloud for your data services and considering adding a private cloud or locally managed data center, your biggest concerns will be to protect the data as it moves between your privately controlled services and the public cloud you're already using.

Data migration readiness

When it's time to migrate away from using a single cloud solution or your own data center to a hybrid cloud solution, be ready for some challenges. You're going to face the (sometimes subtle) variations between cloud service providers. These differences can include security products and measures, protocols for creating roles, or an inability to communicate with custom cloud resource that can turn into a management nightmare.

Different cloud service providers offer different native features. This may be why you're choosing a hybrid cloud solution, but you need to be aware of these features and work these into your migration plan.

Making a plan

Start by creating a team of stakeholders who know and understand how data is being used within the organization. It's not enough to just involve the IT team — they might be knowledgeable, but it's the end users or stakeholders who *really* know the applications and are thus likely to ask the hard questions about why you might want to move them to the cloud. This group, which is sometimes officially organized into the Cloud Business Office, should take a look at your applications and data and decide whether they're too old to move — in other words, whether they're written in COBOL and running on an old mainframe (hopefully, not with cards). See which systems might be approaching failure because of a lack of resources. These might be ripe for the first move.

TIP

Use the *6 Rs framework* to evaluate each of your applications. These six "Rs" comprise the framework:

>> Retire

>> Retain

>> Repurchase

>> Rehost

>> Replatform

>> Refactor

Sometimes it's best to ditch applications that are just too costly to upgrade for the move to the cloud. In these cases, you have to decide if there is a more modern version that can take the place of the outdated application, or if you have a dev team, if it can be recreated with modern technology (with embedded security of course!) Some applications can be retained and will move directly into the cloud. Others may require newer versions and require a repurchase. The advantage of using more than one cloud platform could be that applications that will not run on one cloud platform may just find a home on another where they run with little or no tweaking.

Once you have a list of the applications and your plan for moving them, replacing them or living without them, you can begin moving them, usually into a sandbox, a temporary test location to make sure they operate correctly and the outputs they produce are what you're expecting. Automated test applications can help with this.

TIP

Don't move everything at once. Move slowly through your migration plan. Test each application carefully before moving to the next. Trying to move too much all at once can mean overwhelming your migration team with errors that are difficult to troubleshoot because you aren't sure which application is causing them. See the section on using a migration calendar.

Picking the right cloud service

The offerings of cloud service providers are numerous. Make sure you understand the components offered by each one, including

>> Data storage solutions, such as various database types (SQL, noSQL, object-oriented, LDAP)

>> Cloud management tools

>> Cloud monitoring tools

>> Security software

Imagine you're buying a car. You want to know things like the car's gas mileage or how far it will drive on a battery charge or which features it may come equipped with. It's the same situation with selecting a cloud service: Make sure you know your own requirements before you go shopping so that you don't just grab the first service with a fancy name or logo. Understand your security requirements, your network latency, your need for disaster recovery, and of course, costs.

TIP

Carefully consider the security plan offered by cloud service providers and how they will mesh with your own security plan or security monitoring software.

Using a migration calendar

Do *not* plan to move everything all at once. Creating a hybrid cloud should be a nuanced and carefully executed plan. In the first migration step, you created a plan with your stakeholders. Make a schedule that allows you the time to do proper integration and testing. Give it time to settle so that your stakeholders feel comfortable with the change and you're certain all the security measures have been put in place before moving on to the next part of your migration plan.

Making it happen

When you're ready to begin migrating, *stick to the plan.* Delays can become costly and confusing to the end users. It's important that they maintain a strong trust in the process. The alternative means that they abandon the plan and go off on their own and you're back to data silos.

Dealing with compatibility issues

Compatibility issues arise largely when expanding your local applications into the cloud. There are many good reasons to move them up into public clouds, but invariably you run into the issue where the cloud is running a different stack from the one you run locally.

Compatibility issues aren't usually showstoppers, but they can become gotchas if you haven't planned for them and then suddenly your well-thought-out move into the cloud has come to a standstill.

REMEMBER

Using virtualization makes your environment *hardware agnostic,* meaning that you can avoid many compatibility issues.

One step along the way to migrating to a hybrid cloud might be to start with a private cloud. This gets your environment operating in a virtualized world and you may experience fewer compatibility issues when your applications are moved to the cloud. It also allows you to implement things such as virtual networking.

Using a Package

In this section, I show you that it isn't necessary to do all the engineering of a hybrid cloud deployment yourself. You can find ready-made packages that will handle that task for you.

HPE Hybrid Cloud Solution

The HPE Hybrid Cloud Solution application (www.hpe.com/us/en/solutions/ hybrid-cloud.html) offers a mature software solution that enables you to create a cloud-first environment where you have completely migrated your computing resources into the cloud. It puts your applications in the right environment and then creates seamless and secure communications between your private and public cloud. Your applications are run in containers, which improves their efficiency as well as their agility and portability. This application integrates well with Google Cloud Platform, AWS, and Azure.

Amazon Web Services

AWS (https://aws.amazon.com) is an excellent choice for your hybrid cloud when you've selected AWS for your public cloud. This ensures that applications running on your private cloud have the best integration with the public AWS cloud.

VMware virtualization software (www.vmware.com) is employed in the private cloud. This solution is the vendor of choice for many companies that use virtual machines in their data centers. VMware Cloud (https://vmc.vmware.com/home) is co-engineered by AWS and VMware and is the only hybrid cloud solution fully supported by VMware.

AWS also provides Kubernetes clusters for deploying and managing containerized applications.

Microsoft Azure

Azure (`https://portal.azure.com/#home`) has both hybrid and multicloud solutions. The Azure applications manage, secure, and govern servers, Kubernetes clusters, and applications wherever they live. This can be in a multicloud environment, out on the edge, or in your own private cloud.

A nice feature of the Azure suite of products is that it allows for a unified sign-on for the cloud, mobile devices, other computing devices, and onsite applications.

REMEMBER

Humans are the weakest link in your security. Offering a simple and unified sign-on helps eliminate the need for multiple passwords.

The hybrid cloud solution is just one tool in the chest and may or may not be the right choice for your company. If you start down the path toward a hybrid cloud, your team planning should quickly point out whether this is the right choice. Make sure you do the asset assessment and select the right vendor.

IN THIS CHAPTER

» Recognizing the dangers of email

» Keeping data loss at a minimum

» Securing cloud data from theft

» Dealing with disasters

» Taking chaos in stride

Chapter **10**

Data Loss and Disaster Recovery

C loud security is about more than protecting your data from hackers — it's also about securing the data from loss caused by theft or disaster. Data loss prevention (DLP) has a simple goal: Keep important data safe, whether from leaving your business in an unauthorized manner — walking out the door, you might say — or totally lost because of some random disaster. It's a major issue for security administrators because of the landscape and the scope of the challenge — particularly when the landscape includes multiple cloud environments.

A great percentage of data loss comes from within and not from external hack attempts. As unpleasant as it might sound, you're faced with protecting the data from the intentional or unintentional actions of people who might actually have approved access to such data from phones, laptops, desktops, and Apple Watches. Most businesses are burdened with needing to protect hundreds or thousands of network access points.

When it comes to data loss prevention, you should know that a disaster situation generally produces one of these three outcomes:

>> Everything comes to a screeching halt until the problem is corrected and the data is recovered.

>> Your company can continue operating, by way of work-arounds, at a reduced level. This happens only when a company has shown forethought and invested sufficient time and effort in developing recovery plans.

>> The problem can cascade and make a mess so big that it can't be cleaned up.

This last scenario is sadly the one that many companies end up in. While this scenario is not that common, it can cost companies a great deal to overcome.

DLP and disaster recovery go hand in hand. If you can't get to your data for some reason, it's lost to you until you can access it again. So, preventing data loss is an admirable goal, but recovering from data loss and disasters that prevent you from accessing your data (whether it has been encrypted by malware or even something simpler, like you forgot to renew your domain name) requires planning. Yes, it happens. In 2015 Google.com was accidentally put on the market for $12. The leaders of several large companies have forgotten, over the years, to renew their domain names or their SSL certificates, rendering access to their data impossible. Human error can lead to data loss and potential disaster.

REMEMBER

Having a disaster recovery plan is useless if you don't test it occasionally. It's like reaching for a fire extinguisher, only to learn that it has sat empty for years.

All data loss is a disaster — regardless of the amount. This chapter discusses some of the methods used in making sure you can recover from a data loss disaster.

Linking Email with Data Loss

Any discussion of data loss prevention needs to include the most likely way your company can face a data loss disaster: your email system. Not that long ago, the world was not as digitally oriented as it is today. Communications still occurred over the phone or by physical mail (*snail mail*) and package delivery. The next step might be recalled as the intermediary step of sending floppy disks, CD-ROMs, and even thumb drives full of information via snail mail.

Email, for several years now, has been the primary way that we humans send information to one another. This situation is slowly changing, as apps that encourage collaboration are adopted, keeping at least most of the data we transfer somewhat secure. But we haven't entered the post-email era yet, which means that email is still used daily to transfer some of the most sensitive information imaginable — and without giving it a second thought.

Most folks at least realize that email is *not* encrypted and are at least relatively aware of emails being compromised in transit — a data-in-motion problem. The thing is, the security of email doesn't end with such data-in-motion problems — it's also a data-at-rest problem because most people save their email communications for years. Depending on the type of email service you use, this archive of sensitive data might reside on your phone, your computer, or in the archives of an email service provider such as Gmail or Yahoo. (Remember AOL?)

Data loss from malware

Much more important than the data-at-rest or data-in-motion problems that crop up now and then is the far more ubiquitous problem of human gullibility. ("There's a sucker born every minute," as the phrase associated with PT Barnum succinctly puts it.) Spam brought with it more than a simple annoyance, filling up your inbox. It also brought some of the most devious scams known to humankind — ones that can sometimes bring with them devastating consequences.

If you're reading this book, you're most likely fairly sophisticated and savvy when it comes to spotting fraud in your email. It didn't take too many years until you were wise to the fact that no Nigerian prince has 4.7 million dollars they were willing to send you if you'd just give them the banking information where the money could be sent. But, as a reminder, not everyone in your company is you, and if the Nigerian prince scam no longer worked, it would not continue appearing in your email. It keeps appearing because one person always thinks, "What? Me? A millionaire? I always *knew* this day would come."

Exploits to steal your information, like the notorious Nigerian prince scam, are known as *phishing* attempts, and their deviousness knows no bounds. What if, for example, you receive an email from your bank, informing you that your password has been stolen and needs to be changed immediately for your security? The email also helpfully provides you with a link to change your password. Clicking that link takes you to a *spoof* site, which looks exactly like your bank's website. A form asks you to enter your old password for verification and then enter a new password twice. It may even provide one of those strong password generators. Of course, it's real — real bad. Someone now has your bank account password.

Take this scenario one step further and imagine the email that says, "Your corporate account has been suspended due to suspicious activity. We need to ascertain that you are who you say you are. Please provide a correct user ID and password and the mobile phone number so that we can send you a two-factor authentication code." Oops! Now they have your corporate login and the phone number used for authentication.

The nefarious ransomware

Worse than scams are the malware that allows people to take control of your network in order to encrypt critical data so that it can be ransomed back to you. Law enforcement has gotten better at recovering the cryptocurrency used to pay ransoms, but more than the money, you want your data back. Here is some of the history of the most notorious ransomware attacks.

The first known ransomware attack occurred in 1989. As of the writing of this book, that was more than *three decades* ago, and ransomware is still going strong. The scam was perpetrated by Joseph Poll, PhD, a research scientist studying the AIDS virus. After sending disks in the mail to other researchers around the world (because email was rarely used in 1989), he claimed that the disks contained an AIDS risk assessment tool. Anyone using the disks was 100 percent certain to be infected, not by AIDS, but by malware, *PC Cyborg*, which had the capability to encrypt critical data and then demand a ransom. Though the actual messages may change, Figure 10-1 gives you an idea of the heart-wrenching message people see on their screens.

FIGURE 10-1:
Ransomware attacks have crippled many companies.

The year 2013 saw the start of the terrible *CryptoLocker*, which infected nearly 250,000 computers and exacted millions in ransom. In 2016 a ransomware attack crippled the San Francisco Municipal Transportation Agency by attacking the ticketing and bus management systems. In 2017 the world saw *WannaCry*, which not only extorted money but then failed to release the data. The 2021 Colonial Pipeline shutdown was one of the most recent and *deplorable* ransomware attacks. According to the FBI's Internet Crime Report for 2020, losses to ransomware totaled $29.1 million from 2,474 complaints (www.ic3.gov/Media/PDF/AnnualReport/2020_IC3Report.pdf).

Though multiple methods for the spread of ransomware exist, the most common is the innocuous email message. Malware can be hidden in an email attachment that looks like something as innocuous as a normal morning briefing document. Ransomware is increasing rather than disappearing. Rather than gaining ground on defeating ransomware, it has become more sophisticated. Ransomware is one of the most critical data loss threats you can experience.

Ransomware and the cloud

Cloud data storage isn't immune from ransomware. Files in the cloud are commonly synced with local files by way of one of the many desktop and mobile file-syncing applications, such as Microsoft's OneDrive and Dropbox. That means that, when the files on your local computer are encrypted, files stored in the cloud are also encrypted.

Larger corporate clients may also use a storage gateway solution that also syncs files. AWS Storage Gateway is just one example among many. *Syncing,* as described by AWS, lets you "seamlessly connect on-premises applications with cloud storage." The trouble with the *seamlessly* part is that it "seamlessly" enables ransomware to infect the data you've entrusted to AWS.

The tiered storage solution also poses a potential problem for cloud storage and ransomware. *Tiered storage* is a solution that moves seldom- or never-used data to archival storage in the cloud, saving companies the cost of continually increasing local storage capacity and giving them the scalability they need. This is one of the great benefits of using the cloud, though it doesn't mean that the data you store there hasn't already been encrypted. But tiered data storage may be one of the solutions. Employing a tiered data storage solution may provide the backup you need to recover your data because it doesn't sync with your production data and will remain protected from attempts to encrypt it maliciously.

Crafting Data Loss Prevention Strategies

Data loss prevention involves more than simply installing some applications and dealing with the fallout as they start generating alerts. True data loss prevention is a strategy, like most of the security strategies described throughout this book. You'll find some of these strategies a bit repetitive when comparing them against other discussions of data protection, but they bear repeating in the context of data loss prevention.

Here are some steps you need to take in developing your DLP strategy:

1. **Complete a risk assessment.**

   Not all data has the same risk level attached to it. Therefore, you should not expend the same amount of energy or capital trying to protect it. The level of risk is based on the impact of the loss or theft of the data. By the way, don't think, just because you've implemented the perfect backup strategy, that your data is risk free. You don't want to lose the data in the first place, and a data breach, where the data is stolen or released to the public, can inflict long-term damage on your business.

2. **Create a data classification system that has a corresponding tag system to identify data in a stratified risk manner.**

   Protecting data is much easier if you can see that something is *secret* as opposed to *public,* instead of trying to discern a more chaotic and less understood classification, like this one: "The <poo> hits the fan if this is released!" A good classification system is also a requirement of most regulatory compliance directives.

3. **Create a data flow diagram that clearly points out when data is at risk, whether it's in motion and needs to be encrypted or at rest and needs further protection.**

   This diagram can be extended to include information about the data in the diagram, spelling out which permissions or sharing rights are associated with the data.

4. **Develop or purchase solutions for monitoring data in motion.**

   Employing a cloud access security broker, as discussed later in this chapter, is an excellent first step in protecting the data in motion between your users and their cloud applications. A similar application should be installed in your local- or wide-area network to protect the data in motion there.

5. **Employ Exact Data Match technology to spot data misuse or theft without generating noisy false positives.**

   An example of when a false positive alert might be triggered by a data monitoring application is social security numbers. Your HR department may have to transfer the social security numbers of its employees when filing tax information, which is an authorized and expected use of these numbers. But matching numbers against actual social security numbers of customers allows you to spot misuse only when one of those is unexpectedly transferred across the network.

6. **Develop a set of security policies that clearly spells out, at a fine-grained level, the types of access allowed for files, people, databases, and applications.**

   The same policies will most likely govern local resources as those protected in the cloud. These human readable and easily understood policies will help you create these policies in various applications.

7. **Avoid overextending yourself.**

   Trying to take on the entire organization and all its data at one time is a recipe for disaster. Take small bites and protect the most sensitive data first. Then you can slowly introduce your data loss prevention strategy to users in small tranches rather than try to educate everyone in the entire organization simultaneously.

TIP

When selecting a DLP solution, or set of solutions, try to find one that meets most of the challenges. Very few solutions will fix all problems. The goal here is visibility without the swivel chair effect, where the network operators are swinging to and fro between real-time monitors. You want the fewest number of dashboards, view screens, or other monitoring platforms as possible.

Data loss prevention should also be integrated with other IT security solutions, such as your AIOps solutions. If possible, find a solution vendor that offers a broad variety of applications — so that even if they aren't wrapped up in the same application, they will most likely operate in a similar manner, look, and feel. This strategy makes monitoring easier, enables integration between platforms, and reduces the learning curve for all involved.

After coming up with a data loss protection strategy and classifying your data, you need to take the next step and install the technologies you'll use to implement the plan. This section covers some of the backup strategies for data generally in a perimeter-protected network. The following section covers cloud data loss protection. You need both technologies for a complete DLP system.

Backing up your data

The most obvious solution to data loss, and loss due to a ransomware attack, particularly, is to have a backup of your data. The type of backup you choose to make can be the key to your success in recovering your data in a reasonable amount of time.

REMEMBER

Reasonable amounts of time are relative. For instance, in the Colonial Pipeline ransomware attack, company leaders chose to pay the ransom even though they had backups of their data. They believed that the decryption tools provided by the ransomware perpetrator would be faster than recovering their data from backups, so they ponied up the money. It turns out that Colonial was wrong. The ransomware tools ended up being quite slow, so they had to turn to their backups anyway. Time was of the essence because the east coast wasn't getting its gasoline supplied while Colonial was down. Still, recovery from backups took a considerable amount of time while markets took a dip and customers began idling in their vehicles in long gas station lines.

Tiered backups

If the term *backups* calls to mind those old (and by now, fairly useless) off-premises tape backups, there's a whole new world out there waiting for you. Tiered backups are part of that new world.

The idea behind tiered backups is that, whereas it's true that backing up your data is a no-brainer, *how* you back up that data is not. Backup is no one-size-fits-all solution, so using a tiered backup strategy improves your backup system and your overall data security. In developing such a strategy, here are the factors you need to consider:

>> How much data you back up

>> How often you back up

>> The complexity of the types of data you back up

>> The security risks associated with your data

You need to plan a strategy that allows your IT department easy and direct access to backup data in an organized and simple manner for rapid recovery. You may need to recover large swathes of data or only a single record from a database that may have become corrupted.

Backup data is generally categorized into priority tiers based on the type of data:

>> **Tier 1:** Sales, marketing, manufacturing, and project data

>> **Tier 2:** Financial and accounting data

>> **Tier 3:** Important business application data

>> **Tier 4:** Everything else

If you focus on the first two priority tiers, you'll have maximized your backup strategy. Tier 1 is data that's critical to the operation of your business. It may not include trade secret intellectual property files unless they're used in the ongoing operation of the business. Tier 2 consists of your accounting files that are used daily, not last year's financial records. Tier 3 contains information that lays out your intellectual property, and past-year financial information. Tier 4 contains documents such as business correspondence. Organizing your data by priority allows you to see that the amount of data that needs to be regularly backed up, even daily, is quite small. This operational data should be kept at the ready and easy to recover compared with Tier 4 data, which might get backed up less frequently.

The strategy you use for backing up various tiers differs depending on your required recovery time. For instance, Tier 1 data, critical to the ongoing operation of your business, should be recoverable within an hour. Other tiers may be able to withstand longer downtimes and therefore don't require the same backup recovery time frame. For a discussion of recovery times, skip down to the RTO and RPO section below.

REMEMBER

Segmenting your data into tiers allows you to make intelligent decisions about their backup-and-restore strategies.

You can create as many or as few tiers as you want; no one is regulating this point and no best practices are associated with it. Another benefit of organizing your data into tiers is that the strategies you choose will likely have different costs. Regular backups with high-speed recovery have a different cost basis than something backed up monthly and with a recovery time tolerance measured in days.

Data bunkers

Offline storage of your data in a data bunker is another way to create backups that remain safe. Although not as accessible as other backup-and-restore mechanisms, they are clearly safer. Data storage in a bunker is a one-way transaction. Data goes in and stays in. The data stored in a data bunker cannot be changed after it's there, which makes it safe from ransomware attacks.

Data bunkers offer services that include *tokenization* of your data (replacing private data with tokens) as well as encryption. (The latter is a must-have item.)

In addition to simply keeping your archived data safe, it assists you when it comes to compliance. For example, when doing business in the European Union, GDPR compliance is required. Here are a few companies that can help you if you decide to go the data bunker route for your backup strategy:

- >> **Commvault:** www.cdw.com/product/commvault-complete-backup-recovery-for-virtualized-environments-license/5182986

- >> **Data Bunker:** https://databunker.org

- >> **IBM:** www.ibm.com/cloud/disaster-recovery

- >> **Pure Storage:** www.purestorage.com

TIP

Protect your company from ransomware attacks by storing your data in a data bunker.

Disaster recovery

DLP isn't always about not losing the data; sometimes, it's about getting it back after it's lost. It's kind of like having a cat: You miss it when it's gone, but as long as it shows back up, you're happy. It's the same with data.

TIP

Create a disaster recovery plan. Here is a sample, straight from the US government:

www.ready.gov/it-disaster-recovery-plan

Most of the data vault and backup solutions offer a disaster recovery solution. IBM offers Disaster Recovery as a Service, DRaaS. Here are some features of its disaster recovery:

- >> Automated recovery to avoid errors

- >> Risk-based approach to data recovery

- >> Cloud-based systems that eliminate the need for local disaster recovery servers

Disasters can happen because of more than just hackers trying to take down your company. Simple events like network outages because the bulldozer down the street has just severed your fiber optic connection to the Internet happen as well. Servers can fail, hard drives fail, data center cooling systems fail, floods happen, earthquakes quake, and so the list of potential disasters can become scary and endless.

Minimizing Cloud Data Loss

Cloud data loss prevention (CDLP) is a solution that maintains the most sensitive company data, stored in the cloud in a way that it's safe from breaches, whether it's from an external attack, insider snatch-and-grabs, or — the big one — human stupidity of the kind that misconfigures something and in so doing allows inadvertent access to your data.

Why Cloud DLP?

An increasing percentage of all enterprise data is being stored in the cloud. Clouds offer low-cost storage, handle all the overhead, bear some of the security burden, and allow for rapid expandability (scalability). The benefits of using cloud storage are huge. But because the storage takes place outside your network, it's like sticking an icepick into the balloon: The bubble bursts because now you have more than one environment to protect. In a medium-size business, the number of cloud services might be in the hundreds or thousands.

The way you protect data in the cloud by using a cloud data loss protection (CDLP) system is similar to, but not exactly the same as, the DLP solution you've engaged for your local business environment.

Cloud access security brokers

Cloud access security brokers (CASB) are solutions that act as intermediaries (brokers) between users and cloud services such as SaaS applications as well as IaaS and PaaS environments. They also provide a way to enforce security policies and help you on the path toward security compliance.

A CASB is a mashup of other technologies, such as

>> Security information and event management (SIEM)

>> Data loss prevention (DLP) solutions

>> Data encryption

REMEMBER

PaaS are not kits for dying Easter eggs — they are Platforms as a Service.

CASB provides visibility

A CASB can let you know who is using your cloud data and how it's being used. CASB solutions will allow you to

>> See data usage patterns, including who is using the data and data usage analytics. Machine learning algorithms can spot suspicious activity using these analyses.

>> Clearly see how data in the cloud is being used by applications such as Salesforce, Google Workspace, or Microsoft 365.

>> Track file risk by knowing who is sharing your data files, how they are being used, and who in your company owns the files.

>> Explore logins you've flagged as suspicious.

>> Research data loss prevention alerts.

This is all done using dashboards that provide an overall look into data storage and applications such as email and web servers.

CASB solutions can automatically tag your data. Tagging your data is important, on several levels. For the purposes of disaster recovery, tags can make it simpler to create data tiers for easy identification of risk. Based on these tiers, you can identify the right backup-and-restore solution. (For more on tagging, see Chapter 6.)

REMEMBER

The security policies you've created to protect your locally stored data can be extended to protect your cloud data using a CASB application as an enforcement tool.

TIP

Configure policies for all your endpoint types, including desktops, mobile devices, and even IoT devices.

These are the types of services a CASB is designed to handle:

>> **Monitoring uploads and downloads for confidential information disclosure**

Reasonable amounts of confidential information may be normal. You can set policies that determine these levels, and AI can spot unusually large, private data releases.

>> **Encryption or, based on policies, quarantining your company's sensitive data**

>> **User activity monitoring or signs of access from high-risk user accounts**

>> **Antivirus checks**

The CASB broker software also watches data that passes through it and flags anything it sees as suspicious, such as personally identifying information like phone numbers, social security numbers, or credit card data. It can encrypt your data to provide maximum security — either all your data as it moves to and from your cloud applications or only the most sensitive data. CASB applications either have built-in encryption capabilities or use the native encryption capabilities of the cloud service provider. They may even be able to use third-party encryption applications.

TIP

Encrypting your data not only keeps it safe but also assists with meeting regulatory compliance requirements. You should manage your own encryption keys for maximum protection.

Many, if not most, cloud applications don't encrypt the data they collect. Using a CASB solution, you can add this extra layer of protection to ensure that breaches don't reveal private or confidential information.

The limits of CASB

Cloud access security brokers sit between end users and cloud applications, monitoring the data that is sent between them. This is a bit like a firewall, but it doesn't meet all the functionality a firewall has to offer. Firewalls monitor and filter port traffic at the network level. Although unaware of the data content, they do provide a much broader type of protection than a CASB. Firewalls can protect against attacks at the protocol level — the HTTP protocol used for the web, for example. Firewalls can also block access from specific IP addresses or IP address ranges. This is a way you could isolate traffic from specific geographical locations. That's definitely not the function of a CASB.

REMEMBER

CASB applications form only one part of your data loss prevention solution: They protect the cloud portion of your data infrastructure. You need to integrate CASB with the DLP applications you select to protect your perimeter-protected network. Your intranet carries sensitive information similar to the kinds of data being protected by the CASB solution. You will find that your security policies protecting the two environments are nearly, or exactly, the same. They should form a strong pair of technologies to secure every part of your IT environment.

Recovering from Disaster

No one wants to think that their company will have an IT meltdown. Yet it happens and you need to prepare for it with more than simply having backups or a plan. You need to have a solution that is well-tested regularly.

Recovery planning

Disaster recovery is the process of getting your company back up and running after a disruption. Speed is of the essence. Because the reasons for disruptions vary greatly — whether it was malware, human error, equipment failure, or natural disaster — you need to have plans in place to recover. Even with all the ways disruptions can occur, there are still only two basic types:

>> **Forecasted:** Events you can reasonably expect to happen. For example, if your company is in Florida, you can expect hurricanes.

>> **Unforecasted:** Disruptions you did not expect. A sad but good example of this is the Covid pandemic.

It's impractical to create a plan for every single thing that could possibly go wrong. It's best to just sum them up into "buckets" such as data loss, hardware failure, power failure, structural failure, or human error that results in any of the above.

Business continuity

What you're planning for is business continuity. You want your business to resume operating as quickly as possible. This may require something as simple as replacing a hard drive, or it may require something as major as failing over to another business location, commonly known as a *hot* site — that failover location that has all your current data and where you can pick up business immediately.

A *warm* site is a location equipped with the hardware and networking infrastructure to pick up where the business stopped but likely won't have the latest backup of data. DNS routing also needs to happen, to make sure that traffic to the data center is rerouted. This is more cost effective than maintaining a hot site but requires that a sizeable investment be made in equipment and building space that may sit idle when not in use.

A *cold* site is a place where a company can resume business but may not have equipment installed, may not have the network infrastructure, and may not have the most current data, requiring that a restoration of data be completed from the most recent backup. This kind of site can be nothing more than an empty warehouse with electricity and phone lines running to it. It's considerably more cost-conscious than warm and hot sites, but it would take a considerable amount of time to restore business continuity.

Having a good deal of your business in the cloud, whether it's where you run your business applications, and/or store your data, can help you regain business continuity — pronto. That's if your cloud service provider has not also experienced the same disaster. In fact, continuity in the eyes of the customer may never have even been disrupted, and business access to your cloud applications could be continued using mobile phones or pads.

RTO and RPO

RTO (Recovery Time Objective) and RPO (Recovery Point Objective) are your business goals when recovering from a disaster. RTO asks: How quickly can you recover? Your plans should set goals for recovery time depending on severity and what you've put in place to recover. Not meeting the RTO objective likely means that you'll be job hunting at the beginning of next week — not because you were fired, but because your company didn't recover and the boss used the golden parachute.

The RPO is the duration between when the disaster happens and the last data backup. Long RPOs mean that you have likely experienced data loss during the event requiring recovery. Shorter RPOs indicate that you're backing up in a short cycle or continuously, as in distributed cloud and cluster storage where the same data is sent to multiple locations.

The bottom line in considering the cycles of your backups is answering the question, "How much data can you afford to lose?"

Coming up with the recovery plan itself

As with just about anything in a big company, you need a team of people ready to respond when disaster strikes. Each team member should know exactly what their responsibility is, should failure occur. Even more important is that each team member should take part in mock scenarios to practice their skills so that they become second nature.

TIP

Create a multitiered contact system — in the event of a severe disruption, your company may not have access to a phone system. Sending email messages may not be possible. Depending on the state of the local power grid, neither may text messages be possible. That doesn't mean you need to learn *semaphore* (flag signaling). But it does mean that you need to have a communications plan in place that meets the needs of the scenario. You might want to consider a solution like the one provided by Regroup (www.regroup.com), which provides its customers with a mass notification system. Another popular mass notification system is Everbridge (www.everbridge.com).

The plan itself should clearly state the steps that need to be taken to bring about business continuity. This might involve driving to the backup site, contacting people close to the backup site, and having them begin operations. Each different situation carries with it a unique set of steps that should be taken. The required level of communication between disciplines within a company will be extraordinary, but if carried out successfully will lead to better recovery results.

REMEMBER

When making your recovery plan, always consider repercussions resulting from the exposure of sensitive data. When bad things happen, not everyone is thinking about cybersecurity risk and security. It should be part of your plan.

TIP

Automating your disaster recovery makes great sense as long as you don't attempt to automate it completely. Automation has not yet achieved the ability to know, ahead of time, every possible thing that can go wrong and so, in the long run, all the automated procedures you've put in place can ultimately fail. (More on this topic in the "Chaos Engineering" section, later in this chapter.)

Make certain that your recovery plan is broadly available. You can put it in the cloud and have it mass distributed to members of the recovery team at the moment of crisis. Even when team members have practiced dry runs of various failure scenarios, it helps to place the steps directly in front of them. You can send messages like this: "Do this and contact so-and-so. Here is the RTO, and it's been this number of minutes since the last backup. Get busy!"

Testing your plan

Having a disaster recovery plan and installing the technologies to mitigate disaster by either having backups or archiving data in a vault is all great. A substantial edge can be achieved over those trying to do your company harm, whether internal or external, if you have the ability to recover from the damage that's done. The question is, does your plan work? Many companies spend a significant amount of money planning for and building DLP systems without ever knowing whether they work and whether they work *well enough*.

Creating a regular test of your data recovery plan can provide you with the knowledge and satisfaction that your plan actually works. It also gives you a metric that would otherwise be unknown: How quickly can your company recover from a data loss? If you have decided to create tiered backups, test each of these tiers to see whether recovery times are satisfactory for each. You may need to adjust the technologies used to maximize the ability to recover quickly. No one likes to plan for failure, yet you still need to make sure that if a major failure does occur, you're ready — and ready in such a way that the impact to your company is negligible.

TIP

Plan for your backup to fail.

Does your failover plan have a backup? When your company has planned to continue running in the event of a data loss disaster and to switch operations to a hot site that allows business to continue as usual, you have to ask yourself what you'll do if your failover plan also fails. It doesn't take much imagination to come up with a scenario where your Internet connection to all your potential hot sites just isn't available. Then what? I suppose that you can pull out your phone and start the hot spot and connect via your cellular carrier. (Though this was meant as a joke, it's actually similar to one potential solution: It's possible to point a dish at a satellite and have continued Internet coverage.)

Here are a couple of companies that offer solutions:

>> **Ground Control:** www.groundcontrol.com

>> **Skycasters:** www.skycasters.com

REMEMBER

Even if every plan and every backup plan passes their rigorous tests with flying colors, your business continuity still isn't assured. For example, if part of your scenario is to replace hardware that simply isn't available because the backup hardware was in the part of the building, swirling around like Dorothy Gale's house in *The Wizard of Oz*, you'll run into challenges you didn't expect. Enter chaos engineering.

Chaos Engineering

If you've abandoned cable TV along with network TV, chances are good that you stream shows from Netflix. But entertainment isn't the only cool concept to come out of the streaming giant. In 2005, its engineering department came up with chaos engineering as a means to ensure system resiliency. The technical definition that evolved says that *chaos engineering* involves experimenting on distributed systems to build confidence in its capacity to withstand the turbulent conditions of a production environment. That's a fancy way of saying "Take your production systems and start breaking stuff to see what happens."

After you've started breaking the components of your production system, you quickly see where the vulnerabilities lie; the next step is to (hopefully) fix them. Of course, the idea is that you don't just go in and break stuff without the hope of recovery. This is how you find out exactly how well your plan for recovery will work for you.

The idea that has grown from this concept of chaos engineering is that we've begun relying on agile development — that quick-and-dirty, get-the-job-done-and-fix-it-later type of development. It's not really all that quick-and-dirty now because systems have matured in the DevOps world to create a robust system of rapid development and release. But chaos engineering asks the question "How robust is it, really?" The fact that cloud computing has created a complex distributed system of engineering hasn't helped. (Think of a house of cards in a windstorm.)

Complex distributed systems carry on a nightmarish system of communications that borders on near collapse all the time. Throw in some random failures and — boom — you have chaos.

REMEMBER

Configuration settings can make or break a system. Imagine if your failover configuration settings are incorrect. When the system does fail, your malconfigured setting just makes things worse and the whole house of cards can be transformed into a game of 52-card pickup. This is just one example of many possible configuration failures that can send a failing system into complete failure. That lone configuration setting can end up being the weak link.

Practical chaos engineering

As humans, we learn from our mistakes (theoretically). This is the heart of chaos engineering — learning from mistakes by way of observation in a controlled experimental manner. Break it, watch it, fix it. Chaos engineering consists of these four basic steps:

1. Define the normal output of a system.

   Pick a day that your system seems to be humming along and say, "That's normal." Measure it as amount of traffic, numbers of messages, database updates, or whatever else you can measure to determine normal.

2. Imagine, in your experiment, that things are expected to remain normal in both your control group (the one you measured as normal) and your experimental group (the one you play with to see what happens).

3. **Break things.**

   In your experimental group, disconnect hard drives, pull the plug on machines, turn off network routers, misconfigure DNS settings, or mimic whatever other activity might actually happen in the real world.

4. Examine the differences between your control (properly operating) environment and your experimental one and then you can observe what happens.

   There may be consequences you'd never thought of as a simple thought experiment.

In Step 1, where you're measuring what normal looks like, be thorough. The better you can identify normal, the better you'll know when it's not. It's like having a child who has walked into the room a million times but this time the look they give you alerts you to the fact that something is wrong. That kind of insight only comes from having observed a system over a period of time. See Figure 10-2 to see the simplicity of chaos engineering.

FIGURE 10-2: Chaos engineering is powerful yet simple.

Step 2 basically states that you expect both your normal operating system and the one on which you will break things remains the same. So, when you do break things and systems change, you can see where your experimental system deviates from the norm.

To pull off Step 3, you need to sit down and create a list of potential failures. We humans tend to shy away from this kind of pessimistic thinking. This comes from the older idea of scenario thinking where, if you can imagine something happening, you aren't then surprised when it does. People tend to fear the unknown, and it's difficult to plan for the unknown if you've never given it a thought.

This list of potential failures becomes your test bed. Now you can see in real-world experiments what will happen when things go wrong. You'd never wish that your system administrator suddenly developed a medical condition from the stress of a system failure, but it could happen. In that case, what's the plan? Never thought of that? Now you have.

Step 4 is where you get to figure out how to make things right — bring them back to normal, in other words. In a worst case scenario, you might have to fail over to your underground bunker, located deep in the desert, because storms are inundating the coast and have shut down power while tornadoes have uprooted your ISP and the roof of your data center.

Listing what could go wrong

Put on your thinking cap and imagine all the things that can possibly go wrong; it's best to do so in an orderly manner. Start with your infrastructure. What happens when disks fail? If they aren't in a RAID configuration, what's the plan for making it more resilient to failure? Then start adding problems such as power supply failures, memory chip failures, firmware chip failures, and cable and connector failures to the list. These are the failures you will find it most difficult to predict, but you *know* that they can and will happen.

After you've created a list of possible weak links in your infrastructure, it's time to look at the bigger picture. What happens if your data center experiences a colossal failure? The big oak tree in the parking lot suddenly falls onto the building, collapsing the roof so that the water lines break and begin flooding the room full of servers. (This one might be a bit tougher to actually experiment with in real life and might need to remain a thought experiment.)

Your network connections are critical to the functioning of your entire enterprise. Consider all the things that can go wrong with networking. For example, your DNS becomes wonky and your domain is accidentally canceled and put on the auction block, only to be purchased by a Chinese doll-making firm that won't sell it back to you. The ISP trunk line is cut by the Department of Water and Power because they forgot to call themselves and ask where they could dig. You forgot to pay the bill and your ISP shut you off.

Failures can be delineated, trending from disastrous to not so bad. Perhaps 30 percent of your sales come from social media marketing and someone at Facebook has decided that your ad does not meet the guidelines and suddenly your sales plummet to zero. Another way to rank potential failures is to consider how often these real-world potentialities might happen. If hurricanes are on your list, the consideration might be greater if you're in Florida rather than Wisconsin.

Seeing how bad it can get

On an early spring day in April of 1986, routine testing began on the nuclear reactor at Chernobyl, Russia. The goal of the test was to see what would happen to one of the systems if power flow were reduced. The failures began to cascade and attempts to bring the system back to normal failed because of an unforeseen buildup of xenon in the core, keeping anyone from raising the reactor's power. As the test progressed, all the safety and emergency systems were shut off. That's chaos engineering in its highest form: An unexpected power surge triggers the operator to attempt an emergency shutdown, but the rods jam as they reenter the core — and the rest is history.

Chernobyl, though terribly tragic, is the perfect example of unforeseen circumstances in the most controlled of environments. The same was true for the Fukushima Daiichi nuclear disaster in 2011. Who had imagined that a magnitude 9 earthquake and resulting tsunami would create one of the worst nuclear disasters in history?

Nuclear disasters may seem a bit outside of what might occur in your network, but they are excellent examples of what might have been averted if someone had asked the question, "What will we do in the event of a magnitude 9 earthquake?" After all, Northern Japan regularly experiences high-magnitude earthquakes.

Attaining resiliency

When crafting your chaos engineering experiments, you should attempt to work with actual operational data in an environment that mimics your production environment. You can test on your actual production system but with the knowledge that it may upset your customers. When testing on live production systems, make efforts to limit the impact.

REMEMBER

Only a system tested in the crucible of real-time data gives you accurate results.

Not all testing is possible with live data. While the results may not be as accurate as a live test, this doesn't let you off the hook. Don't let testing your system be a one-time event. You should test the system nearly continuously, and therefore automate it. Both the experimental failures and the measurement of what happens as a result are completely hands-free. Continuous testing results in a substantial amount of data accumulation, which can be great data to feed an AI that can predict future failure scenarios.

TIP

Automating your disaster recovery makes great sense as long as you don't attempt to automate it completely. Automation has not yet achieved the ability to know ahead of time every possible thing that can go wrong and so, in the long run, all the automated procedures you've put in place can ultimately fail. (More on this topic in the "Chaos Engineering" section, earlier in this chapter.)

3

Business as Usual

IN THIS CHAPTER

» Managing data protection

» Instituting cloud security validation and multifactor authentication

» Handling hardware security modules

» Working with key management services

» Exploring crypto service gateways

Chapter **11**

Using Cloud Security Services

The number of cloud security services increases daily with the ever-changing cloud landscape. It's almost impossible to keep up with all of them. If you've done your homework, you know what the risks are and you know where your vulnerabilities lie. Next comes the job of figuring out the cost effectiveness of either providing the services you need in-house or visiting the marketplace for solutions.

Though you may be responsible for providing security for your cloud environment — particularly, your data — you aren't required to have at your fingertips all the capabilities you need. Keep your business goals in mind. Unless your business is cloud security, it's sometimes best to leave that task to people who eat, live, and breathe cloud security. They have the equipment, the expertise, and the skilled manpower to do the job — and they tend to keep up with changes in the industry because that's their business.

You can pick and choose from a broad array of services to ensure your cloud and local data security as well as help you meet compliance regulations.

Customizing Your Data Protection

Managed data protection services offer specialized security protection for your data. This differs from most generalized information security services in that they focus specifically on protecting one of your most important assets: your data. These services help you meet some of the following demands:

>> Maintaining security in a rapidly changing security landscape

>> Assessing data for risk levels to help you prioritize data security

>> Managing user data interaction to overcome accidental or purposeful data corruption or breaches

>> Managing compliance regulation conformity

WARNING

When flexibility goes up, security levels go down. This is one of the basic truths about using cloud services. Those providing much greater flexibility make security more challenging.

One typical solution is offered by Cloudrise (`https://cloudrise.com`). It automates data protection and privacy solutions, security for business applications, and visualization tools with rapid incident response and report.

Validating Your Cloud

One huge challenge for businesses is to keep pace with the burgeoning number of cloud resource types offered to users every single day. The continual release of new products and resources by cloud providers makes it a difficult task for a business to validate and certify each of these new changes.

Prancer (`www.prancer.io`) helps you keep up with this heavy requirement by doing the heavy lifting of maintaining your security compliance throughout your entire cloud environment. These folks will even work directly with your development team to see that security is enforced in your DevSecOps group writing Infrastructure as Code (IaC) configurations. (It's these misconfigurations that pose a huge risk to your organization if not managed well.)

Using its static code analyzer, Prancer uses Policy as Code to enforce the security of your IaC and live cloud resources by performing policy checks for compliance using the more important compliance regulations or even your own custom company-security policies.

Multifactor authentication

Multifactor authentication (MFA) has become one of the de facto ways to authenticate users logging in to company resources — particularly, cloud SaaS applications. You're required to further authenticate your identity established by a user ID and password by responding to a phone call or text message or by entering a one-time passcode.

One popular MFA system is the SurePassID (`https://surepassid.com`). Here's a list of some of its features:

>> Hybrid and on-premise deployment

>> Offline desktop login with two-factor authentication (2FA)

>> Firewall configurations that include network pathing and replication schemes

>> User login and logout audits

The system integrates with your existing security information and event management (SIEM) system and helps you comply with some of the most stringent compliance regulations.

WARNING

SMS one-time passwords are vulnerable to man-in-the-middle attacks and are thus no longer compliant with multifactor authentication. Because messages sent by SMS have become insecure, passcodes sent by SMS can no longer be trusted.

One-time passwords

One-time passwords (OTPs) are randomly generated passwords that are used only a single time. This type of password system overcomes the vulnerability of passwords that have already been breached, passwords that are weak and easily discoverable, and passwords that have been stolen. These one-time passwords, known as *tokens*, come in one of four types:

>> **Soft:** Delivered using a mobile phone app

>> **Hard:** Delivered using a key fob

>> **On-demand:** Delivered by SMS and email

>> **FIDO U2F:** Inserted as a fob into a USB port

    The canine-sounding acronym stands for Fast IDentity Online Universal 2nd Factor.

SOFT TOKENS

An example of a soft token is the application Google Authenticator. After downloading this app to your phone, you can add applications that use this type of 2FA. Once added, they continually update your app with new tokens that are created using the keys of each application.

Some applications, such as Facebook, have their own authentication OTP generator. Suppose that you've elected to use two-factor authentication in Facebook. To be able to log in to Facebook from a new device, you have to use the Facebook mobile app to get a new code from the code generator found on the Facebook menu. Only after entering the code located there into the device requesting 2FA do you then authenticate the new device.

Mobile phones are fairly ubiquitous — in fact, by this point it's probably more correct to say that many techies can't live without them. This makes using soft tokens from an app pretty simple. The codes generated by the app are time-based and therefore don't require a connection to the Internet to create codes. Being *time-based* means that the passwords expire quickly — usually, every 30 seconds. This feature protects you from password replay attacks, where passwords are intercepted by a hacker and later used to access private resources such as a bank account or network login.

Here are the downsides to using this technology:

>> Mobile devices can be stolen, and if someone manages to slip past your device's security PIN, they then also have access to your two-factor authentication code generator.

>> Phishing attacks may intercept your code in a fake request and then use your code within the 30-second time frame to log in and authenticate as you.

>> Mobile phones are still vulnerable to attacks that can allow snooping of your phone activity.

HARD TOKENS

Hard tokens are small digital fobs (shown in Figure 11-1) that are often placed on keyrings to prevent them from getting lost. This device generates a one-time password from a cryptographic seed also shared with the server. The advantage over a soft token is that a hard token isn't connected to a network that can be attacked. Instead, it's air gapped and stand-alone. (Something is considered "air gapped" when it is not connected to an insecure network; it's a measure used to protect devices from external attack.)

FIGURE 11-1:
Fobs, often
placed on
keyrings, provide
one-time tokens
without the need
for a mobile
phone.

These little devices are power-friendly with batteries lasting up to about seven years.

These are the downsides of hard tokens:

>> **Expense:** The little devices aren't cheap.

>> **Administration:** Someone needs to physically hand out the device and keep track of who has them.

>> **Easily lost or stolen:** Even though putting them on a key ring helps keep track of these small tokens, keys are also lost. Of course, if found it's useless without knowing your user ID and password.

Though these seem like perfect little devices, they're still vulnerable to man-in-the-middle attacks because you still need to enter the code it generates into an application. When codes are generated, they expire after a short period of time. If an attacker intercepts your code, they could immediately use it to impersonate you. Saving the code for later use fails. Intercepted codes are the weak link. The passcode is secure right up to the moment where it needs to be used. Still, hard tokens are the standard of the industry, even after decades of use.

ON-DEMAND TOKENS

Soft tokens and hard tokens each have their uses. A simpler system, on-demand tokens, is useful for occasions where you may need to authenticate someone only during their first login. These tokens are sent via either SMS message or email. The advantage of using an on-demand token is that, in addition to authenticating the person, you've authenticated one of their contact methods.

Once a user has logged in with a user ID and password — often, for the first time — the application they're logging in to sends them a random code that it generates on its own. This code is then sent either to the user's SMS mobile phone number (if they entered a mobile phone number) or to their email (which is standard info to ask for when someone signs up for a transaction). These codes aren't time-based, like the other two methods I describe. Instead, the user has a set period in which to enter the code into the application before it expires. The expiration tends to be longer than other types of token generators because you have all sorts of issues to consider, such as network lag and the time it takes an email to be delivered (and then located in the spam folder where it inevitably ends up).

Some of the benefits of using on-demand tokens include the fact that it's simple and inexpensive and requires no administration, like a hard token — and it can be used without a smartphone. (SMS messages can be received on phones with older technology.) On-demand tokens depend on the fact that there is no shared secret between the device and the server that can be exploited. The server simply sends random values. The number of digits sent varies on the level of assurance your system needs.

The downside of using on-demand tokens is that they just aren't all that secure. Too many people and systems are involved in the creation and delivery of the code that usually isn't delivered cryptographically. They also aren't recommended for systems that require regulation compliance, because the codes are easily stolen and simply receiving an email doesn't authenticate an individual, because fake email addresses are far too simple to set up. Instead, the National Institute of Standards and Technology (NIST) suggests that you use push notifications (in-app pop-up messages) to a device that makes certain the user is in possession of the device.

FIDO U2F TOKENS

You probably know about the little USB fobs that wireless keyboards use. FIDO U2F tokens look just like those. What they do is provide a token automagically when you attempt a login at a site that supports this technology. After you've entered your user ID and password, you press a button on the USB device and, like magic, you're authenticated.

Of all the token types, this one is the most secure. It uses public key cryptography to create a client-server real-time challenge-response between the client (your web browser) and the server. It protects against

>> **Phishing:** No codes to type so phishing isn't a thing.

>> **Session hijacking:** Keeping criminals from stealing a session id or session cookie because these are not relied on for authentication.

>> **Man-in-the-middle attacks:** Avoids the ability to intercept your network traffic because the server will detect anomalies in the response and deny transmission.

>> **Malware attacks:** Malware can't fake the encrypted challenge-response.

Also, if you lose the little guy, it has no identifying information on it to reveal who might own the device. It works only with sites where you've already registered.

One interesting feature about this type of security is that the protocol allows for two devices to be registered to every account. This means that if you lose one device, you're not totally locked out of your account.

The FIDO U2F token method is often used as the primary authentication method. Once authentication has been achieved and you have trusted devices, soft tokens can be used. If they should ever fail or become lost or stolen, you can then reuse the FIDO USB device to authenticate your account on a new device.

Here are some of the downsides to FIDO U2F:

>> **Cost:** They can cost upward of $20 each.

>> **Support:** It's still a new technology, so it doesn't have widespread industry support yet.

>> **Size:** It's tiny (not even the size of a keyring fob), so it's easily lost.

>> **Dependability:** USB ports weren't designed for daily devices to be inserted and removed, so this type of port can experience degradation over time.

>> **Mobile support:** It isn't fully supported for mobile phones. (See the note below about Yubikeys.)

When it comes to mobile phones, which have no USB ports, you can still use FIDO U2F. TapID Mobile Account Security lets you tap NFC-enabled phones the same way you might use a card to make a payment. This solution isn't quite ready for prime time, though.

A popular solution is offered by Yubiko www.yubico.com/. Their Yubikeys work fantastic and come in a variety of form factors including mobile Lightning connectors.

Managing file transfers

When data is moved from one place to another, whether it's sent via an application or an email or by FTP or another file transfer mechanism (data in motion), it's at considerable risk. You should feel that risk in your bones, the same as when you were a child and feared monsters under your bed. When you got up and headed into the next room with your parents, you felt at risk until you got there. Your company faces file transfer risks when it moves sensitive data within the company, to vendors, and to partners that need the data.

Most cloud solutions have a mechanism for sending data in an encrypted form to and from the users or other devices. Secure file transfer is a topic you rarely hear mentioned, for that reason. It just works. But sometimes you need to go beyond just sending and receiving data. This is when you need some forensic evidence of a transfer, or the transfer needs to be tracked to make absolutely certain it was successful. Also, there may be occurrences when you need a level of encryption or safety beyond that offered by the standard SSL/TLS processes.

To solve this complex data-in-motion problem, you need to use a secure file transfer mechanism. One of the companies offering this service is Progress (www.ipswitch.com), with its MOVEit Managed File Transfer application. This SaaS program offers compliant and secure file transfer of sensitive data.

Progress also offers a secure File Transfer Protocol (sFTP) server known as WinSock FTP (WS_FTP). WS_FTP was one of the first widely distributed FTP applications on the Internet. Though not as popular as it once was, FTP in general is still used today after 50 years. There is still a need for secure file transfer, but these services have largely moved to the cloud. ExaVault (www.exavault.com) has just such a cloud FTP platform.

Data in motion and file transfer have largely been replaced by simpler file transfer mechanisms — Secure Sockets Layer (SSL)/Transport Layer Security (TSL), for example, which is used by most cloud providers for security in their data connections. MediaFire (www.mediafire.com), a popular cloud storage and file sharing application, uses this type of secure transfer made simple with a drag-and-drop interface, as shown in Figure 11-2.

FIGURE 11-2:
A simple
drag-and-drop
interface lets you
move and share
files using built-in
SSL/TLS security.

HSM: Hardware Security Modules for the Big Kids

A hardware security module (HSM) is a physical computing device that safeguards and manages digital keys and performs encryption and decryption functions for digital signatures as well as strong authentication and other cryptographic functions. These modules traditionally come in the form of a plug-in card or an external device that attaches directly to a computer or network server. A hardware security module contains one or more secure cryptoprocessor chips for fast cryptographic processing. This replaces servers with math cards that weren't designed for this kind of heavy math computing. An HSM is a smarter solution and is much more scalable than building server farms for the purpose of cryptography.

The secret behind HSMs is that they have been hardened and made tamper resistant to such an extent that they can be trusted to protect your company's most sensitive data by cryptographically storing private keys. (See Figure 11-3.) These modules are thus able to perform a variety of cryptographic functions, including generating, managing, and storing the keys used for public/private key encryption and for digitally signing documents and code.

FIGURE 11-3:
A typical HSM,
with tamper-
resistant tape.

Here are the typical functions of an HSM:

>> Key storage

>> Key exchange

>> Encryption

REMEMBER

An HSM contains special cryptographic hardware that uses a security-focused operating system tested to a standard set up in the Federal Information Processing Standard publication 140-2 (FIPS 140-2 certified, to use the jargon of the security industry.) Despite that fact, network access to an HSM should still be limited and controlled. In a zero trust environment, almost no one should have access to the HSM.

Looking at HSM cryptography

Cryptographic keys are strings of random letters and numbers. Because computers aren't really designed to create random strings, you need special processes to generate strings that are truly random. An HSM has this special cryptographic chip that excels at generating this level of randomness that results in strong, random keys.

The HSM hardware is designed to perform mathematical processes for developing random keys at scale. This requires that the cryptographic chips be capable of amazing math performance, generating in the millions of digital signatures per second. Hardware devices such as the Futurex HSM (www.futurex.com) have some of the fastest processing speeds. Another company to look at is Cryptomathic (www.cryptomathic.com.) It provides an array of key management products with functionality such as

- ≫ The ability to route data to hardware security modules

- ≫ Key management in a bring-your-own-key (BYOK) scenario, where enterprises choose to create and manage their own keys.

- ≫ Digital signing credentials management

Managing keys with an HSM

HSMs are purpose-built for the protection and management of cryptographic keys. Organizations that make heavy use of cryptography because of the amount of encryption they use generally make use of multiple HSMs.

REMEMBER

Cryptographic keys are used for encrypting data, digitally signing documents, and even signing code developed by your developers. This ensures that signed code has not been changed and that you know who the author is — without a doubt.

Key management systems are designed to control access to these keys and update keys when needed, all within the security policies set by the corporation. Many of these security policies will be dictated by security compliance regulations. With an HSM managing keys, you can be assured that they're safe and at the same time easily managed.

REMEMBER

Following a zero trust policy means that only the most trusted individuals should have access to the HSM. Remember that they become the weak link because they are the system's only true vulnerability.

In keeping with the highest level of security, an HSM also maintains a full audit as well as log traces. This enables a forensic investigation in the unlikely event that the device is somehow compromised.

A little bit about keys

HSMs are designed to generate and store both symmetric and asymmetric keys. The difference between the two is simple. *Symmetric* encryption has a single, private key. It might seem a little like a password, but it's more than that — it's the key used to encrypt the data and, consequently, you'd use the same key to decrypt it.

This same kind of cryptography was used as far back as ancient Sparta in 600 BCE, when messages were sent using a leather strip that was meaningless unless you had a special stick that revealed the message when you wrapped the leather strap around it. (See Figure 11-4.) Later, Julius Caesar made use of a substitution cypher requiring that you knew which letters were switched with others in order to understand the message. It was about 1500 years later when Giovan Battista Bellaso came up with the first encryption key. (It's an excellent trivia question for nerds.)

FIGURE 11-4:
A scytale revealed a message when leather was wrapped around a specially designed stick.

The problem with symmetric encryption is that both the encryptor and the decryptor need the same key, which means it has to be transferred between them. Some of the greatest old spy novels of days gone by included the subterfuge used to transfer symmetric keys. Advances were made in encryption right up to 1997, when the Data Encryption Standard (DES) encryption that had been used since the 1970s was finally cracked.

Twenty years before DES was cracked, a pair of crypto researchers — Whitfield Diffie and Martin Hellman — published a paper that laid out the idea of an encryption pair of keys then known as the Diffie–Hellman key. This was the basis for asymmetric cryptography. In 2000, the AES Advanced Encryption Standard became the gold standard. But it's still a symmetric key. This type of key is commonly used to encrypt data where there's no need for anyone other than the person who encrypted it to be able to do so.

Asymmetric encryption uses a public key to encrypt data that can be decrypted only by someone who has the corresponding private key. This strategy is particularly important in a world like the Internet where data must be sent encrypted, without both user and sender needing to have the private key. Encrypting data in motion is a perfect use for asymmetric encryption.

Your private key can also be used to encrypt data that can be decrypted using the public key, something that brings about non-repudiation, proving the sender is who they say they are.

TIP

Bitcoin and other cryptocurrency

Yet another type of encryption is *elliptic curve cryptography* (ECC), an advanced type of public key cryptography that can make use of shorter keys without a resulting decrease in security. This type of algorithm is used to encrypt blockchains that form the distributed storage mechanisms of cryptocurrencies like Bitcoin. Because knowing the key to your Bitcoin is necessary to unlocking its value, these keys must be securely stored, and an HSM is the perfect place to store them. Cryptocurrency is generally stored in an electronic wallet compatible with the type of currency you're storing, and this wallet can then be stored on the HSM.

Building in tamper resistance

An HSM isn't worth much if you can tamper with it. It's not impossible to break in, but most of them have certain safeguards and after-the-fact detection, including

>> Visible tampering indications

>> Tampering logs to provide forensic evidence

>> Alert systems to notify automated security systems or system administrators

An HSM can take additional measures beyond the physical detection, logging, or alerting that can make an attack on an HSM more difficult (automatically deleting the keys it's protecting when tampering is detected, for example). Of course, such measures can prove to be a problem if use of these keys is critical to your business continuity. You don't want to lock yourself out of your own systems.

To manage high-throughput cryptography, which is compute-intensive, HSMs are equipped with secure cryptoprocessor chips that also work to prevent tampering and bus probing by encrypting bus traffic. (The bus is the hardware equipment over which data travels, so this device protects against anyone trying to read the data by physically connecting to the hardware.) The secure cryptoprocessor will likely have its own tamper resistant packaging (the term used is *potting*) that makes it less necessary for the rest of the HSM to have tamper resistance. It's like breaking into the box just to find a brick. Physical tamper evidence is usually a type of tape, easily torn, indicating that someone has tried to tamper with the item. It's the same way your spouse knows that you were the last one to use the plastic wrap — the evidence is obvious.

Using HSMs to manage your own keys

Managing your own keys is the most secure way to maintain cryptographic keys. Entrusting them to a third party is asking for trouble and may even be a no-no for some regulation compliance.

Most HSMs have a single purpose — managing secret keys. With tamper systems ready to zero out a key if tampering is detected, you'll want a secure backup of your keys. HSM units can securely back up the keys they manage in order to secure portable devices, such as secure smart cards.

TIP

IDFactors (`https://idfactors.com`) makes trusted smart card equipment suitable for backing up the keys stored in your HSM.

Meeting financial data security requirements with HSMs

Financial data is some of the most sensitive data you can create. It forms the backbone of the US economy, and a failure caused by a cryptohack can lead to global financial devastation. This description is more than a fairytale: On June 19, 2011, the Mt. Gox cryptocurrency exchange in Japan was hacked. More than 2600 Bitcoins were transferred when the Mt. Gox auditor credentials were stolen. At today's prices, that's almost $162 million. The second time Mt. Gox was hacked, in 2014, was even worse. At the time, it was responsible for about 70 percent of all the Bitcoin trades in the world. It was later learned that around 750,000 Bitcoins were stolen. Today, that amount would be $47 billion. These are late-2021 prices.

The cryptoexchange hacks are some of the most amazing examples of financial crime, but you don't need to steal billions to create significant financial consequences. If nothing else, when banks are hacked — and don't forget that a great deal of a bank's transactions are now digital — confidence in the institution is lost and major depositors often leave for another bank. For this reason, financial data security is heavily regulated. Equipment such as HSMs are generally certified to international standards or the US FIPS 140-2 standard. This level of certification ensures that the equipment can withstand even the most aggressive attacks and gives bank officials and depositors the assurance they need.

DNSSEC

One of the underlying security technologies is one you really don't have to pay much attention to because it's built into the foundations of the Internet. The Domain Name Service (DNS) is the system that uses aliases (URLs) to stand for numeric IP addresses. Being able to modify these aliases to change which IP addresses they point to is an area of Internet security that has been addressed using cryptography. For example, OpenDNSSEC makes use of an HSM to manage its cryptographic keys. (For more on OpenDNSSEC, see the next section.)

DNS has been one of the weak links in Internet security and is often the root cause of many devastating exploits. Familiarize yourself with this critical piece of IT infrastructure because its security (or lack thereof) is of critical importance to you. DNS translates domain names into IP addresses with the help of domain registries. Many of these registries sign their zone files — the master file that matches URLs with IP addresses — with a cryptographic key and then store the keys in an HSM. Before this level of security was employed, DNS wasn't secure — many exploits used to breach security were made possible by hackers spoofing DNS.

Work began on a solution to the DNS security problem back in the 1990s. The result, deployed in early 2007, is known as the DNS Security Extensions (DNSSEC). DNSSEC uses digital signatures to secure authentication in DNS communications. Every DNS zone has its own key pair (public and private). Using PKI (public key infrastructure), the two components of DNS (the zone server and the resolver) use these keys to authenticate one another. HSMs are used by certificate authorities (CAs) and domain registration authorities to generate, store, and manage key pairs.

There are two components to DNSSEC:

>> **Data origin authentication:** This involves making sure the information is actually from the authorized zone. If authentication fails, the resolver assumes that there is an attack and disregards the attempt.

>> **Data integrity protection:** This involves making certain that the data wasn't changed en route. This is possible because the data is signed and can be verified using a key.

DNS resolving is done using a tree-structured layer of zones with a root zone at the top. Each zone is signed with the root zone signature the most trusted, or *trust anchor*. Each layer is then subsequently signed creating a layering of trust.

TECHNICAL STUFF

The top five DNS attacks use DNS tunneling, ransomware, distributed denial of service (DDoS), identity reconnaissance, and DNS service vulnerability exploits.

OpenDNSSEC

OpenDNSSEC (www.opendnssec.org) is an open-source application that maintains your DNSSEC keys and the signing of zones. It works by taking unsigned zones and adding the necessary digital signatures and other DNSSEC records. Once this information has been added to the zone, it's then sent on to the authoritative name servers managing that zone.

The data flow in the OpenDNSSEC system is shown in Figure 11-5.

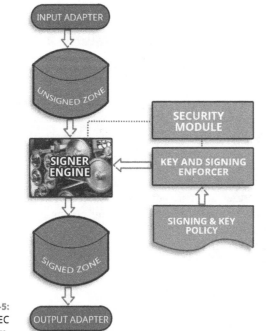

FIGURE 11-5: OpenDNSSEC flow diagram.

Evaluating HSM products

When selecting an HSM, you want to make sure they work, no matter which cloud service provider you're using. You want to look for an HSM that is secure, fast, and scalable. Because of the limited marketplace, you have only a few HSM vendors to choose from. These are the best known:

>> **nShield:** www.entrust.com/digital-security/hsm/products/nshield-hsms/nshield-connect

>> **Thales Group:** https://cpl.thalesgroup.com/encryption/hardware-security-modules

>> **PKI Solutions:** www.pkisolutions.com

Thales Group is the brains behind the SafeNet Luna SA HSM, shown in Figure 11-3.

The devices themselves are pretty simple boxes. You may want to select an HSM because of the associated software capabilities. For example, the nShield monitor and nShield Remote Administration products connect HSMs and remotely monitor the HSM for performance and uptime. An HSM also helps you do infrastructure planning by showing you load trends and usage statistics. As an additional level of security, the HSM also reports on tamper events, warnings, and alerts. The Remote Administration application allows you to administer the HSM via a secure interface. This way, you aren't tied physically to the device, and you can administer it remotely.

Looking at cloud HSMs

An alternative to using a hardware HSM is to employ a cloud HSM. Some of the major cloud providers such as Google and AWS allow you to host your HSM in the cloud, freeing you from the responsibility of managing the device. In the case of Google Cloud and AWS, you can host your encryption keys and complete your other cryptographic operations using a cluster of FIPS 140-2 Level 3 certified HSMs.

Here are some benefits of using a cloud HSM:

>> Increased security

>> Scalability

>> Reduced management requirements

>> The reassurance that comes from not having your device in a vulnerable building

HSM solutions certainly aren't the cheapest way to go, but for large corporations that rely on the highest level of security or for those that manage secret and private information that must be protected by cryptographic means, HSMs are currently the ultimate solution.

There are not that many HSM providers. Here are a couple:

>> nShield offers an HSM as a SaaS application.

>> The Thales Group offers its Luna Cloud HSM.

KMS: Key Management Services for Everyone Else

If going the HSM route or even using a cloud-hosted HSM is more than you need for managing your keys, you have an alternative, known as *key management services KMS*. Encrypting keys give those who have access to them direct access to private and privileged data. They're a bit like super passwords, but more, because these keys have the ability to unlock things that are deeply locked away.

Definitely consider a key management service if you have any investment in cryptocurrencies. You can store your wallet credentials there as a means of protecting your investment.

SSH compliance

SSH keys can provide access to your critical assets. The Secure Shell (SSH), part of the Linux operating system and all its variants, was originally created in 1995 and became an Internet standard in 2006. SSH became the standard way to access remote systems securely. This public key cryptography key pair is the most common way users authenticate themselves when logging in to remote servers.

The increased level of authentication provided by SSH overcomes the weaknesses of standard username-and-password combinations, which are generally plagued by poor password maintenance and behavior. In an SSH authentication system, you can use passwords as a second authentication factor, giving you two-factor authentication.

Recent research suggests that longer strings of unusual words form better passwords than shorter strings of numbers, letters, and special characters.

The first step in setting yourself up for SSH access is generating your own set of keys, both the public one and the private one that you give to no one and protect at all costs. You then post your public key in the system to which you want to log in. It becomes part of your user account and, if your public key is ever made public, it matters little to you because it can't be used in any meaningful way.

When you first create your SSH key pair, you're given a few choices. One is whether to protect your keys with a password. This extra level of protection is helpful but not foolproof. Another is the type of key format you want to use — RSA or ECDSA. RSA (based on the RSA algorithm) is the older format and remains fairly strong. The newer form, ECDSA (short for Elliptic Curve Digital Signature Algorithm) uses, as its name implies, an elliptical curve encryption like the one used to protect Bitcoin. Whether you choose RSA (the old standard) or the newer ECDSA, you have the option of choosing the length of your key.

There are trade-offs to key length. Longer keys are far more secure than shorter ones, but the trade-off is that when you use the key to encrypt or decrypt something, it does take somewhat longer.

REMEMBER

Your system administrators, when protecting your systems with SSH key authentication, should disable standard password login capability.

Once you have set up your system to allow access using only an SSH key, you then need to make sure your SSH logins are logged for the purpose of auditing and compliance regulations. Keep zero trust in mind when limiting access to individuals based on need and risk.

SSH audit logs are important for their ability to feed data to applications like those in an AIOps-managed system, as shown in Figure 11-6. These applications use AI to spot potential user security issues. For example, it spots unauthorized actions taken by a user and takes further action to deny further access, revoking their authorization until you can investigate the incident. Audit logs are also a requirement of most compliance regulations.

SERVER .... **SECURITY MONITORING**

Audit Log

SIEM Application

SSHd ▶ Syslog

FIGURE 11-6:
The SSH daemon feeds data into the syslog, which is sent to the SIEM monitoring system to generate alerts or automated actions based on policy.

When using AWS, the SSH audit trail is performed by Amazon's CloudTrail application. This tracks which users accessed which encryption keys, which resources they were used for, and when they were used.

The AWS KMS (Key Management System) can be integrated with other AWS services so that you can encrypt things such as data at rest. This is done using envelope encryption, where a data key is employed to encrypt the data and then that key is then encrypted by a KMS key that is then stored in the AWS KMS application.

There are a couple of different KMS key resources you can create with AWS:

>> **Automatically create an AWS-managed KMS key.** Permissions for the resource are managed by the AWS service for which it was created.

>> **Manage the KMS key yourself.** This type of key gives you maximum control over the permissions and the key lifecycle.

The encryption-key lifecycle

Encryption keys are like salmon: They have a complicated and detailed lifecycle. As you may know, salmon begin their lives as young fry that flow downstream to the ocean, where they grow up in a saltwater environment. As adults, they swim back upstream. If they aren't eaten by bears or other predators, they lay eggs, fertilize them, and then . . . are eaten by more bears. Encryption-key lifecycles are even more complicated. Not all the following lifecycle stages are mandatory:

>> **Key generation:** This one is mandatory because this is when the key is made.

>> **Key registration:** You must register your key.

>> **Key storage:** Unless you have a photographic memory and don't mind typing 2048 characters, you should store the key.

>> **Key distribution and installation:** You need to distribute and install your public key to make the key pair useful.

>> **Key use:** This is not mandatory but sort of defeats the purpose of creating a key if you're not going to use it.

>> **Key rotation:** Keys normally have an expiration, like milk. When they expire, they are destroyed and new keys are created in their place.

>> **Key backup:** It's possible to create a password-protected backup of your encryption keys. It's not a bad idea to also encrypt your backup.

>> **Key recovery:** There is generally an encryption key that enables you to restore another production key. Without it, you're just not getting the encrypted data back.

>> **Key revocation:** This optional lifecycle stage doesn't actually destroy the key. It's simply a message to users of a particular key that it's no longer valid.

>> **Key suspension:** Suspending a key means removing it from memory so that the key isn't written to disk during a memory write. The key can still be used later.

>> **Key destruction:** This permanently destroys the key — just like that salmon being eaten by a bear.

Key management can be complicated and require several layers of encryption and keys. StrongSalt (www.strongsalt.com) has an Encryption as a Service (EaaS) offering that allows you to have a keyless and decentralized management system.

Setting Up Crypto Service Gateways

A *crypto service gateway* (CSG) is a middleware application that acts like a router for encryption service requests. You can think of it as Cryptography as a Service. Each request is routed to the HSM or crypto service module best suited to handle the request. Having a centralized service over HSMs that, to everyone's misfortune, have been distributed silo fashion throughout an organization makes good sense. It shortens the time and effort it takes to make policy decisions, such as which encryption standard you'll use. (Standards do change, and when you want to change to keep up with the Joneses, you'll want an easy way to do it.)

A CSG also makes auditing a cinch. More compliance security audits are required each year. Having a centralized system creating visibility throughout your cryptographic environment saves you considerable time and money. This is particularly important in financial institutions, where encryption is a normal part of all transactions.

With a CSG, you'd be able to

>> Seamlessly use HSMs from different vendors

>> Easily scale your organization because HSM management is centralized

>> Deliver cryptographic applications to production in shorter times

>> Enable load share between HSMs

>> Establish centralized and simplified audit mechanisms

REMEMBER

The CSG doesn't actually do any key management. It acts to redirect requests for crypto services. Key management will still be done in your HSM or KMS systems.

TIP

Cryptomathic, a major player in the security field, makes a CSG system: www. cryptomathic.com/products/key-management/crypto-service-gateway.

IN THIS CHAPTER

» Keeping calm and carrying on

» Knowing the enemy

» Instilling employee etiquette and data security

» Avoiding cloud native breaches

» Guarding against insider data theft

» Dealing with data spillage

Chapter **12**

When Things Go Wrong

I talk a lot in this book about the types of events that can go wrong right alongside a lot of talk about the technologies used to either prevent these mishaps or deal with them after they've happened. This chapter goes into greater detail on the challenges you face in protecting your IT environment, particularly when it includes cloud services. The good news is that, in a shared security model, the part of the model that includes clouds covers considerably less territory than the hazards you have to look out for in a traditional security environment.

If this sounds like a pep talk, that's because it is. Information security is overwhelming at best and twice as complicated when you've chosen to muck up your perfectly good perimeter security to take advantage of the awesome perks provided by cloud service providers.

Finding Your Focus

The job of orchestrating network security can be overwhelmingly complex. It works best to take a 50,000-foot view of the situation to best direct your efforts toward a plan that works for your company. What does your company do? If it does things that collect gobs and gobs of private data, your focus should be on data. On the other hand, if your business is developing Software as a Service or other cloud services, your focus will be entirely different.

Finding a focus might be easier if you start by looking at which compliance regulations govern how your company handles its security. Rather than look at these regulations as the big and scary hoop you have to jump through, let them comprise the starting point. In a way, compliance regulations can make the job of finding your security focus easier by giving you a step-by-step guide to exactly what the end result must be. This is not unlike a paint-by-number painting: You're given an outline and now you just need to paint within the lines.

When you have your focus, the next step is to put in place as many automation systems as possible. For example, if your company develops software and is using an agile development methodology, you'll want to automate testing. This way, the security is baked right into the development cycle and not tacked on after the fact.

REMEMBER

Automated security testing doesn't have to end with the development cycle. In fact, it shouldn't. You should also continue with automated security tests after a product has been released.

You may be thinking, "I've tested my software, so everything should remain good." Two observations: One, nothing stays the same, and the environment in which your software runs may change and introduce vulnerabilities that didn't exist at release time. Two, no one develops perfect software. No one!

When your company provides services rather than a product, you should still consider things like penetration testing and regular security reviews of your systems. Your website applications might be vulnerable to attack, giving hackers access to your customer information.

REMEMBER

The likelihood that your company will experience a data breach is high — take steps to limit this situation, and protect your systems when it does happen.

Stealing Data 101

One of the worst kinds of breaches, and one of the most common, involves stolen data. To guard against data theft, this section talks about some of the strategies used by data thieves. The technologies used to steal data go much further than low-tech means such as shoulder surfing — looking over a person's shoulder, in other words — and copying passwords found precariously stuck to the monitor. Social engineering should be high on your hit list of nefarious schemes to protect against. Spam should be right up there at the top of the list as well.

REMEMBER It is believed that as much as 94 percent of all malware is delivered by spam email. Several good antivirus programs — Malwarebytes, Kaspersky, Norton, and McAfee, to name a few of the top programs — are worth whatever they charge.

You'll have a better idea of how to protect yourself if you know some of the more common data theft strategies. I start you out with landing, expanding, and exfiltration.

Landing, expanding, and exfiltrating

The strategy behind almost any data theft — whether it's from a disgruntled employee or from a former employee who still has access to the company's data or from some random hacker trying to grab your data to sell it to the highest bidder — is usually the same: The person must first hack in (or misuse their credentials to log in), figure out what content they have access to, and then figure out how to transfer the data out of the system. This is known as *landing, expanding, and exfiltration,* or getting the data out of the system.

Sticking the landing

When a hacker lands on a platform (usually, in a PaaS or IaaS cloud resource), it means that the exploit was successful and they now have access to your system. You need to keep two issues in mind about landing: The first, of course, is to make it as difficult as possible to land on your systems. Misconfigurations, weak entry points, and the vagaries of human weakness can allow someone access to your network. Even the best configured and protected system still has a human element. Creating a network that is better protected against breach comes from instilling and promoting good employee password hygiene and from educating people about the kinds of phishing scams used to gather their personally identifying information (PII).

REMEMBER Your best defense against insider intrusions is to limit each employee's access to only those resources that are absolutely necessary to do the job. One common recommendation is to even limit the hours that such resources are available. Access attempts outside that window should throw up red flags.

PHISHING FOR ACCESS

Email isn't the only place people try to steal your personal information. It doesn't take too many pieces of information to accurately identify you. One subtle but extremely effective way is to answer those stupid questions on Facebook — don't do it. Some typical questions ("Name a food your home state is famous for") identifies your Facebook ID, whatever Facebook publicly reveals about you from your profile (which is public), as well as the fact that if you said "Cheese," you're most likely from Wisconsin. Here are a few more examples:

>> **What was your family's phone number when you were a kid?:** Answering this question tells someone the town in which you were born, a typical 2-factor authentication question.

>> **Is anyone old enough to remember the national anthem being played just before the TV got shut off for the night?** This question identifies seniors. Seniors are easy pickings.

>> **Who is the most famous person you've ever spoken to?** This can reveal associations, locations, interests.

>> **In a single sentence, what advice would you give your 18-year-old self?** Who knows what kinds of info you could discover about a person from this answer?

Considering what you can learn from Google and social media, you might open yourself up to all kinds of identity theft. Stolen identities can be manipulated to gain access using social engineering to your most critical systems. Inspiring workers in your company to stop giving away personal information in Facebook requires education.

Identity thieves are looking for your name, address, social security number, age, birthday (think about all those astrology questions revealing an approximate birth month), your email address, and any other identifying information they might be able to use for the next stage of their attack. If they can pretend they know you, they might be able to get you to provide your bank card information, your social security number (even limiting it to the last four digits simply gets them closer), or other credential documents.

WARNING

Many people don't realize that their habits off hours can impact their work security — this lesson *must* be taught, however.

Imagine this scenario: An attacker knows your name, the city in which you live, the last four digits of your social security number, and your birth month. That might be enough information to create an official looking request asking you to further verify your identity for continued e-banking, and that request might say something like this: "Take a picture of your photo ID, front and back, and email it back to us, and we will then make sure you have continued access." Of course, this message wasn't sent from the bank, but someone now actually has an image of your photo ID, and it only gets worse from here. Social engineering is the easiest way to gain access to critical systems.

Facebook isn't the only social media site where information can be collected. LinkedIn, a more business-facing social media platform, offers an amazing amount of information that, if used in the wrong way, can set someone up to be phished. You can find information on LinkedIn such as who your coworkers might be. Imagine how powerful it is to be able to spoof an email from a coworker that even mentions the names of other coworkers.

REMEMBER

Social engineering reaches new levels every day. Artificial intelligence programs used by malicious people can even go so far as to craft email messages based on your entire social media and online presence information — even including photos of your kids grabbed from any number of sites, like Instagram.

EXPANDING A HACKER'S REACH

In the next stage, the hacker begins trying to use the credentials and privileges they now have to access other nodes of the network. They will also begin probing the network to look for weaknesses in databases, applications, configuration settings, and anything else they can take advantage of to further infiltrate your network.

TIP

Apply the latest security patches to all your computers to limit the info a hacker might exploit. You might consider a Patch Management as a Service (PMaaS) application such as Bell Integration (www.bell-integration.com/capabilities/run/patch-management-as-a-service).

Hackers don't always act the way they do in the movies, where they sit in front of their computer screens, drinking the latest energy drink until they've managed to breach your system. Infiltration of your network might instead be a long-term effort. Hackers can install *keyloggers* to copy whatever characters you type so that they can steal your password. They can also install *network sniffers* to search traffic on your network for choice morsels of data to steal. Your computers can even be used to secretly store data the hackers stole from somebody else.

REMEMBER

Protecting your network from allowing access to all parts simultaneously is the key to limiting expansion.

Gaining access to your cloud resources can also lead to a backdoor into your local networks and the other way around. Both must be protected equally and be as isolated from each other as possible. This can be particularly challenging in a hybrid cloud environment.

Developing security zones

To limit access to your entire network — cloud, local cloud, standard LAN resources — you can create security zones in it. It's a lot like having watertight doors on a submarine: If one part of the sub springs a leak, you can seal off the watertight doors and protect the other areas of the ship. (See Figure 12-1.) Submarines use steel; networks mainly use network segmentation software.

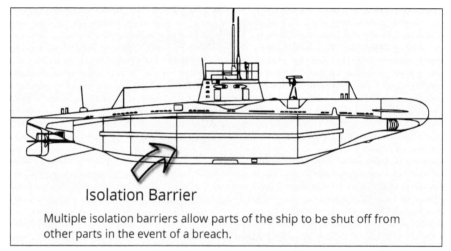

FIGURE 12-1:
Networks can be isolated in the same way submarines and large ships isolate areas in the event of a breach.

Isolation Barrier

Multiple isolation barriers allow parts of the ship to be shut off from other parts in the event of a breach.

TIP

Network segmentation can be achieved using either network segmentation software, routers, or firewalls.

Network routers have the ability to limit network traffic into sensitive areas of your network. One way is by creating a VLAN, or virtual *LAN*. You can think of it as a network within a network, like the old Mickey Mouse balloons where a smaller Mickey head would blow up inside the larger balloon. When VLANs are isolated, computers or devices within this network have no ability to communicate with other devices on the physical network. In fact, they have no knowledge of their existence. If someone then breaches one of these VLANs, the other areas of your network remain safe.

Microsegmentation is a way to create secure zones in either your local or cloud networks. Allowing even more fine-grained access control than a VLAN, microsegmentation was made possible by technologies such as software-defined networks and virtual networks — they work by isolating traffic between servers that normally are allowed through traditional perimeter network protection tools. Following the zero trust model, it's possible to set up policies that limit the types of traffic allowed between devices, by giving them a role and setting the access restrictions. Isolating communication in this way limits expansion by hackers.

TIP

To pull off microsegmentation, you need to have mapped the data paths between all your users, applications, workloads, and devices. Use a good discovery tool to help you identify what or who is connecting to your cloud resources, particularly when these applications are communicating with one another in the cloud.

Network isolation is a standard part of the security provided by all cloud service providers — it's what keeps the data from one customer separated from all the others. It's up to you to provide further isolation within your own cloud. Alternatively, you can use multiple cloud accounts.

Different security zones will have different levels of trust associated with them. This is a standard differentiation (recognized by many security certifications) that requires zone level security.

WARNING

Containers don't provide enough isolation to be considered a security zone, because they all share the same host kernel. They aren't isolated enough so that a motivated hacker gaining access to your cloud couldn't also have knowledge of your containers and gain access to them. Work is being done to truly isolate containers, but it's not ready for prime time.

There are many ways to create your own isolation within a single cloud account. Microsoft Azure, for example, offers a role based access control mechanism. You can choose to use one of the built-in Azure roles — Owner, Contributor, or Reader — or create your own, custom roles. If you've created a role based access control system (RBAC), you can apply those same roles by creating them within Azure.

REMEMBER

When using Azure Storage, your data is further isolated by using public key authentication to access the storage area.

AWS creates isolation using its identity and access management (IAM) system. After identities have been created (IAM User), you can assign roles (IAM Roles). The two types of identities are pretty much the same — they define which resources can be accessed by the user or role.

Google Cloud uses the Kubernetes RBAC system, which is enabled by default. It's possible to use both the Kubernetes RBAC and IAM systems to control access.

EXFILTRATING THE ILL-GOTTEN GAINS

Exfiltration is a fancy word for withdrawal. It's most often used when talking about withdrawing troops from a forward operating area. The same word applies to data: The goal of hackers trying to steal your data is getting your secret data out of your network — often, using malware that creates a backdoor into your system using malware such as a remote access trojan (RAT). SQL database scripting exploits were also a problem for a long time, but that particular danger has faded because most people have upgraded their scripting languages. Old applications using older SQL implementations may still be vulnerable.

Once data has been accessed on your network by way of any number of hacks, the next job is to move that data out of your cloud storage or local computer servers. This task requires that the data be copied to a place where the hackers have access to it, such as

>> **Copying your data directly to an anonymous remote location on the Internet:** This location can be anonymous on several levels. It might be anonymous because it has been copied to a file storage location on a website accessible only via the Tor network (sometimes known as the *dark web*). Traditional tools are often used to copy data in this manner — using Secure Copy to move data across an SSH connection, for example.

>> **Creating a tunnel in your system that can be accessed later, when the user is no longer logged in to your system**: This avoids tying the data movement to a particular account. Some systems are set up to notice when users move large segments of data, particularly when the behavior is deemed unusual. This can be done in the cloud by creating a storage gateway. (For more on storage gateways, see `https://docs.aws.amazon.com/storagegateway/latest/userguide/create-gateway-vtl.html`.

>> **Finding vulnerabilities in FTP servers that allow unrestricted access to files:** FTP has probably seen its better days, and unless you absolutely need it, you might consider not running an FTP server.

Hackers can also create their own socket based transfer systems that bypass the usual file transfer mechanisms. This requires that they scan your network for an open port and then write a small transfer application that uses this port to move packets of data — your data — into their hands.

>> **Sneakernet:** In the case where someone has gained physical access to hardware on your network, moving data might mean simply copying it to a thumb drive and walking away with it.

>> **When you're running a hybrid cloud network and your mainframe may become the weak link:** Mainframes typically have their own file copy mechanisms, like `IND$File`. This can be dangerous because these types of file transfers generally aren't logged. Additionally, IBM mainframes have a system, called Network Job Protocol (NJP), that allows the transfer of data between systems.

It's one thing to try to keep people out of your network. It's an even more difficult job to keep valuable data from exiting after someone has access to it. The best-known example is the hacking of the media giant Sony in 2014, when someone managed to steal 100 terabytes of movie files from the company's servers. Because networks, applications, devices, and user access have become so complex, spotting a simple hidden app that's streaming data like a leaky showerhead is nearly impossible for a security team to spot.

AI applications are better at spotting small and seemingly unrelated perturbations in the way the network operates. When your system collects log and performance data, the AI learns what is normal. When things move outside of that pattern, the AI throws up red flags. The hope in the future is that more AI systems will be built to recognize a breach in progress and defeat it. Dark Trace (`www.darktrace.com/en`) is a British firm that has an AI that purports to stop data theft as it's happening.

Offboarding employees

When employees leave, they often take more than that handy pack of pencils. Loyalty tends to end with the last paycheck. Two items that often walk out the door with the former employee are customer lists and intellectual property. This info is usually valuable to a new employer or an enterprising former employee who has decided to compete. Though employees who are loyal to your company are still risks for pilfering data, you must ensure that employees who are leaving no longer have the ability to access sensitive data.

TIP

Here's an easy-to-remember list of utterly worthless documents: noncompete agreements, nondisclosure agreements (NDAs), a doctor's note written in crayon, bounced checks.

An employee who parts ways with you is one of your biggest insider risks. Taking extra care to manage their departure should be a normal part of saying goodbye. Once the cake is cut in the breakroom, get started following your offboarding procedures. You can find a number of helpful IT checklists for offboarding employees — here's yet another one:

>> **Revoke access to the identity provider.** This can be Active Directory, LDAP, OpenLDAP, or another database type that contains the information your former employee uses to sign in to resources. This also includes any multifactor authentication information. Notice that I said *revoke* and not *delete.* You may need this information later for closing out employee information, gaining access to critical systems created by the employee, and more.

>> **Remove any SaaS account credentials from applications the employee may have accessed in the cloud.** Keep in mind that cloud access is pretty much from anywhere, so this task should be high on your offboarding agenda. Make sure you shut down the user account in the application.

TIP

Many companies pay big bucks for user licenses that are no longer being used — make sure you manage user account licenses.

>> **Remove remote access accounts via SSH or VPN.** These accounts are the most likely to allow someone access to systems where they can do the most harm. Here are some tips for removing SSH users: www.linuxshelltips. com/disable-ssh-user-login.

>> **Change the role of the departing user in any systems where the user has been granted access using a role-based authorization system.** The same goes for all zero trust systems — the trust just plunged to zero.

>> **Redirect the employee email to a supervisor or an administrator, and then change the email sign-in password on the mail server so that the departing employee no longer has access.** Notice that this is a redirect, not a delete. Not deleting the user allows you to access the user's email, and redirecting it means that any important correspondence is directed to the person taking over the former employee's responsibilities.

>> **Nab those packages of pencils before they head out the door.** Seriously, make sure that any multifactor authentication tokens are returned as well as any company hardware — particularly, any that might contain sensitive information or have backdoor login methods installed. This usually includes any intellectual property designs, drawings, lists and other items, in either digital or hard copy format. You can never be sure that the employee made no backups.

REMEMBER

You can go only so far in protecting data from employee theft. Serving search warrants on all departing employees just isn't allowed.

>> **When employees have corporate credit cards, you need to have those returned as well.** Part of this process involves auditing the account after the fact, to see which systems autobill the company card — in case the card was used to pay for a system that's critical to business continuity. It's no fun waking up to find that your domain name has expired because the card no longer works.

You also want to make sure that the credit card information isn't being used without the card. After all, who needs a physical card when you've memorized all the digits?

- **It's old-timey tech, but the phone system must also be updated to disallow voicemail access.** Some voicemail systems allow broadcast messages to be sent. Even though revenge hacking represents a tiny percentage of hacks from departing employees, you do *not* want them sending broadcast messages.

- **Create a look-ahead date.** This is the date on which you take a second look at any credit card accounts, complete a general security audit to make sure none of their accounts has been accessed surreptitiously, and perhaps start canceling accounts that were suspended until someone could take their place and new credentials added. This includes the email account that was simply forwarded.

- **Update any physical access identification systems.** This can be card swipe, biometric, or PIN number door access. It's also a good idea when using PIN access to assign each employee their own PIN so that you don't have to change the number for each and every one every time someone leaves.

TIP

If an employee is being terminated or laid off, you might want to shut down their access to company data resources before making them aware of their change of status.

Get rid of any shared accounts where all users share the same user ID and password. It's a bad security practice, and you should avoid it. (See Figure 12-2.) But, in the event that you did it anyway to save the company some money from not buying seats in Salesforce or QuickBooks, you need to remember to change the password and notify the others of the change.

Lastly, if the employee had access to vendors or customers, you may want to make them aware that they "left for other opportunities." This isn't necessarily an IT function, however: The HR department can take care of matters such as medical insurance, final pay, and other requirements.

REMEMBER

When particularly trusted employees leave who may have had credentials allowing them access to HSM or other key management software or hardware, that's the place to start removing access. As an added precaution, check recent logs to ensure that they didn't make key backups to a removable device.

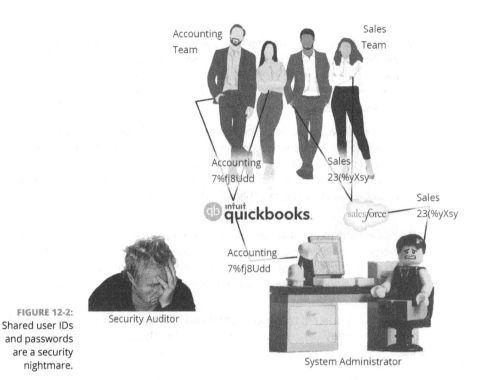

FIGURE 12-2:
Shared user IDs and passwords are a security nightmare.

Preventing the Preventable and Managing Employee Security

Bad things can happen for apparently no reason. You can put disaster plans and technology in place to try to manage that eventuality, but some things happen because they're bound to happen. If you never change the oil in your car, for example, you can expect the engine to just give up someday and quit on you in the most terrible way. Think of it as housekeeping. Perhaps it doesn't seem so sexy; perhaps it's even mundane. Regular maintenance needs to be done to protect your data security, in both the cloud environment and the well-designed perimeter security protecting your local network. This starts with employees. Even your best high-tech security software doesn't help much against an employee gone rogue.

Using any potential security audit as a guide, one of the areas you need to consider is the security risk you experience from your employees. The earlier section, "Off-boarding employees," discusses departing employees and the risk they pose, and this chapter also discusses the risk you run from employee error. Now you must look a little deeper into the people you've hired and determine what they mean to your data security.

REMEMBER

The number-one risk to your data security comes from employees. According to www.helpnetsecurity.com, 60 percent of respondents to a recent survey said that background screening is one of the most important security controls they'd put in place.

In today's work environment, you might be eager to hire *anyone* to fill that empty role in your company. Doing this lackadaisically can spell disaster, though. Your company may have followed all the standard hiring practices — such as having the potential employee interviewed for general hygiene, skill level, and potential fit for your team. Keep in mind that the guy in *The Silence of the Lambs*, Hannibal Lecter, was an excellent doctor.

The background check

Most security audits require that you've taken an extra step beyond getting the standard responses from previous employers telling you that this new potential worker did the job in a perfunctory manner. Many companies, fearing lawsuits, now say nothing negative about previous employees — you have to do your own background investigation. That doesn't necessarily mean that you have to hire a private investigator to follow the person around and take surreptitious photos. But it might. This depends on the level of security required for the types of data your company handles. Your business might be a government contractor that regularly requires a top secret or secret security clearance. In that case, government agencies can do that level of investigation for you.

Proper background screening is an important step when bringing someone into the security blanket you've laid for your company's data. According to the US Equal Employment Opportunity Commission (EEOC), it isn't illegal to ask pertinent questions of a potential employee and require a background check. However, you have to secure the employee's permission before checking their background. You need to

>> Inform the prospective employee that you might use the information you gather to make a decision about hiring

>> Let the person know the scope of your investigation

>> Secure their permission in writing for a background check

>> Certify to the company providing the background information that you won't use it to discriminate against the potential employee and that you have the person's permission to initiate the background investigation.

Confidentiality, NDAs, and other fairly worthless documents

It's perfunctory to make certain new hires sign all the right paperwork, including documents such as confidentiality agreements that ask the employee to keep the company data secret and to return all company equipment, designs, drawings, and other intellectual property information if they leave. Fearing that the employee might use their newfound knowledge of, for instance, customer lists, trade secrets, or other confidential information to compete with your business, you ask them to sign a noncompete agreement and a nondisclosure agreement (NDA). In some cases, employees start new businesses competing with the current employer without even leaving.

Government regulations are strict about what you can restrict a person from doing after they've left your employ. In fact, states such as California have made non-compete agreements pretty much unenforceable. You should check federal, state, and local laws about what you can and can't do when crafting these documents.

Most importantly, these documents, when properly crafted, signed, and hidden away in the HR department file drawers, do absolutely nothing to protect your data.

TIP

Make sure all those necessary documents are signed by the employee, not because signing them will keep them honest (well, more honest), but because security audits will look for the little crossed *t*'s and dotted *i*'s.

Employee training

Employee training is more important than you can possibly imagine. Many of the strategies for cloud security suggested in this book rely on people throughout your company participating in the security plan. To participate effectively, people need to be educated. For example, zero trust is a goal that requires people at multiple levels within your company to understand and participate in limiting data access to only that which is required. This type of strategy can't be managed by IT alone — it must be part of the corporate culture.

Disaster planning involves many people. Educating people (not just once but regularly) on what their role is and what steps to take can mean the difference between suffering total disaster and successfully averting total disaster.

TIP

Employee security training should not be a one-and-done affair. Just as agile software development requires continual security testing, making sure that your employees are on top of the changing landscape of IT security, (particularly when they're using the cloud) is of prime importance.

Education also means letting people know about consequences. What happens when a breach has occurred? It could hurt your business's reputation, causing the company to fold or experience huge customer loss. Your company can fail a security audit and lose its credentials for working on certain projects. These and other consequences that affect the ability of a business to stay in business, or to maintain its standing in the business community, should also have consequences for the people who let bad things happen — when it was their responsibility to protect them. You need to let people know what those consequences might be.

Overall, educating everyone in the company about information security policy helps create a team atmosphere and makes your company a more secure place to work. Admittedly, it does seem almost strange these days to call it a place to work, because many businesses now have completely remote workforces. But it's precisely those remote workers who most need education about how to protect data, because *they* are the ones most likely to use the cloud to perform their tasks, either via a SaaS application or remote access to IaaS systems.

Data loss prevention systems

The US government's National Institute of Standards and Technology (NIST) has the most succinct definition of data loss prevention — trying to change it would be an injustice: "Data loss prevention is an enterprise program targeted on stopping various sensitive data from leaving the private confines of the corporation."

Data loss can be categorized into these two specific types:

>> **Leakage:** This is when data is in the wild and no longer under your control. It has leaked out. Most leaks are perpetrated by attacks on your system by way of the efforts of both external and internal bad actors. (Don't go running off to check rottentomatoes.com for a list of Bad Actors. In this instance, they are the bad people trying to steal your data — usually, to exploit it for some nefarious purpose.)

>> **Invisibility:** This is when your data is no longer visible because it's either lost, encrypted during a ransomware attack, or damaged either purposely or accidentally.

Data loss prevention involves many of the topics covered earlier in this book. At its simplest level, it means making best efforts to maintain your data in a manner that preserves its integrity and secrecy. In slightly less simple terms, don't lose it, don't give it away, don't let people steal it, and don't blow it up accidentally.

TECHNICAL
STUFF

One angle not covered yet is the role of intellectual property protection. This topic is beyond the scope of a book on cloud security, but it should be a checklist item in your information security plan.

The key components of any good data-loss prevention scheme should include these actions:

>> **Managing your data** in such a way that you have a plan and stick to it, by implementing policies and security measures.

>> **Taking the steps (in data discovery) to determine what data you have, its sensitivity, its risks, its location, its owner, and its storage situation** — perhaps in an SQL database located in a virtual machine (VM) somewhere in the cloud, to take just one example.

>> **Monitoring data usage,** which is important to its continued safety. Knowing the patterns of usage can help you identify anomalous behavior patterns that can identify potential breaches before they happen. It also helps you put in place the necessary technology to protect the data as it moves from the cloud to local users or applications.

>> **Protecting your data,** which is the goal of any company that has data: Even the local ice cream truck has data. You need to have a plan for protecting your data as well as what you're going to do if it becomes compromised.

Navigating Cloud Native Breaches

A *cloud native breach* is a successful attack by hackers that results in customer data being stolen. (It's important that you spell *breach* correctly, because *breeches* are pants and the only way to fix them is to send them to a tailor.) Cloud native security encompasses applications, platforms, and infrastructure security. There are many layers to this kind of security, spanning the operating system, the network (including any software-defined networks), applications, virtual machines, and containers.

TIP

With a complicated landscape for security, try to develop an integrated approach so that you aren't trying to fight battles on multiple fronts.

Most of the security breaches in network and cloud security come from mistakes made by employees. The next section focuses on that topic specifically and on ways you can minimize those mistakes.

Minimizing employee error

To err is human. Everyone's heard that phrase, if for no other reason than to make themselves feel better after making a mistake. The security firm Tessian (`www.tessian.com`) performed a research study with a Stanford University professor, Jeff Hancock, that elucidated the fact that human error is responsible for 88 percent of all data breaches.

Knowing that 88 percent of your challenge in preventing data breaches lies with preventing human error should make your head spin like poor possessed Regan in *The Exorcist*. Let's say that the researchers were way off and that the real number is 44 percent. That's still 44 percent. Alarm bells should be going off now because the solution to the bulk (between 44 percent and 88 percent) of all data breaches can be prevented by eliminating human error.

Removing human error

The easiest way to remove human error is to remove humans from the equation. This strategy leads to the hole-in-the-bucket problem. (If you aren't familiar with this problem, take a moment to listen to Harry Belafonte and Odetta sing all about it at `www.youtube.com/watch?v=AthT8kw7CIo`.)

The obvious solution to human error is automation. The problem is that automation rules and instructions must be entered by a human and are prone to human error. This exact problem occurs when setting up the rules and settings that make Configuration as Code possible. Scripting configuration and then saving it to a code repository so that it can be checked out and used again and again is simply genius. Though the system effectively uses the configuration settings each time something is configured, if the settings are wrong, they are equally wrong every time. But, unlike in manual configuration, these scripts can be debugged, refined, and modified over time until something useful pops out on the other end.

Sometimes, human error isn't so much error as it is the effects of change. Things change, and the software realm changes daily. Configuration settings necessary to configure a product can change, or the software can change versions or simply expire and then it can no longer be used. It's a lot of work to keep configuration scripts updated, and after all the low-hanging fruit for scripting daily configuration settings are dealt with, you may experience diminishing returns when trying to keep everything updated.

When your environment has largely moved to the cloud, just about everything can be scripted. Creating these Configuration as Code scripts to manage your environment lowers person-hours and reduces error by debugging the scripts.

TIP

There are positives and negatives to using Configuration as Code. Overall, it saves time and money and reduces overall errors after the scripts are debugged.

Seeing what happens when configurations go bad

In January of 2021, VIPGames exposed more than 23 million records of around 66,000 individuals because of a cloud misconfiguration. This data included information such as usernames, email addresses, IP addresses, hashed passwords, and social media login information. Some of the worst data breaches have come from misconfigured platforms because they are so prone to error. First, there are many platforms, and often on many different cloud configurations. Configuration settings are a lot to keep up with. Doing it manually opens you up to error. It's a much better idea to script your configuration tasks.

Automating SSH key management

Historically, key management has been a manual process that lends itself to errors and theft. Because SSH key management literally manages the keys to your kingdom, you want to make sure this is done well and with a minimum amount of human interaction.

For remote access to most Linux systems, SSH keys are required. Because SSH keys are a form of identity authentication, managing them becomes vital. You many not necessarily want to leave that task in the hands of overworked system administrators who've just returned from a six-pack lunch. SSH key management can be challenging in a large company where keys need to be rotated (changed) regularly for maximum security. Larger companies also have larger employee turnovers requiring keys to be removed. Thycotic (`https://thycotic.com`) makes the Thycotic Secret Server, which can manage and automate the task of managing secret keys. This system manages the keys and interoperates with identity management systems that do things like manage the roles associated with an employee. This can be a critical part of offboarding an employee, as covered earlier in this chapter.

In addition to users having SSH keys, machines must also have SSH keys to allow them access to critical data. A great deal of effort has been spent on protecting human identities, and little effort has gone into machine identity and authentication. Machines now access data more often than humans. What does it take to protect machine identities when such identities are everywhere? They include IoT devices, VMs, containers, and cloud resources. Having a platform to manage machine identities to protect them in the same way human identities are protected becomes a requirement. Venafi (`www.venafi.com`), a major player in this growing field, has a platform for managing machine identities.

Guarding against insider data thefts

Insider data theft is more common than you may realize. In most cases, people are trusting by nature. They want to trust those they work with — fellow employees, contractors, freelancers, vendors, customers, and anyone else within the scope of your daily work who has access to your data, whether via a SaaS application or connecting into your network by way of cloud resources like IaaS and PaaS services.

According to the Verizon Data Breach Investigations report, in 2021, in smaller companies with fewer than 1,000 employees, 44 percent of the breaches came from internal threat actors. Many of these come from privilege abuse. In companies with more than 1,000 employees, that percentage dropped to 36 percent. The greatest number of these breaches were for financial gain. Take these figures seriously when considering how to best protect your data resources, locally and in the cloud. In a nutshell, between one-third and one-half of the people you work with (when including partners) will take actions that allow your data to be stolen for financial gain — by someone abusing their access to data. I don't mean to say that all these actions are being taken maliciously. In fact, the greatest percentage of the breaches are originated by organized criminals looking for weak links into your networks, and insiders are appealing targets. According to a report by Experian, 80 percent of these breaches are caused by employee negligence. The earlier section "Automating SSH key management" mentions how accidents by employees cause serious problems. It goes further when you're talking about sheer negligence or even sabotage.

The kinds of data that are being stolen consist largely of credentials and personal information. The challenge to someone trying to secure this kind of data becomes clearer. To protect your company's valuable information from attack by insiders, you must implement systems that identify when the people you work with are negligent and allow others to abuse their access privileges to steal credentials and personal information for financial gain.

REMEMBER

A huge percentage of data breaches occur because people in your organization are sloppy with password protection and data security in general.

The classic response to insider threat is prevention. This concept can mean anything from better password control to AI-based user behavior analytics to spot when things appear wonky. But prevention is never 100 percent effective, and a fine line always exists between onerous data protection rules and ease of employee access, particularly in a work-at-home environment. Make things too difficult and you have a new kind of problem. Some users just can't access the system because the process is too complex. Even worse is that the more creative ones will find ways around your best-laid plans. Simply put, prevention can go only so far.

AI-based user behavior analytics sounds like the obvious answer. After all, it's automated. But this is only partly true — spotting unusual behavior is the automated part. Someone must respond to all the alerts generated by these systems, and a great number of them end up being false positives. You'll find yourself looking for a needle in the haystack. Will it find a potential attack? Yes, but that's like looking for a gun toting terrorist at an NRA rally.

REMEMBER

AI can help you find the problems as they occur, but it's only a tool to be used by security operators — who will need to follow up on each of the alerts. This strategy can be time consuming. Some people farm out this task whenever possible.

The next approach, as already suggested, is to get rid of data you aren't using so that it doesn't sit there as a target. This exercise works only if you've carefully tagged and classified your data and you know exactly where it is and how and by whom it's being used. (Like that ever happens.) It's an admirable goal, but because data is created every moment, this type of exercise can also fall short. Thousands of people in hundreds of cloud applications creating who-knows-how-much data means that some of that data will be ignored because the business is to create data, not spend all your time grooming it with metadata — adding descriptive information such as tags, in other words. The cloud has also created a new mindset that is a pushback against this practice. Data never needs to be erased, because unlimited storage exists, and who knows when we might need it? Yes, the cloud has created a hoarder mentality that isn't going away anytime soon.

The past few years have seen the growth of new tools that promote working in partnership with others. Tools like Slack (`https://slack.com`) have become commonplace, and information sharing is part of that culture. *Zero trust* philosophies — giving access as little as possible and only when needed — seem to work against this newer, open, sharing mechanism of working together.

The way to thread this needle seems to be to use a hybrid approach. (See Figure 12-3.) Watch how your data is being used — protecting it when you can, erasing it when you can, encrypting it always, watching your user behavior, and taking all the traditional approaches to limiting risk from poor data etiquette.

Preventing employee data spillage

Data *spillage* is the same thing as data *leakage* — the unintended release of confidential data, in other words. The statistics show that in at least 80 percent of cases, the release of private information is unintentional. This doesn't only mean that someone taped their password to the top of their computer screen because passwords change so often that it's difficult to remember the current one. Yes, this happens. It also means misconfiguring applications to deliver private data unintentionally or adding bugs in application code that retrieves more data than was intended. This happens when SQL, the query language for databases, contains the wrong syntax.

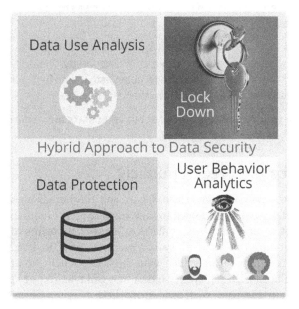

FIGURE 12-3:
A hybrid approach to data security gives you the best results.

Accidents happen, but what happens next can make all the difference. Make sure you follow the steps in this next section to reduce the impact of a data breach.

Cleaning up after the spill

Refer to your incident response plan. If you don't have one, you need one. Chapter 11 goes into more detail about developing an incident response plan. Here are the basic steps you need to follow in response to a breach:

1. **Identify the breach.**

   Once a breach has been identified and authenticated as a real breach and not a false positive, move on to the next step.

2. **Respond to the breach.**

   Take actions that seal the breach and remove account access, and then begin searching for elements of the breach that may have been left behind to make breaking in again easier.

3. **Limit the scope of the breach:** Once you know about an active breach, you need to lock down your sensitive data even more than it already may be, in order to limit what the attacker can access.

4. **Take countermeasures to limit the ability of reinfection — further attack, in other words.**

5. **Put a forensics team on the job to determine as much as possible about the breach.**

   Forensics teams gather the data that may be used in further legal actions, either by your company or against it. It's never pretty. They may also uncover areas of the breach you didn't know about at that time that can help you seal the breach further and stop any further data release.

6. **Talk to your corporate counsel about what state and federal requirements you may need to follow.**

Announce the breach publicly

Once the barn door is open, so to speak, and the horses are out trampling the neighbor's daisy patch, you need to take steps to alert others to your breach. This action serves several purposes. It alerts other security teams to the type of attack you've experienced so that others can work to avoid it. It complies with most requirements that you announce your breach publicly. It also makes anyone affected by the data breach aware so that they can take steps to protect themselves from devastating impact, such as identity theft.

REMEMBER

Always contact the appropriate law enforcement agency in the event of a data breach. When personal and medical data is released, you also need to notify the FTC. They may require you to contact the media according to the Health Breach Notification Rules.

If your breach has released social security numbers, contact the major credit reporting companies, who will advise you on which steps to take to mitigate the damage there. Many companies offer free credit monitoring services to those affected by the release of the SSNs.

TIP

Clearly assess what information has been released. There is no reason to contact customers in cases where only their names or non-identifying information has been released.

Responding to EU breaches

Data breaches that involve the release of private information of people living in the European Union have additional response requirements. Because businesses no longer operate within single geographical borders, you should be aware of and plan for these requirements. You can read the requirements here: `https://gdpr.eu/article-34-communication-of-a-personal-data-breach`.

Minimize the impact

You can take additional steps, as described in the following list, to help minimize the impact of a data breach (nothing can entirely mitigate the damage to your business, but you want to minimize the potential damage to the people who have entrusted you with their private information):

>> **Contact search engines to let them know of your breach.** Fill them in on the kinds of data that may have been released so that they can assist in making sure that if someone releases your private data to the public, it will be difficult for others to locate.

>> **Begin searching the Internet for your data using known keywords.** This strategy is unlikely to yield any results — particularly, if you've contacted search engines before this step. It's still important to be thorough.

>> **Watch for ransom demands.** Unlike traditional ransomware that encrypts your data, some attackers will steal your data and threaten to release it unless a ransom is paid.

>> **Contact the FBI (**`www.fbi.gov`**).** According to the FBI website, it's the lead federal agency for investigating cyberattacks and intrusions.

>> **Contact your cloud service provider.** In a shared security responsibility, the provider may have security resources that you don't have, and they may be able to assist you in locking down your assets and locating the perpetrator.

IN THIS CHAPTER

» Recognizing some common industry and government frameworks

» Getting to know SASE architecture

» Learning the guts of a SASE implementation

» Discovering the Cloud Native Application Protection Platform

» Getting a handle on the government NIST framework

Chapter **13**

Security Frameworks

More than at any other time, cloud adoption has reached new levels. Because of the demand of the remote-work paradigm that was forced on businesses at the beginning of the Covid-19 crisis, cloud adoption was shoved onto even those most unwilling to change. Many companies, after making the leap, have seen the benefits of having remote workers and have continued this work-from-home paradigm. Some businesses have chosen a hybrid architecture of both in-office and home-office work. In both cases, cloud adoption has created an additional burden on existing network architectures and spawned a cloud connectivity challenge of unusual proportions.

This chapter covers some of the common industry and government frameworks that were designed to bring some order to this chaos, Gartner, the Connecticut-based technology research and consulting company, refers to these frameworks as strategies designed to impose order and empower security departments by using specific integrated application technologies that attempt to roll many security requirements into one. AIOps, covered earlier in this book, is both a framework and an application suite. (It has migrated away from the framework model and more to a suite of applications model, which is why I cover it separately.)

In this chapter, I describe SASE and CNAP frameworks and how they pull together key technologies into a single framework. I also talk a bit about the NIST risk management framework for government agencies and companies that contract with these agencies.

Looking at Common Frameworks

Quite a number of cloud security frameworks are out there, covering security at levels ranging from the highest level of government secrets to privacy related frameworks to general industry cybersecurity frameworks. No single solution fits every need, and frameworks are designed to walk you step-by-step through the process of protecting your data, making sure nothing is left out. Because this process isn't a simple one, some of the frameworks can cause more work than necessary. In those cases, make your best effort to meet the goals set forth in the framework. It's the same with applications that provide security: There is no magic bullet. The best you can do is try to find the framework and applications that do what you need them to do in an efficient and cost-effective manner.

Keep cloud security in mind because many of these frameworks are a bit long in the tooth and don't discuss cloud security with any specificity, and they tend toward a perimeter security model. With that in mind, the following introductions should help you find the framework that might best fit your needs.

Keep your budget in mind when considering some of the following frameworks. Some are free and community-created, and some can cost into the millions of dollars.

COBIT

Control Objectives for Information and Related Technology (COBIT) is an Isaca framework (www.isaca.org) heavily adopted throughout industry for information security. (Back in the day, Isaca was known as the Information Systems Audit and Control Association, but now it insists that everybody call it just Isaca. The organization is clearly modeling itself after Cher and Madonna.) It's industry- and business-type neutral, so it bills itself as capable of meeting the security needs of most businesses. Its primary goal is information and data security, so it's of particular importance to organizations that must comply with privacy regulations or for companies whose focus is IT-related products and services.

The COBIT framework tackles these four main components:

>> Planning and organization

>> Acquisitions and implementation

>> Delivery and support

>> Monitoring and evaluation

The fourth component is the key, in that the method used in this framework tracks the performance of all IT systems in your business. It helps you gauge how well your business processes align with your security goals.

Within these four component parts, the COBIT framework sets out principles of operation, such as putting the stakeholder first when it comes to deciding the success or failure of any project. If it doesn't do what stakeholders want, it needs to be done again.

REMEMBER

Agile development methodologies use the same idea of putting the stakeholder first and making them an integral part of the development process.

Another principle of COBIT is that it's meant to meet the needs of the entire organization and not simply the security needs of IT. Its principles and methods govern the entire organization, bringing them into a single and guided focus. This doesn't preclude using other frameworks (some of which are mentioned in this chapter) alongside COBIT in order to achieve further security goals.

COBIT also has the stated principle that governance should be separate from management. IT governance is a different animal and should not be confused with management. Governance has a completely different sets of goals, methods of monitoring performance, and things to get done that are not always in alignment with the management goals of making a nice widget or providing the best service. Governance creates a best-practices standard that companies must comply with when handling certain types of private data. Governance compliance is then often policed through mandatory security audits.

SABSA

Sherwood Applied Business Security Architecture, or SABSA (https://sabsa.org), is a framework and methodology for achieving information security while balancing the needs of businesses to achieve their goals. It may not be as industry-neutral as COBIT, but it's in use by organizations with some serious security goals, including banking, nuclear power production, government, and information and communication companies.

SABSA is an integration of frameworks, methods, and processes with these features:

>> **Attributes profiling:** A system of name-value pairs of attributes that describe factors such as security risk

>> **Risk and opportunity management framework:** A framework that helps you manage *business risks* — that elusive smooth path to achieving your goals

>> **Policy Architecture framework:** The development of policies into executable code

>> **Security Services-Oriented Architecture framework**: A SABSA framework for providing security services

>> **Governance framework:** A framework for managing governance and compliance issues

Federal Financial Institutions Examination Council (FFIEC) Cyber Assessment Tool (CAT)

Banks and credit unions use the FFIEC CAT that was created by financial regulators. It's not a hard-and-fast model, unlike other frameworks. It gives the security staff the freedom to create their own maturity and risk models as well as their own controls catalog.

Using this framework, organizations can measure their continued success in achieving security goals. This ability is particularly robust in the FFIEC CAT framework. For further information on FFIEC CAT, download the government's write-up about it at www.ffiec.gov/pdf/cybersecurity/FFIEC_CAT_May_2017.pdf.

Federal Risk and Authorization Management Program (FEDRAMP)

The US government developed the sweeping and governmentally complex Federal Risk and Authorization Management Program (FEDRAMP) for cloud service providers that hope to contract with the government. The program is based on a modified version of the NIST Risk Management framework, covered at the end of this chapter. Unlike SABSA, which is noncommercial, FEDRAMP is a commercial framework that mirrors what the Federal government does internally to manage risk. Many providers find the cost of, and difficulty in, implementing FEDRAMP to be prohibitive, but you might find that it fits your needs. Check it out at https://marketplace.fedramp.gov/#!/products.

Personal Information Protection and Electronic Documents Act (PIPEDA)

Similar to the privacy laws set forth by the European Union in its GDPR legislation, the Canadian government also set out policies that govern privacy. These policies are known as Personal Information Protection and Electronic Documents Act (PIPEDA). The goal of PIPEDA is to protect the personal privacy of its citizens; anyone wanting to do business in Canada (either physically in Canada or over the Internet) must comply with PIPEDA.

To learn more about complying with PIPEDA, check out the comprehensive guide at www.priv.gc.ca/biens-assets/compliance-framework/en/index.

WARNING

The PIPEDA is not optional when doing business in Canada. You must comply or else you face severe penalties.

Payment Card Industry — Data Security Standard (PCI–DSS)

The credit card industry deals with personally identifying information, credit card data, and related transaction information every single day. It should come as no surprise, then, that it has developed one of the most comprehensive and strict frameworks governing the privacy of such information, The framework is owned and governed by a consortium of credit card companies that includes Visa and Mastercard, American Express, Discover Card, and JBC. The consortium is known as the Payment Card Industry Security Standards Counsel. (That's as difficult to remember as your credit card number; it's PCI, for short.)

Unlike frameworks and policy standards managed by government agencies, the PCI–DSS standard is industry-self-governed, and one they imposed on themselves to engender trust in using credit cards.

For more on PCI-DSS compliance, check out this wiki at https://cio-wiki.org/wiki/Payment_Card_Industry_Data_Security_Standard_(PCI_DSS).

GLBA

The Gramm-Leach-Bliley Act (GLBA) is not so much a framework as it is a government law (thus, the *Act* at the end of the name). This requires financial institutions, and anyone acting like one, to demonstrate how they protect private information as it's disseminated. Like the medical requirement, HIPAA, which most people are familiar with by now, the GLBA has requirements such as your telling your customers exactly what you'll do with the private information you're being entrusted with. Of course, they must give customers the right to opt out of allowing their personal information into the hands of third parties.

The GLBA is managed by the Federal Trade Commission (FTC), in case you ever wondered what it is they do along with federal and state banking regulators.

SCF

The Security Controls Framework (SCF) is a *meta* framework (a framework built of frameworks, in other words) designed to manage cybersecurity and privacy issues. It's composed of about 750 controls categorized within each of 32 domains. These include topics such as

>> Asset management

>> Security and governance

>> Disaster recovery and business continuity

>> Capacity planning

>> Change management

>> Cloud security

>> Compliance

>> Privacy

The SCF website (www.securecontrolsframework.com) explains that this framework is designed to do more than just assist companies when it comes to meeting compliance. It aids in building in security after which compliance will follow.

DFARS 252.204-7012/ NIST 800-171

When you want to do business with the US defense agencies, you need to comply with Defense Federal Acquisition Regulation Supplement (DFARS) Clause 252.204-7012, affectionally called "Huh?" It lays out the requirements for all contractors and subcontractors to follow in safeguarding data that flows through their computer systems. It also specifies the reporting requirements should a breach occur. Think FBI on your doorstep.

This is not one of those frameworks that you have meetings about and decide how to implement. This framework has hard-and-fast requirements, and, as with most government policies, you'll need help complying. Here is a company that offers just that: https://nist800171compliance.com.

TIP

Off-the-shelf versions of Microsoft 365 don't meet DFARS 252.204-7012 security requirements.

ISO/IEC 27000 Series

The International Standards Organization (ISO) / International Electrotechnical Commission (IEC) 27000 Series or, if you want to sound cool, the ISO27K, is a set of information security standards that many consider to be the best framework for industry best practices. It's called a series because this framework of many documents generally starts with ISO 27XXX. To get you started with this series, you should take a look at ISO/IEC 27001:2013, which lists the requirements for information security management systems (ISMS). More than a dozen standards within the series cover everything from asset security to intellectual property protection.

The amount of information covered in this family of standards is vast. You can get started looking at 27001 here: `www.iso.org/isoiec-27001-information-security.html`.

CIS Critical Security Controls

The Center for Internet Security's (CIS) Critical Security Controls `www.cisecurity.org/controls` is a prioritized set of actions that work to protect your company from cyberattack. It's useful as both an implementation plan and a base for assessing how well you've achieved your security goals.

Critical Security Controls is a community-developed framework based on actual experience in fighting cyberthreats. Like many frameworks, it's task-based and starts off by having you inventory your assets. (Tag them, of course.) It also includes continuous vulnerability management, privilege administration, system maintenance, and log analyses.

The framework itself has 18 controls that contain 153 safeguards organized into implementation groups. Each control contains actionable guidance to defend against cyberattack. CIS also points you to additional products and services to help you defend your organization against hackers.

CIS Benchmarks

Another community-developed guideline from CIS, the Benchmarks framework is a series of configuration guidelines designed to assist you in developing your cybersecurity. Within these guidelines are various frameworks to adopt a *defense-in-depth model.* This model integrates people, technology and operations at every layer of an organization to bring about information security. The controls within the CIS Benchmarks were developed in collaboration with the consensus within the community of IT experts and CIS SecureSuite members — these people, from companies of all sizes, have access to additional tool sets and resources.

You can download the CIS Benchmarks documents for free at `https://learn.cisecurity.org/benchmarks`.

Common Criteria

ISO/IEC 15048, more commonly known as the Common Criteria, is an international standard for computer security certification. It's made up of concepts and cybersecurity principles and an evaluation model.

The framework spells out guidelines for creating a *security target* (ST) — a statement of security needs for a specific target of evaluation, in other words. (Or, if you prefer, "Here is a thing that needs to be secured.") What do you need in order to secure it? The thing to be secured is the target of evaluation, and the list of security needs is the ST, which includes items such as threats, assumptions, security objectives, and security requirements.

Because it isn't enough to simply follow guidelines once, the Common Criteria provides a model for continuous evaluation.

TIP

Part of developing your security plan should include having stakeholders participate in writing protection profiles (functional security requirements) as recommended by the Common Criteria.

In support of the Common Criteria, there is an international treaty signed by most Western nations known as the Common Criteria Recognition Arrangement (CCRA), where each signatory has agreed to recognize evaluations against the Common Criteria. This creates a base standard for cybersecurity assessment among nations. For more on the Common Criteria and CCRA, see `https://commoncriteriaportal.org/index.cfm?`.

FDA regulations on electronic records and signatures

The US Food and Drug Administration (FDA) has an interest in regulating the electronic records and electronic signatures for organizations such as medical device makers, biotech companies, drug companies, and other FDA-regulated businesses. The particular regulation, 21 CFR Part II (often just called Part II) requires these companies to follow stringent guidelines for making sure they can provide audit trails, system validation, secure electronic signatures, and complete documentation of all developed software and systems used to handle private and sensitive data.

This is an extremely complicated and onerous regulation that has been challenged by many of the companies to which it applies. In response, the FDA has agreed in one of its guidance documents to take "enforcement discretion."

ITIL

The Information Technology Infrastructure Library (ITIL) is a set of guidelines and practices for the proper integration of IT Service Management (ITSM) and IT Asset Management (ITAM) into the operations of your business. This guideline is technology- and industry-neutral and can be used by businesses of all sizes.

TIP

Implementing ITIL internally in an organization does not require a license for its use.

The five books that make up the ITIL cover the stages and processes of the entire IT service lifecycle; they are generally regarded as seminal works, on which many of the other security guidelines and frameworks have been based.

Figure 13-1 shows the circular nature of the ITIL lifecycle.

FIGURE 13-1: The ITIL lifecycle begins with strategy and moves out into implementation and then continuous improvement.

Introducing SASE Architecture

The job of Secure Access Service Edge (SASE) is to make network infrastructure simpler by combining both networking and security into a single architecture — one based in the cloud that eliminates centralized hubs with spokes as an architecture. The cloud has changed the way computers interact. Now everything works in a decentralized fashion.

SASE was developed because existing network security just wasn't up to the task of all the emerging technologies and the move toward distributed and cloud-based applications and data. The old hub-and-spoke network architecture became overwhelmed with workloads moving to and from the cloud and the sheer number of devices connecting to applications and data. That's because today's data traffic is no longer headed to centralized data centers. Work is happening in the cloud or offline in apps and then uploaded to the cloud.

REMEMBER

The amount of data on the move between data centers, remote users, SaaS applications in the cloud, storage in the cloud, and IoT devices has increased and will continue to increase. The cost of protecting data transfer using old technologies is expensive compared to the finance model and security of the cloud.

SASE is the convergence of existing wide-area networking and security concepts into a cloud-delivered integrated service. Figure 13-2 shows the two sides of SASE that make up the overall architecture. Its underlying security philosophy is zero trust, which moves the focus away from perimeter security to hyperfocusing on the security of individuals (users) and devices — clearly a move in line with the move to the cloud.

TWO SIDES OF SASE

NETWORK	SECURITY
SD-WAN	WAN SECURITY
ROUTING	BROWSING PROTECTION
DYNAMIC PATH SELECTION	SaaS SECURITY
LATENCY OPTIMIZATION	WEB SECURITY
NaaS	REMOTE ACCESS
	FWaaS
	IoT SECURITY

FIGURE 13-2: SASE is composed of both network and security principles.

TECHNICAL
STUFF

There is a component of SASE that comprises only the security side of SASE, known as the Security Service Edge (SSE).

Cloud-centric data patterns differ from older data patterns where data was collected in a wagon wheel pattern and headed to a centralized hub. Now every user connects directly with a cloud application using everything from a watch to a desktop, and all the time, not just when using business-specific applications. Smart speaker devices like Alexa and Nest (formerly, Google Home) provide constant data that includes video, music, the time-and-weather, information retrieval, podcasts, and thousands of related services. You may not picture such devices at the office, but now that the office is largely at home, you will see more of these types of connections to public cloud services.

The sassy side of SASE

The objective of a SASE architecture is to apply policy based security to the interactions between users and devices. Users and devices are identified, and then security policies associated with them are used to control access to applications and data. This happens no matter where these entities are physically located. The entities can be users, groups of users (such as a company department), hardware devices, applications, services, or locations out in the cloud.

SASE ends in E, for Edge. The concept used in a SASE framework is to push information processing closer to the user. This is the underlying concept of edge computing. Moving processing closer to the user also means pushing the granting of access and security closer to the user as well. This improves network latency, first by being distributed and no longer experiencing the bottleneck of a centralized server, and second because the processing is physically closer to the user. It also avoids using a less-secure VPN technology to connect with on-premises services and devices.

Access to applications by users and devices is granted based on the identity of either the user or device, the context in which it wants access, corporate security policy guidelines, and continual risk assessment based in zero trust (access allowed if and only when it's needed).

The benefits of employing a SASE implementation are that you need only a single cloud-based system to manage the security of your devices wherever they're located. It was also built with zero trust as a philosophy rather than trying to shoehorn it in later. This immediately becomes simpler because now you've done away with many different point solutions, many of which were unable to talk to one another because they were being run within a silo — an area cut off digitally from others in your company, in other words.

Sassy makeup

A number of components make up a SASE framework. Each one replaces stand-alone applications and makes them part of a single framework hosted in the cloud. Companies using SASE should be employing a cloud-first mentality.

Though SASE is vendor-neutral and various companies offer SASE solutions, there are some basic technologies (formerly stand-alone applications) that make up a SASE framework solution. Here's a brief list:

>> **Secure web gateway:** The secure web gateway (SWG) enforces corporate security and acceptable use policies and provides protection when using the web. It's middleware that sits between the user/browser application and the website they're attempting to form a connection with. The SWG app then examines the target and decides whether it meets the policy guidelines and blocks access when it doesn't.

>> **Firewall as a Service:** Hosted in the cloud, Firewall as a Service (FWaaS) replaces or expands on the uses of traditional hardware and software firewalls by expanding the capabilities beyond perimeter security. Firewalls weren't designed to manage cloud traffic or handle encryption natively. These two features make them completely outdated. Not only that, because they aren't based in the cloud, it's difficult to scale them should you experience a sudden increase in traffic.

FWaaS is scalable, handles encryption, and was designed to handle traffic to the cloud. It's also more secure because it inspects the traffic between users, applications, and devices. They have built-in intrusion prevention systems, provide DNS security, and provide centralized management, making it easier to manage a large enterprise with multiple cloud service providers. This was commonly implemented as a stand-alone application.

>> **Cloud access security broker:** Cloud access security brokers (CASB) work to enforce security policies in traffic between users at your premises or their bedrooms (home offices) and the cloud by monitoring user activity and providing continual risk assessment. They also include malware protection functionality. The functions of a cloud access security broker include giving the security staff increased visibility, threat protection, data security, and compliance monitoring:

• *Visibility:* Visibility is the key to any cloud security platform. Making sense of the multitude of users, data centers, applications, connections into the cloud, and the many cloud environments can only be done practically by using an integrated dashboard that lets you see how everything is working together. This kind of application also helps you control the fine-grained access policies that allow users and devices to view and change sensitive data.

CASB visibility also extends to the ability to discover shadow IT situations. It's not always possible to control which applications users choose to employ in the cloud, but it's important that the applications be known and have security policies control access to the applications. This brings these situations out of the shadows and enforces security.

TIP

Educate users in your company on the importance of letting the IT department know about the applications they use. With the idea that it's easier to get forgiven than to get permission, getting that forgiveness is important so that it's possible to either employ the application's security policies or wrap the application in a manner so that its protections fall within your guidelines.

Visibility also extends to viewing and managing ongoing security risks. It's possible to see unusual behavior and flag it, throw up an alert, or even automate responses to security risks such as shutting down the connection. An example of this would be unusual access to an application by a user who has no reason to use this type of application. Of course, this should also be controlled using a zero trust model of granting access only when and if it's needed.

Threat protection: Built into CASB systems is malware threat protection and behavior analytics. This provides protection beyond merely controlling who has access to which application. When hackers break into your cloud or network, they look to spoof their way into applications for access to sensitive data.

Weirdness protection is a term first coined here in this book. Weirdness is anything out of the ordinary — they, whoever they are, ask you to report strange behavior on buses and subways. It's the same kind of thing. CASBs look for weirdness in your system by studying user behavior or flagging unusual files that just may not belong. It's a little like seeing the suitcase left alone at the airport — the CASB system then throws up alerts or remediates the weirdness.

Threat protection also includes all the ordinary protections you would expect in a cloud security system, like these:

- Antimalware
- Account defense mechanisms
- Application security
- Ransomware protection
- URL filtering of malicious links

This list of protections isn't exhaustive, partly because by the time you're this far into the book, it's likely that other types of malware have arisen to give you headaches.

- *Data security:* CASB systems offer a broad range of standard security protections, including data encryption, tokenization, and zero trust or similar access control to private data.

  Another area of data security handled by CASB systems is data loss prevention. Labeling data is one of the functions offered by a CASB. Once data has been labeled, you can use these labels to assess risk and control access to the data. A great deal of the work required to label data and enforce access policies can be automated, freeing you to get lunch once in a while.

- *Compliance:* Compliance is one of those burdens that many companies find to be time consuming, costly, and in some cases more than they can handle. There are two results to this scenario: Either the company automates compliance, or they just don't do it until they get caught, because private data has found its way into the wrong hands.

  A better way to handle compliance is on the front end. That means you create policies that comply with the regulations and then do everything you can to make sure that your policies are followed. Policy compliance can be largely automated, also something that must be done on the front end. And yes, there is Compliance as a Service (CaaS) through companies like Accenture (www.accenture.com/us-en).

  Compliance is one of those far-reaching areas of security that ranges from the obvious medical information and finance-related regulations to the regulations covering international business to the privacy regulations of individual countries or blocs like the European Union. Unless your business is large enough to have an entire group of people manage compliance, it might be best for you to farm out this task to a company that manages these types of compliance. They can help you create the policies necessary to feed application frameworks like CASB.

>> **Zero trust network access:** Zero Trust Network Access (ZTNA) makes zero trust a reality by controlling access to applications, data, and services using the concept of least privilege. This differs from the traditional VPN access from user to server by providing more fine-grained access restrictions. A VPN is a bit more like a barn door: Once you're in, you get the hay, the cows, the sheep, and the chickens.

The ZTNA system first authenticates the user and then creates a secure tunnel to applications for which they are authorized. Creating this encrypted tunnel means that IP addresses are no longer made public, adding more security protection. This type of zero trust implementation means that if hackers gain access to your network, they can't scan the network to gain greater access. They are in the dark.

TIP

Though it's possible to set up a ZTNA as a stand-alone application, a cloud-hosted ZTNA gives you far more flexibility and best latency efficiency.

>> **Software-defined networking:** A software-defined wide-area network (SD-WAN) uses software to control network operations rather than network hardware such as traditional routers. Using an SD-WAN virtualizes networking in the same way that virtual machines (VMs) virtualize computer server hardware. This saves a lot of money and allows instant scalability.

Dynamic path selection directs network traffic using algorithms to choose the best possible path based on the quality of service (QoS) requirements of the application. Some applications, like video, require low latency and high throughput, and others, such as moving text values, have lower demands.

The Cloud Native Application Protection Platform

The Cloud Native Application Protection Platform (CNAPP) is a unified platform that combines several security applications into a single solution. These platforms generally include these features:

>> **Artifact scanning:** An *artifact* in this context is a software program, a library, a compressed archive file, or another file used for application deployment. Scanning them is obviously a good idea. Though cloud service providers have scanning solutions as a stand-alone application, a CNAPP platform integrates this functionality. Artifact scanning monitors your container registry and artifact registries.

>> **Cloud Workload Protection Platform (CWPP):** This one manages cloud workloads (and is covered in more detail in the next section).

>> **Cloud Infrastructure Entitlements Management (CIEM):** This functionality manages identities and access privileges. It follows the strategy of least privilege, fitting nicely into a zero trust philosophy.

>> **Cloud Security Posture Management (CSPM):** This functionality provides vulnerability protection as well as protection from human error when applying configuration settings. CSPM is a means to identify risk, assess it, prioritize the risk, and then adapt to it. This function is sometimes known as IaC configuration scanning.

>> **Kubernetes Security Posture Management (KSPM):** KSPM is meant to complement a CSPM solution, providing the same type of configuration setting errors but in Kubernetes containers.

Working with CWPP

Cloud Workload Protection Platforms (CWPP) manage the workload associated with operating in the cloud. This includes networking, computing, and storage. Cloud workloads have security needs that differ from the same services in a local network environment. A CWPP system manages these workloads in a multicloud environment that includes local clouds, public clouds, and a hybrid of the two. Chapter 9 covers the various cloud types in more detail.

Trying to move applications that have been running in your local environment to their new home in the cloud and expecting them to run the same is an unreal expectation. That's why you need CWPP.

Discovery is the first benefit provided by CWPP. This application works to discover workloads of all types running anywhere in your environment. Once the discovery is complete and the application has a list of the various workloads, each one is then examined to determine whether any vulnerabilities are associated with the workload. This is done using your predefined security policies and any known vulnerabilities.

TIP

CWPP makes recommendations to secure your workloads with various solutions, including network segmentation, antimalware applications, and run-time protection.

Advantages of CWPP

There are a number of advantages you'll experience when implementing CWPP into your cloud security plan, whether you're simply using the cloud for SaaS applications, storing your data there, or actually developing applications meant to run in the cloud. CWPP applications integrate into your DevOps development pipeline. This enables the applications you develop to be automatically configured for workload security.

Because CWPP is a cloud application, you also experience the same benefits you get with any cloud solution. It scales up and down as needed and fees are pay per use.

Like many cloud-based security solutions, you gain visibility by providing a single point of access that oversees the entire network, both on-premises and in the cloud. This type of solution blends well with zero trust implementations and artificial intelligent solutions such as AIOps.

Managing with CSPM

Cloud security posture management (CSPM) is an important part of CWPP. Because misconfigurations are one of the major issues with cloud security, you need a system like CSPM to scan for configuration errors. In addition to straight-up errors, it makes certain that your configurations match your corporate security policies as well as any compliance requirements your company may face.

Because the number of configuration settings has grown to unmanageable and massive proportions, it's ripe for automation. A CSPM system automatically finds and corrects most configuration errors and thus increases the security of your system.

REMEMBER

Most network breaches involve misconfigurations.

Checkpoint (www.checkpoint.com) has both a CWPP and CSPM solution. Its CloudGuard Workload Protection application can provide security to serverless and containerized cloud applications.

McAfee has its MVISION Cloud Native Application Platform, or CNAPP www.mcafee.com/enterprise/en-us/solutions/mvision.html), which performs the same functions: discovery, risk assessment, and integration with DevOps, all with a zero trust philosophy. Aqua (www.aquasec.com) also has CNAPP solutions.

NIST Risk Management Framework

The NIST Risk Management framework, like other similar cybersecurity frameworks, has a multistep process for the implementation of security. This framework is the basis for meeting the requirements of the Federal Information Security Modernization Act (FISMA) discussed in the next section.

These are the seven steps of the NIST RMF:

1. **Prepare.**

   Preparation to manage security and risk.

2. **Categorize.**

   Create a list of resources and categorize the risk associated with each.

3. **Select.**

   This step is unique to the NIST framework. In this step, you must select the set of NIST SP 800-53 controls necessary to protect your system based on the Categorize Risk Assessment step.

4. **Implement.**

   Planning is only half the battle. You must make the dream come true. Oh, and document what you've done.

5. **Assess.**

   Check it all out to see whether everything is operating as planned.

6. **Authorize.**

   The brass get to step in and do their part, authorizing the launch of the system to operate. *Note:* This is not an agile system, where you do a little, test a little, and then do some more. This is a full-on government framework: Plan it, build it, test it, and launch it.

7. **Monitor.**

   This step simply monitors the security system for risks to the system.

For complete documentation on following this framework, visit `https://csrc.nist.gov/projects/risk-management`.

Federal Information Security Modernization Act

Part of the NIST Risk Management framework, the Federal Information Security Modernization Act of 2002 (affectionately known as FISMA), is a requirement for each federal agency to "develop, document and implement" agency programs that provide information security. This includes businesses, contractors, and other government agencies that do business with the one complying with FISMA.

In 2014, the law was amended to eliminate unnecessary reporting requirements. Together with the Paper Reduction Act, FISMA focuses on efficient and cost-effective risk-based security. It's composed of a number of NIST publications, as shown in Figure 13-3.

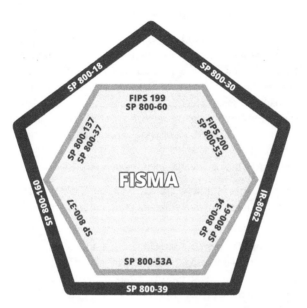

FIGURE 13-3: FISMA is composed of a number of NIST publications.

The first requirement is to create a security plan. This next section talks a bit about the Cybersecurity Strategy and Implementation plan.

Cybersecurity Strategy and Implementation Plan

When working with the US government or as a government agency, you may be asked to put your cybersecurity strategy and implementation plan (CSIP) in place. Unlike some of the other frameworks that have a set of technologies to adopt, this is more of a "Develop a plan and then figure out how to meet the plan" type of direction. (I always say, "Use what you have first, and then find new stuff.")

There are five major points you need to consider when making your organization ready for CSIP:

>> **Prioritize:** Prioritize the protection of your assets. Determine which hardware you have installed, which cloud systems you use, and which other related hardware such as network hardware, firewalls, and key storage systems you

may have set up. You need this information for FISMA reporting. Part of your asset list should include the asset name, who is authorized to get it or use it, where the asset is located, what it is, or what it does. The better the effort you put into this step, the better the outcome of the entire plan. It won't be perfect, because things change too quickly and the amount of stuff out there is overwhelming. Make a best effort.

>> **Timely detection and rapid response:** You need to set up systems that allow you to make rapid detections and then allow you to respond to incidents quickly. Rapid detection requires automated systems. Detection is something AI does exceptionally well. The US Department of Homeland Security (DHS) has its Einstein system, which is a signature based malware-detection technology. Because it's signature based, Einstein cannot identify zero-day threats — vulnerabilities that software vendors only recently became aware of. Use technology that employs behavior-based algorithms and AI to find zero-day attacks taking advantage of these previously unknown exploits.

Rapid response means that you have a well-oiled incident response plan and team. This includes staff and stakeholders. Don't just dust off the old plan and call it macaroni.

>> **Rapid recovery from incidents:** Once you've identified the threat and stopped it, you need to recover from the impact of the attack. This includes problems such as damaged data, reputation damage, any stolen data, and the need to determine who was impacted and how to reach them.

>> **Recruitment and retention of qualified personnel:** You often find the best people in universities. If they're just coming out of school, you may even be able to afford them — but you must be competitive. One way to do this is to keep your staff engaged. This is particularly true for people working on a contract. Short-term contractors tend not to attract the cream of the crop. You'll get people who get in and get out quickly, creating churn and loss of skills gained from experience and/or training. Longer contracts give contractors the satisfaction of knowing that they don't need to hunt for a new job right away, and you gain from the skill of a retained worker. See Figure 13-4.

Make sure you budget for training. Technology changes at such a fast pace that training regularly keeps the team up to date.

>> **Efficient and effective acquisition and deployment of existing and emerging technologies:** If you have followed the steps in the previous section, you have a pretty good idea of what you already have at your disposal to implement your plan. Use what you have and then look at newer technologies that may enable you to handle security in a more efficient and powerful way.

FIGURE 13-4:
Retain
contractors by
giving them
longer contracts.

You'll notice distinct similarities between the government security frameworks and those proposed by Gartner. The long and short of it is that you need a plan, you need to act on the plan, you need to continually test your implementation, you need to update the plan, and then you need to test it some more and regularly revisit the plan with fresh eyes.

REMEMBER

Revisit your plan at least once a year and put your heart in it because a well-thought-out plan can save you a great deal of heartache later.

Chapter **14**

Security Consortiums

t's never easy to do the hard things by yourself, so it's good to know that some amazing international, national, and local groups of people are quite willing to help if you need advice about how you can best meet your security concerns. To be completely successful with your cloud and network security, join one or more of these consortia and participate with them in bettering security for all. Most of the groups discussed in this chapter have helpful training programs and working groups in specific areas that might interest you based on your industry or security needs. For example, if your company is facing a security audit, you might get some of your staff certified as auditors or join a group that helps you prepare for audits.

Because this book is largely about cloud security, this chapter starts with an alliance specifically dedicated to cloud security. I do talk a bit about information security generally now and then, so the last part of this chapter introduces some of the other, more general groups you may want to join.

Doing the Right Thing

As a member of the Cloud Security Alliance (CSA, `https://cloudsecurityalliance.org`), you're part of the most advanced organization promoting best practices for secure cloud computing. You don't necessarily need to be a member to learn about the best practices proposed by the CSA. It has a group of documents that are regularly updated. By answering a few questions, you can download these documents from the blog website. Here is one of its series on application containers and microservices:

```
https://cloudsecurityalliance.org/blog/2021/08/18/
secure-containers-and-microservices-series
```

As a reminder of some of the best practices I discuss in this book, here are some recommendations for you to follow:

>> **Make a plan.** Without a strategy, you're doomed to fail. Certain frameworks can assist you in the development of a good plan. Follow a framework that best fits the kind of business your company is in, and then make it your own.

>> **Select a cloud service provider you can depend on for security and reliability.** This is a shared security responsibility, so it's a bit of a marriage when it comes to providing security.

>> **Train your employees.** So much of what goes wrong happens because of poorly trained employees. Configuration mistakes alone make up many of the reasons breaches can occur. Good training is imperative.

>> **Remember that visibility is the key in cloud security.** If you can't see it, you can't protect it. Shadow IT can overwhelm your security staff, making a secure cloud environment nearly impossible.

>> **Employ a zero trust philosophy whenever possible to limit access to cloud resources as much as possible without impacting your ability to do business.** Good authentication is important.

>> **Recognize that there is no longer a perimeter and that every user device that connects to the cloud is a point of vulnerability.** Make certain, as much as possible, that the bring-your-own-device culture that now exists doesn't defeat your attempt at cloud security.

>> **Encrypt everything you can.** Data is the thing you most want to protect in cloud security. Make certain to use best practices when it comes to data at rest as well as on the move.

>> **Discover!** Track down everything you have to deal with, including applications, users, devices, IoT thingies, partners, vendors, or anyone else who may access your cloud systems. Then label them. Determine the risk associated with each of these, and associate risk labels with each of them, making security management possible.

>> **Use technologies such as cloud access security brokers (CASBs) to enforce good authentication and access based on risk.** One of the must-have technologies is the use of AI systems that can mine your data and provide you with the support you need in a complicated environment such as the web. (AIOPs is awesome.)

>> **Employ good DevSecOps.** Don't let security be a development add-on.

Try to get a handle on your information security now because some of the predictions for the future show that the sheer numbers of users and devices will soon become overwhelming. The *Cisco Annual Internet Report* (2018–2023) makes this prediction: "The number of devices connected to IP networks will be more than three times the global population by 2023."At the very least, follow the steps shown in Figure 14-1.

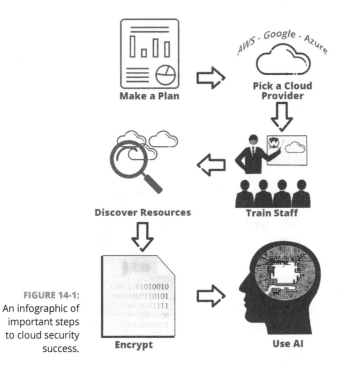

FIGURE 14-1: An infographic of important steps to cloud security success.

Membership in the Cloud Security Alliance

You lead a busy life. This is simply true of anyone in the infosec world and mostly true for people in cloud security. Being busy becomes a bit of a *Catch-22* — kind of like that conundrum where you can't get a job without experience and you can't get experience without a job. Participating in organizations such as the Cloud Security Alliance can help ease the burden by providing some of the best-and-latest information you need for securing your cloud resources. On the other hand, you may be thinking, "Who has time to participate in an organization?" You'll find that participating is easy, either via forums or even local chapter meetings. Everyone who participates is at least as busy as you and making time to be part of this organization or others will greatly enhance your capabilities. Your participation also helps others, allowing you to share your experience and knowledge with others.

It's possible to participate in the CSA via either a company membership or a personal membership. Both memberships provide the same access to information, training, certification, and chapter membership.

Company membership

One significant action you can take for your company's security is to participate in a community that supports constant education and support for best practices in cloud computing and security. This also helps you organize staff training, which should remain a regular part of your business plan. You may find training programs that not only assist your immediate security staff but also assist people in adjunct areas or even stakeholders.

You can choose from these three levels of business membership:

>> **Enterprise:** The enterprise membership level is primarily for consumers of cloud services. If your company uses the cloud for storage or uses SaaS applications, you'll want to stay current with best practices for securing this interaction, particularly with so many people working remotely.

>> **Solution provider:** The solution provider level of membership is perfect for companies providing cloud-based solutions or security. This is a great way for DevSecOps teams to participate with others in the same field. DevSecOps is rapidly changing, and one of the simplest and most efficient ways to stay abreast is interacting with a community.

>> **SaaS solution provider:** The SaaS solution provider level of membership is for companies offering Software as a Service applications. Benefits to this type of membership include

- Access to a support desk

- Tools to improve the security of your application with guidance from CSA

- Notice to others that you care about the security of your application, by getting listed in the CSA STAR Registry

- The ability to display the badge that lets others know your SaaS applications are created by people who care about their security — and that you have qualified as a CSA Trusted Cloud service provider.

The benefits of being a SaaS solution provider don't end there. Trust is one aspect that can set your application apart from others. For more information on this particular membership, check out `https://cloudsecurityalliance. org/membership/solution-providers/#saas-section`.

Individual membership

Individual membership gives you a wide range of ways to participate with the Cloud Security Alliance. You can participate by actively joining online discussions in the forum known as Circle, or you can join a local chapter of the CSA and meet with others in person to either share your own experience or expand your own knowledge from others in your chapter. You can also take part in research working groups where you get to share your knowledge and assist in the exploration of the latest cloud security knowledge and then help disseminate it by way of local chapter participation. Figure 14-2 shows the different types of individual membership programs within the CSA, and this list fills in some of the details:

>> **Circle:** Circle is CSA's online community forum, where you can communicate with others who are dedicated to better cloud security. Actively participating in CSA through Circle allows you to be part of a number of research initiatives. It's also a great way to stay in touch with local chapters in your area. Of course, this is the best way to keep up to date on CSA happenings and member benefits.

Chapters: In a chapter, you can participate and rub shoulders with other local infosec professionals. These experts, and perhaps you, volunteer to bring about better knowledge of cloud security in the local area. Active participation includes activities such as research to discover novel ways to increase cloud security, security education, community cloud security awareness projects, and CSA outreach. People who participate actively in the CSA chapters are seen as leaders in the field and can help people further their careers.

>> **Research working groups:** CSA working groups are the go-to source for best practices, research, and tools for providing security assurance and privacy in the cloud. CSA's diverse membership of industry practitioners and corporate members has converged and is continuously cycling through researching, analyzing, formulating, and delivering arguably the most advanced research

and tools available across the cloud security spectrum. All research is developed according to the phases in the CSA research lifecycle.

Here's a list of some working groups:

- Threat intelligence
- Emerging technologies
- C-level guidance for top decision makers
- Assessments and audits
- Security services
- Industry-specific topics
- Security DevOps
- Architectures and components
- Privacy

Check the CSA website for additional work groups or ones that have been added after this book was published.

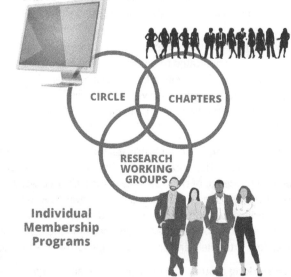

FIGURE 14-2:
Participate as an individual member in any of these programs.

Getting that Stamp of Approval

A certification means much more than getting to spend time away from work or earning a piece of paper to hang on your cubicle wall (for those still going to the office). Certification enables you to keep up with the latest technologies and assures the company you work for that you know what you're talking about. It also assures vendors, partners, and customers that their private data is in the hands of someone who is certified to be competent at handling cloud security.

TIP

The CSA is not the only organization offering the courses I discuss here. Later in this chapter, I list several other organizations, many of which offer similar or even more expansive training and certification.

CCSK Certification

The certificate of cloud security knowledge (CCSK) can assist those hoping to land a great job as a cloud security specialist *and* enhance the career of someone already working in the field.

You can prepare yourself for this open book exam in one of two ways (or both, I suppose): Study from the booklet provided or take a certification course. This certification course provides the best-and-latest knowledge necessary for complying with global cloud security requirements. For more information, check out https://cloudsecurityalliance.org/education.

CISA: Certified Security Information Systems Auditor

The CISA course is an ISACA www.isaca.org course that covers the essentials of information security auditing practices. Topics include these:

>> The information systems auditing process

>> Governance and management of IT

>> Information systems acquisition, development, and implementation

>> Information systems operations and business resilience

>> Protecting information assets

Make sure your staff stays up to date on the latest information on maintaining security by having them keep up with continuing professional education programs and maintaining their certifications.

CRISC: Certified Risk and Information Systems Control

This credential focuses on IT risk management. It establishes a foundation in best practices to identify, analyze, evaluate, assess, prioritize, and respond to risk. Learn more about this certification program here:

```
https://www.isaca.org/credentialing/crisc
```

You must be able to demonstrate work experience in the field of IT risk management along with passing the exam to gain this certification.

CCAK: Certificate of Cloud Auditing Knowledge

You can learn the essentials of cloud auditing in this course. Companies that are required to be audited for security because of compliance requirements will definitely want to have people skilled in handling these audits. Failing an audit can have dire consequences for a company.

Cloud auditing is different from traditional IT security auditing. The sheer breadth of the cloud and its many types and choices in services make cloud auditing different. You'll want to make sure your business, when requiring security audits, is staffed with certified cloud auditing personnel. Information security officers should also be armed with this information and should gain certification to support their well-rounded knowledge of cloud security.

You should have cloud security and security auditing experience before attempting to study for (and take) the certification exam. Though experience is important, no previous certification is required for taking the test. The test, which is self-paced, is only $495 for nonmembers. Once you sign up, you have a year to take the test.

Advanced Cloud Security Practitioner

The Advanced Cloud Security Practitioner training is essentially CCSK training in overdrive, expanding on the standard hands-on training. This class is a deep dive into practical cloud security and DevSecOps. Meant for people working in larger enterprises, this course sets you apart from traditional infosec by giving you skills in the kinds of abstraction and automation that define cloud computing. After completing the training, you will know how to

>> Architect enterprise-scale cloud environments

>> Manage the security of an enterprise-level cloud implementation

>> Employ the latest DevSecOps information to build secure applications and maintain their security

GDPR Lead Auditor and Consultant

When doing business with the European Union (EU), you may want to have certification that supports your security efforts when it comes to dealing with EU security regulations. The EU General Data Protection Regulation (GDPR) certification training qualifies auditors for the CSA Code of Conduct, part of which requires you to be able to show your compliance with the GDPR regulations.

TIP

The EU is not the only country that requires this level of security and privacy for its citizens. The GDPR is a good basic model for the requirements of almost any other country with this type of security compliance requirement. Becoming familiar with the GDPR will ready you for working with other countries.

Information Security Alliances, Groups, and Consortiums

Participating in groups that are focused on information security prevents you from having to reinvent the wheel. These groups embody the expertise of some of the top infosec researchers on the planet. Almost all of them also have training and certification programs that will assist you in compliance requirements. Others are simply the perfect place to go for assistance when creating infosec plans. Table 14-1 lists some of the most well-known information security alliances, groups, and consortiums.

In addition to the organizations listed here are groups for specific countries and some of the larger metro areas in the US. Make sure you seek these out and participate.

TABLE 14-1   Security Alliances, Groups, and Consortiums

Organization	URL
Anti-Phishing Working Group (APWG)	`https://apwg.org/apwg.org`
Association for Executives in Healthcare Information Security (AEHIS)	`https://aehis.org/aehis.org`
Association of Certified Financial Crime Specialists (ACFCS)	`www.acfcs.org`
Center for Internet Security (CIS)	`www.cisecurity.org`
Chief Information Security Officer Executive Network (CISO)	`https://cisoexecnet.com`
Computing Technology Industry Association (CompTIA)	`www.comptia.org`
Cyber, Space, & Intelligence Association (CSIA)	`http://cyberspaceintel.org`
Cybercrime Support Network (CSN)	`https://cybercrimesupport.org`
Cybersecurity Advisors Network (CyAN)	`https://cyan.network`
Federal Information Systems Security Educators Association (FISSEA)	`https://csrc.nist.rip/organizations/fissea/home/index.shtml`
Forum of Incident Response and Security Teams (FIRST)	`www.first.org/first.org`
Identity Management Institute (IMI)	`https://identitymanagementinstitute.org/identitymanagementinstitute.org`
Infragard	`www.infragard.org/infragard.org`
Institute of Internal Auditors (IIA)	`https://na.theiia.org/Pages/IIAHome.aspxna.theiia.org`
International Association of Privacy Professionals (IAPP)	`https://iapp.org`
International Association of Security Awareness Professionals (IASAP)	`https://iasapgroup.org`
International Consortium of Minority Cybersecurity Professionals (ICMCP)	`www.cyversity.org`
International Information Systems Security Certification Consortium (ISC2)	`www.isc2.org`
Information Systems Security Association (ISSA)	`www.issa.org/issa.org`

Organization	URL
Internet Security Alliance (ISA)	`https://isalliance.org/isalliance.org`
IT Information Sharing and Analysis Center (IT-ISAC)	`www.it-isac.org`
National Cybersecurity Alliance (NCSA)	`https://staysafeonline.org/`
National Cybersecurity Society (NCSS)	`https://nationalcybersecuritysociety.org`
National Technology Security Coalition (NTSC)	`www.ntsc.org`
Risk Management Association (RMA)	`www.rmahq.org/?gmssopc=1rmahq.org`
Security Industry Association (SIA)	`www.securityindustry.org`

Words for the Road

Being part of the Cloud Security Alliance or another similarly attuned organization as a member makes you part of a community of people dedicated to securing cloud computing. The support you receive is invaluable, and the various certification courses you can take will give your cloud security team the information they need as well as provide the assurance to others that your team is well-trained and proficient at handling private information in the cloud.

But don't just take it from me. Learned monks of the Middle Ages were saying much the same thing, as the following quote makes clear:

Nos esse quasi nanos gigantium humeris insidentes.

—ATTRIBUTED TO BERNARD OF CHARTRES, 12TH CENTURY

This quote is best known as a quote from a letter of Isaac Newton's from 1675, where he states, "[I]f I have seen a little further it is by standing on the shoulders of giants. I take Newton to mean that "we discover truth by building on previous discoveries." This remains so true today: There is no reason you have to re-create the wheel. Participate with others in the amazing challenge of cloud security. Participate in several of the organizations listed in this chapter. This will enable your team to stay abreast of current technology and solutions, make them aware of new threats as they emerge, and collaborate to defeat the bad guys.

The Part of Tens

IN THIS PART . . .

Plan your cloud security improvement strategy.

Investigate cloud security solutions.

IN THIS CHAPTER

» Assessing the risks

» Involving the right team

» Setting up configuration management

» Adopting AIOps

» Instituting DataOps

» Getting to know and love zero trust

» Restricting access

» Managing compliance

» Becoming involved in the cloud security community

» Preparing for the future

Chapter **15**

Ten Steps to Better Cloud Security

This chapter is largely a review of the concepts covered in this book that make up the top ten steps you should take to build better cloud security. You can even use this list as a starting point for creating a basic cybersecurity plan that includes your use of clouds (private, public, or hybrid) in your IT landscape. One recommendation that doesn't appear in the list of steps is to find a framework that gives your effort structure. This keeps a monumental task manageable. The ninth step in this chapter is to get involved in a cloud security community. Don't try to do it all on your own — use the resources that are already out there.

Scoping Out the Dangers

The landscape of a network that includes cloud environments is complex and difficult to protect effectively. This is a change from the time when all you needed to do was throw up a firewall and your network was protected.

To protect a cloud-based environment, you basically have to pick and choose what you need to protect and then what doesn't need as much protection. To do this, you need to inventory everything and everyone involved. This process in itself can be a difficult challenge — but it's a necessary one.

Start by inventorying your assets, including data, applications, devices, and network hardware. A device might be anything from an IoT device to a server or from a phone or pad to an iWatch if it connects to your network in some way. Once you have a list, you need to assess what the risks might be with each asset. Create a uniform set of tags to help you add consistency to your assessment. These tags can be as simple as Scary Bad, Kinda Bad, Not So Bad, and Ho Hum. It's your job to determine how fine-grained you want to make your assessment — the more complicated you make it, however, the harder it might be in the future to create security measures to protect groups of similarly tagged assets.

Once you have analyzed the risk associated with each asset, you must make a calculated decision about what to do that best protects the asset. You generally have these three options:

>> **Accept:** Accept the risk and spend your time and effort coming up with a plan to counter that risk.

>> **Transfer:** Offload the risk to someone else by transferring the asset. For example, if you have a data storage system, you might consider transferring that storage to a cloud storage system that handles the security and protection for you. At a base level, this strategy avoids the requirement for providing physical security.

>> **Remediate:** Make plans for how you will handle the risk yourself.

TIP

Consider all risk your own, even in a shared risk agreement. Once you start expecting someone else to handle risk for you, it disempowers you from taking your own action and starts a never-ending blame game.

Once you have completed your device and data risk assessment, you have to start assessing risks with the people who will have access to your system. You can start with the highest risk, which is always those closest to you. It may seem counterintuitive to have the least trust in those with whom you work most closely, but it's usually those people who have access to the most private data and can potentially cause the greatest harm.

Employees with limited access to your system can still pose a risk because hackers often use the account access of people not as likely to be conspicuous or who don't have higher risk profiles. In these cases, it's a good idea to limit access as much as possible.

Contractors, partners, vendors, and customers also pose a security risk, so you should include them in your assessment, which should describe how they might be a risk. What scenarios might feasibly happen that would cause a breach by way of one or more in this group of people? This question can help you build the right security mechanisms. It's a fine balance when restricting access and allowing business to move forward unencumbered.

Inspiring the Right People to Do the Right Thing

Responsibility for information security may *begin* with the IT department, but this is definitely not where it *stops*. This concept of responsibility started changing with the introduction of the Sarbanes–Oxley Act of 2002 — the one that made the CEO responsible for financial record keeping. The focus is definitely different when the CEO has to put their signature on documents certifying financial documents. This is a time when executive management became more responsible for all that happens within a company, even IT security. Back in 2014, for example, a large data breach led to executive upheaval at Target.

Cloud security is a team activity. It's a little like picking your team in grade school: You want all the best players — and then some who are just friends. Create a team that includes these "players":

>> IT security staff

>> Cloud management staff

>> Privacy and compliance managers

>> Stakeholders

>> Risk managers

>> DevOps

>> The person who always brings the doughnuts

REMEMBER

Don't let your team become too unwieldly. Your cloud security team may not be the same team as your incident response team or your disaster recovery teams. Those are a bit more specialized and require regular training together in the event of a breach or a disaster that needs to be recovered from.

Your incident response team may require extra people, such as personnel from Legal, to help with the public response and reporting requirements. You may have specialized incident response staff for compliance reasons. (You may not need the doughnut guy for this one.)

The disaster recovery team needs to be a well-oiled response team that may cover people from each department in your company. This team may also interface with outside disaster recovery services you've employed. Pick this team carefully and train often. There have been suggestions that you even train in a *live-fire* scenario, where you invoke an actual disaster just to see how your company responds. This technique might be going a bit too far for some companies.

The most important thing to establish after you have a team in place is a dependable means of communication. For incident response teams, this may be a team messaging system that allows secure file transfers between group members. It may mean a shared view of an AIOps dashboard.

TIP

AIOps applications generally include the ability to assign tasks for certain events along with an integrated messaging system. This is helpful when you want to automate that functionality.

Keeping Configuration Management on the Straight and Narrow

The need for a good configuration management system cannot be understated. The largest percentage of breaches occur because of errors in configurations. A configuration management system allows you to

>> Control configuration changes

>> Track configuration changes

>> Audit configuration changes

Why manage configurations? Because you're human. Humans forget things, overlook things, and make errors. That's one of the reasons for controlling, tracking, and auditing changes — you may need to track changes back to the source to patch a security hole.

The complexity of cloud computing, with virtual machines and containers coming and going, has created the necessity to automate configurations, because doing it manually is no longer possible. Automating discovery means that you can save these changes as they happen into a configuration management database (CMDB). Investing in a good CMDB can save your posterior as well as possibly save your company.

REMEMBER

Not only does misconfiguring virtual machines cause a security nightmare, but configuration settings also control how efficiently they operate.

Without a good configuration management system, your disaster recovery efforts are probably futile. A good system can help you get back to where things were before the disaster, having control over the tens of thousands of settings (or more!).

TIP

Good configuration management applications sometimes include patch management systems. You definitely should keep all your devices up to date with all the latest security patches. It doesn't make sense to do this manually when you can automate this process.

Adopting AIOps

The complexity faced in today's networks far exceeds the ability of many teams to keep up with dynamic changes in the network taking place every second. (It's like one of those horror movies where the walls and doors keep changing.) AIOps uses deep learning AI algorithms to help you

>> **Create visibility:** Essential in managing complex networks and often include automated discovery systems.

>> **Change management:** Automatically updates the CMDB that is essential in tracking users and devices in a complex network.

>> **Simplify alerts:** Stops alert overwhelm and provides background information on the history of the alert, dependent systems, and suggestions on how your response team should react. This frees your team by giving you faster resolution times.

The great thing about AIOps is that, because it's a philosophy and a technology solution, you can add as many applications as you need in order to round out your entire security management system into a single dashboard.

A good place to start in implementing AIOps is with Splunk (www.splunk.com). This enterprise-level system manages the many facets of AIOps. For larger enterprises, you may want to consider ServiceNow www.servicenow.com. Its cloud-based AI learns from the data of a large number of clients and provides some of the best insight into alerts, cutting the time it takes to resolve them.

In complex networks, the problem of being bombarded by alerts can constantly overwhelm your security staff. Using AI allows you to create a hierarchy that shows a single alert, listing all consequential alerts within. Solving the primary issue takes care of most of the other alerts automatically.

Getting on board with DataOps

Because cloud security is also data security and because data security is also application security, solving the problem at the source can save a great deal of time. So, be sure to build information security into your applications. Following a DevOps paradigm increases the effectiveness of your team.

Testing is built into the rapid continuous integration and continuous delivery pipeline. Following the DataOps paradigm ensures that security is built-in and not tacked on after the fact — a recipe for failure if I ever saw one.

TIP

Don't let testing stop with the development cycle — continue testing and monitoring applications for security issues after their release. This feedback should then filter into the pipeline. What you end up with is continuous improvement.

Befriending Zero Trust

Zero trust may sound like the name of a movie that includes zombies, but it is a sound philosophy for implementing authentication. The basic idea of zero trust is that both people and machines connect to network resources with the minimum level of security access necessary to get the job done and that authorization is checked at every step.

REMEMBER

Never trust. Always verify. This is the basic tenet of zero trust.

Zero Trust is difficult to employ when trying to shoehorn it into existing and legacy systems. There are wrappers you can use, but it's better to see wrappers as a stopgap measure and move into applications and resources that are built with zero trust in mind from the ground up.

TIP

Make sure your network and cloud resources have a single and secure authentication method. It's difficult to manage several authentication mechanisms successfully. Use authentication systems that are built on the concept of least privilege.

Because zero trust is not an authenticate-once-and-you're-done idea, you need to continually monitor your systems to ensure that THEY don't come under attack from trusted insiders.

Get started with zero trust now because it won't be long until the majority of systems are accessed by way of zero trust network access (ZTNA). This will slowly phase out access systems that are complicated and difficult to manage — like VPNs.

TIP

Employ network segmentation techniques to overcome lateral movement by hackers. Segmentation stops a hacker's attempt at discovering additional areas of a network to exploit once they've broken in.

Keeping the Barn Door Closed

Whether you choose to follow zero trust or create a DIY security paradigm, you'll want to restrict access to the network, to devices, and to applications as much as possible. Once a hacker lands in your network, you want to shut down their ability to discover applications, access data storage, or gain more access authority than the level where they gained access. For example, in a Linux system, they may crack someone's password and then look for exploits that will give them root access and carte blanche to your data.

One way to restrict access to Linux based systems is to use a public key to authenticate the user. These are much harder to crack than a password — and are ultimately more secure. Another approach for all operating systems is to use multifactor authentication for access. User IDs and passwords are too often stolen in the course of a day. The trading app Robinhood recently disclosed that millions of customer names and emails were stolen. Though it was unclear whether any financial data was stolen, once they have your name and email, hackers can potentially use that to track down your password.

Since there have been so many data breaches revealing your username and password, you should probably take a look to see if it's happened to you: Enter your email into the website `https://haveibeenpwned.com`.

Complying with Compliance Mandates

Managing compliance isn't just a nice-to-have extra; it's a requirement for most companies handling private information — particularly, health, legal, and banking companies. You need to do one (or both) of the following:

>> Develop a compliance team consisting of security and legal staff.

>> Contract with a company that specializes in compliance management, audit management, and legal issues.

Being successful at managing compliance starts at the top. The CEO is the manager of corporate culture and thus should support the idea that compliance is critical to the success of the company. In this type of culture, you can engender the security principles necessary to meet compliance without its being a constant struggle at audit time.

Hire a skilled compliance officer and don't skimp on paying them what they deserve. Failing compliance audits can quickly cost the company a great deal in fines or worse — a loss of ability to do business — so it pays to invest in the right people upfront. When it comes to risk and business continuity, this is high on the list.

Compliance departments often deal with more than cybersecurity compliance: They often handle everything from SEC trading laws and antitrust matters to export regulations and many more. It's easy for this group to become overwhelmed and therefore need the support of the entire company in meeting compliance. For this reason, the code of conduct to meet cybersecurity compliance should be clearly communicated. Don't make it only a handout that you distribute to new hires. Make it part of the overall culture. Print it on the paper coffee cups, if you must. Imagine looking into the bottom of the coffee cup and seeing this: Have a nice day. Change your password.

Keep international offices in mind when creating a corporate compliance culture. Classes and compliance documents should be in the local language, for maximum uptake.

You can also consider hiring a consultant to help you achieve compliance. This is a useful option for smaller companies that lack the budget to build a full compliance team. Rather than do it halfway, it's better to farm out this task. Here is a company that does just that: Foresite (`https://foresite.com`).

Joining the Cloud Security Club

Cloud security is an ephemeral matter: It changes so radically in so short a time that it's difficult to stay abreast of all the changes. One way to do that is to spread out the responsibility by relying on a trusted group of security professionals: international, national, or local. For the most part, you can participate in these groups by way of forums and online interaction.

Depending on the status of any particular pandemic, local branches of many of these groups also exist, in addition to many statewide security groups. Chapter 14 has a list of many of the organizations along with their website URLs.

These groups provide more than socialization, networking, and information exchange. They also fill the vital role of providing education. Keeping your staff trained is not only smart — it's also likely a part of any compliance regulations you may be subject to.

Preparing for the Future

Quantum Computing isn't just for the good guys. If you aren't familiar with quantum computing, you soon will be. IBM defines it succinctly:

Quantum computing is a rapidly emerging technology that harnesses the laws of quantum mechanics to solve problems too complex for classical computers.

Once a futuristic technology that would change the world, quantum computing is now here and will become a mainstream topic in a very short time. Some of the largest, well-funded companies like IBM and Google now have working quantum computers that are capable of solving problems. What does this have to do with cloud security?

Almost all network security relies on encryption, whether one-time-pad (OTP) or public key or another flavor of encryption. The encryption is so strong in most cases that it would take computers of today hundreds or thousands of years to crack the encryption. All encryption is crackable given enough time, however. Here is the problem: Quantum computers can do in minutes what would take many years for a traditional computer. Throwing one more monkey wrench into the works here, it's pretty well known that many of the hacks and exploits to our US national and business networks come from nation state aggressors like Russia and North Korea. Add to this the announcement that China claims a quantum computer a million times more powerful than Google's. So now we have a nation state armed with the Jiuzhang 2 quantum computer.

REMEMBER

Bitcoin and other cryptocurrencies are secure only because of strong encryption.

Watch out for post-quantum encryption. Check out this quote from the US Department of Homeland Security:

The transition to post-quantum encryption algorithms is as much dependent on the development of such algorithms as it is on their adoption. While the former is already ongoing, planning for the latter remains in its infancy. We must prepare for it now to protect the confidentiality of data that already exists today and remains sensitive in the future."

—ALEJANDRO MAYORKAS,
US SECRETARY OF HOMELAND SECURITY,
MARCH 31, 2021

Post-quantum encryption is believed to be strong enough to be uncrackable by quantum computers. Though this isn't an immediate way to protect your network, it's something to keep on your radar.

Another change you can look forward to is the continued migration of business services to the edge. Today, cloud computing is at the same stage as mainframes were when computing first became a popular business tool. The move to decentralize has already begun, but it's still in its infancy. Soon, and it won't be long, edge computing will not only be a thing, there will also be competition to see how close you can move that cloud processing to wherever the action is. For example, when you're taking inventory in a warehouse in Philadelphia, you don't want to be sending those bar codes or IR codes to Memphis. The advantages of reduced data travel time and reduction in data path will gradually become more important as folks realize that every mile your data travels is a mile it's exposed,

REMEMBER

For every dollar you spend protecting your data, someone (somewhere, someplace) is spending twice that much to defeat your best efforts. Nothing is perfect. No one is perfect. All we can do is keep trying.

IN THIS CHAPTER

» **Automating security**

» **Inventorying assets**

» **Observing stacks**

» **Protecting your data storage**

» **Analyzing traces and creating data flow maps**

» **Implementing enterprise identity management services**

» **Going the AIOps route**

Chapter **16**

Cloud Security Solutions

loud security, or any kind of cybersecurity, is impossible without the use of technology. This chapter provides glimpses of a variety of applications that provide everything from unified cloud security services and malware detection to AIOps and more. This randomly ordered list of applications is in no way a definitive list but may work as a starting point in your search for the right apps to round out your security platform.

Checkpoint CloudGuard

The Checkpoint CloudGuard (www.checkpoint.com/cloudguard) is a unified cloud security application that lets you automate your security and provides threat prevention and cloud posture management. Cloud security posture management (CSPM) automates the process of cloud security in resources such as Infrastructure as a Service and Software as a Service. CloudGuard provides these security features across a variety of cloud types.

REMEMBER

Never trust — always verify. This is the basic tenet of *zero trust.*

CloudPassage Halo

CloudPassage Halo (`www.cloudpassage.com/cloud-computing-security`) automates your asset inventory. When you have an inventory of the assets you need to protect, it helps you do so by making a vulnerability assessment. It also provides posture management, threat detection, and network security and keeps you in compliance via continuous monitoring.

TIP

Keeping an asset inventory is one of the more critical functions you need to perform, whether it's using Halo or another application that updates a CMDB.

Threat Stack Cloud Security Platform

Threat Stack Cloud Security Platform (`www.threatstack.com`) provides full stack observability using artificial intelligence that generates machine learning intelligence. The platform provides these benefits:

>> Security and compliance telemetry

>> Compliance risk monitoring and detection

>> AI machine learning algorithms for anomalous behavior detection and resolution

>> Integration with third-party security apps and a consultant team

Symantec Cloud Workload Protection

Symantec's Cloud Workload Protection (CWP, `www.broadcom.com/products/cyber-security/endpoint/hybrid-cloud/protection-engine`) was designed to protect your data storage from attack and malware. This application uses

Symantec's long-held reputation as an antimalware business to provide threat protection. CWP for Storage detects threats at runtime by scanning the workload storage. The automated discovery of data stores initiates an automatic scan for malware.

Here's a list of some CWP features:

» One-click deployment

» Instant and scheduled malware scans

» Autoscaling (when used with Azure)

» A unified dashboard across an entire enterprise

Datadog Monitoring Software

Datadog's Monitoring Software (www.datadoghq.com) works well in distributed systems, where it happily collects, searches for, and analyzes all traces. It can manage service performance issues all the way down to the endpoint layer of an individual user with infinite cardinality tagging. It also helps you create a data flow map, which is often critical when it comes to managing data flow in a distributed system.

Features include:

» Aggregated metrics and events from more than 450 integrated technologies

» Slice-and-dice metrics that start from any source using tags

» Data storage with up to one-second granularity for 15 months

» Centralized logging

» API testing

» Visualized network traffic flow

» Threat detection as well as misconfiguration detection

Azure AD

Azure Active Directory AD (`https://azure.microsoft.com/en-us/services/active-directory`) provides enterprise identity management services with single sign-on and multifactor authentication. This system protects your users from nearly all cybersecurity attacks. Its features include

>> Single sign-on

>> Conditional access and multifactor authentication

>> Single identity platform that creates unity between cloud and on-premises systems

>> Developer tools so that you can integrate identity into your applications

With Azure AD, you can create seamless access to thousands of SaaS applications and automate workflows for user lifecycle and provisioning.

Palo Alto Prisma

Palo Alto Prisma (`www.paloaltonetworks.com`) is a cloud-delivered suite of security services that protect public cloud environments, SaaS applications, Internet access, and remote users. Here are some of its features:

>> SaaS security with an integrated cloud access security broker (CASB)

>> Visibility and threat detection in multicloud and hybrid cloud environments

>> A Secure Access Service Edge (SASE) system

>> Secure Kubernetes environments with the CN-series firewall

>> VM-series firewall

Fortinet Cloud Security

Fortinet (`www.fortinet.com`) adaptive cloud security applications work side-by-side with the cloud service provider with security products that provide visibility and management across an entire enterprise. Some of its features include these:

>> Streamlined operations

>> Policy management

>> Improved visibility and lifecycle management

>> Automation

The applications are FortiAnalyzer, FortiManager, FortiCWP, FortiGate, FortiMail, FortiWeb, FortiClient, and FortiSandbox.

ServiceNow AIOps

ServiceNow AIOps (www.servicenow.com) is one of the more powerful AIOps solutions. Its AI-based machine learning system can predict system issues before they happen and remediate them automatically — before they cause problems. You see a marked reduction in critical P1 incidents (major incidents at the "Oh My God" level) and a major reduction in alert noise (the AI automatically groups alerts). This leads to a significant reduction in the mean time to resolution of most incidents.

Here are some of the ways data is fed to the AI for analysis:

>> Health log analytics

>> Metrics from embedded agents learning normal system behavior

>> Event management, where alerts generated from health logs, embedded agents delivering system behavior alerts, and alerts from third-party monitoring applications are handled.

Alerts are correlated, reducing noise and creating a single actionable alert. The AI then provides resolution support by either activating automated processes or by giving the network operator additional information such as suggestions on how the alert was solved in the past, or by finding behavior patterns that are the most likely root cause and showing these in the network operator's dashboard.

Lacework

Lacework cloud security platform (www.lacework.com) secures cloud-based applications whether they're hosted in a container or not. The Lacework Polygraph analyzes baseline behavior and later alerts you to possible behavior anomalies. Behavior analysis catches potential breaches even when there is no malware signature, making it a powerful tool against zero-day threats (previously unknown software vulnerabilities) and internal abuses of privilege (where either an employee has gone rogue and abused their privilege to acquire data or a hacker has gained access to a user's id and abused their privileges).

The Lacework Infrastructure Monitor uses AI to monitor the health of the entire enterprise and simplifies alerts by combining them into a single, actionable alert.

Because configurations are the root of all evil when it comes to creating unwanted security holes, Lacework also includes a Configuration and Audit Control application. This allows you to plug in that security policy you created while reading this book. The application then continuously scans for policy and compliance requirements. Other features include

>> Workload and container security

>> Advanced threat protection

>> Vulnerability monitoring

>> File integrity monitoring

These applications run on the most popular cloud service providers.

Index

Forum of Incident Response and Security Teams (FIRST), 320
Franklin, Benjamin, 69
FTC (Federal Trade Commission), 286, 294
FTP servers, 272
Fukushima Daiichi nuclear disaster, 239
Function as a Service (FaaS), 34
Futurex HSM, 252
FWaaS (Firewall as a Service), 118, 300

G

GAPP (Generally Accepted Privacy Principles), 123
Gartner, 41, 119, 289
Gauntlt, 71
General Data Protection Regulation (GDPR), 104
  compliance, 106–107
  Lead Auditor and Consultant certification, 319
Generally Accepted Privacy Principles (GAPP), 123
Genie, 83
geofencing, 63
GFILanGuard, 41
Git, 83
GIT source code control system, 100
GitHub, 76, 143
Gitrob, 144
Git-secrets, 144
GLBA (Gramm-Leach-Bliley Act), 293–294
God roles, 99
Google
  authentication, 103
  quantum computing, 333
Google Cloud
  Data Catalog, 46
  Discovery Service, 9
  encryption, 59
  hardware security modules, 259
  logging, 136–137, 140
  market share, 79
  network isolation, 271
  patch management, 133
  service level agreement, 10

Google Drive, 128
governance by design, 84
GPS, 63
Gramm-Leach-Bliley Act (GLBA), 293–294
Ground Control, 235

H

Hancock, Jeff, 281
hard tokens, 244, 246–247
Hardware Asset Management (HAM), 210–211
hardware risk assessments, 108
hardware security modules (HSMs), 251–259
  cloud HSMs, 259
  cryptocurrency, 255
  cryptography, 252–253
  data security requirements, 256
  defined, 251
  DNSSEC, 256–257
  evaluating, 258–259
  functions of, 252
  key management, 253–256
  OpenDNSSEC, 257–258
  tamper resistance, 255
hashing, 58
Health Insurance Portability and Accountability Act (HIPAA), 47, 52, 89, 104
  breaches, 109
  compliance, 107–109
  forms, 108
  training, 109
heat and color maps, 21–22
Hellman, Martin, 254
Help Net Security, 277
Hewlett Packard
  HPE Cloud Volumes, 207
  HPE Hybrid Cloud Solution, 216
high interaction honeypots, 96
HIPAA. *See* Health Insurance Portability and Accountability Act
hole-in-the-bucket problem, 281
Homogeneity attack, 49

W

WannaCry, 222
waterfall method
    agile method vs., 66–68
    shift-left concept, 68–69
weirdness protection, 301–302
whitelisting, 61
wide area networks (WANs), 119, 201, 303
WinSock FTP (WS_FTP), 250
Wiz, 93
WWE, 27

X

XML, 136

Y

Yubiko, 249

Z

zero trust, 173–193, 312, 330–331
    challenges of, 190–194
    defined, 173
    features of, 175–185
    implementing, 185–194
    perimeter security vs., 174
    SASE architecture, 302–303
Zero Trust Network Access (ZTNA), 302–303
Zoho Patch Management Plus, 132

About the Author

Ted Coombs is a consultant technologist in Appleton, Wisconsin. He has spent over 40 years as a software developer, information security expert, and forensic computer scientist. He was formerly the vice president of PivX, an information security firm in Newport Beach, California. He currently consults as a futurist, sharing backgrounds in computer technology, anthropology, molecular biology, optic and mechanical engineering, and laser physics. He is semiretired, and in his spare time he creates adventure guides for Franko Maps, writes technology books, and paints portraits.

Dedication

To my grandchildren: Ocean, Forest, and Flower. May the world become a safer place.

Author's Acknowledgments

I would like to acknowledge my family and friends, particularly Thijs, for putting up with my absence while writing this book. I would also like to acknowledge Paul Levesque, who has turned gibberish into a useful text.

Publisher's Acknowledgments

Acquisitions Editor: Steven Hayes

Senior Project Editor: Paul Levesque

Copy Editor: Becky Whitney

Tech Editor: Sara Perrott

Production Editor: Mohammed Zafar Ali

Cover Image: © D3Damon/Getty Images

Take dummies with you everywhere you go!

Whether you are excited about e-books, want more from the web, must have your mobile apps, or are swept up in social media, dummies makes everything easier.

Find us online!

dummies.com

dummies
A Wiley Brand

Leverage the power

Dummies is the global leader in the reference category and one of the most trusted and highly regarded brands in the world. No longer just focused on books, customers now have access to the dummies content they need in the format they want. Together we'll craft a solution that engages your customers, stands out from the competition, and helps you meet your goals.

Advertising & Sponsorships

Connect with an engaged audience on a powerful multimedia site, and position your message alongside expert how-to content. Dummies.com is a one-stop shop for free, online information and know-how curated by a team of experts.

- Targeted ads
- Video
- Email Marketing
- Microsites
- Sweepstakes sponsorship

20 MILLION PAGE VIEWS EVERY SINGLE MONTH

15 MILLION UNIQUE VISITORS PER MONTH

43% OF ALL VISITORS ACCESS THE SITE VIA THEIR MOBILE DEVICES

700,000 NEWSLETTER SUBSCRIPTIONS TO THE INBOXES OF

300,000 UNIQUE INDIVIDUALS EVERY WEEK

# of dummies

Custom Publishing

Reach a global audience in any language by creating a solution that will differentiate you from competitors, amplify your message, and encourage customers to make a buying decision.

- Apps
- Books
- eBooks
- Video
- Audio
- Webinars

Brand Licensing & Content

Leverage the strength of the world's most popular reference brand to reach new audiences and channels of distribution.

For more information, visit **dummies.com/biz**

PERSONAL ENRICHMENT

Staying Sharp
9781119187790
USA $26.00
CAN $31.99
UK £19.99

Facebook
9781119179030
USA $21.99
CAN $25.99
UK £16.99

Guitar
9781119293354
USA $24.99
CAN $29.99
UK £17.99

Investing
9781119293347
USA $22.99
CAN $27.99
UK £16.99

Beekeeping
9781119310068
USA $22.99
CAN $27.99
UK £16.99

Digital Photography
9781119235606
USA $24.99
CAN $29.99
UK £17.99

Meditation
9781119251163
USA $24.99
CAN $29.99
UK £17.99

Pregnancy
9781119235491
USA $26.99
CAN $31.99
UK £19.99

Samsung Galaxy S7
9781119279952
USA $24.99
CAN $29.99
UK £17.99

iPhone
9781119283133
USA $24.99
CAN $29.99
UK £17.99

Crocheting
9781119287117
USA $24.99
CAN $29.99
UK £16.99

Nutrition
9781119130246
USA $22.99
CAN $27.99
UK £16.99

PROFESSIONAL DEVELOPMENT

Windows 10
9781119311041
USA $24.99
CAN $29.99
UK £17.99

AutoCAD
9781119255796
USA $39.99
CAN $47.99
UK £27.99

Excel 2016
9781119293439
USA $26.99
CAN $31.99
UK £19.99

QuickBooks 2017
9781119281467
USA $26.99
CAN $31.99
UK £19.99

macOS Sierra
9781119280651
USA $29.99
CAN $35.99
UK £21.99

LinkedIn
9781119251132
USA $24.99
CAN $29.99
UK £17.99

Windows 10
9781119310563
USA $34.00
CAN $41.99
UK £24.99

SharePoint 2016
9781119181705
USA $29.99
CAN $35.99
UK £21.99

Fundamental Analysis
9781119263593
USA $26.99
CAN $31.99
UK £19.99

Networking
9781119257769
USA $29.99
CAN $35.99
UK £21.99

Office 2016
9781119293477
USA $26.99
CAN $31.99
UK £19.99

Office 365
9781119265313
USA $24.99
CAN $29.99
UK £17.99

Salesforce.com
9781119239314
USA $29.99
CAN $35.99
UK £21.99

Coding
9781119293323
USA $29.99
CAN $35.99
UK £21.99

dummies.com

dummies
A Wiley Brand

Learning Made Easy

ACADEMIC

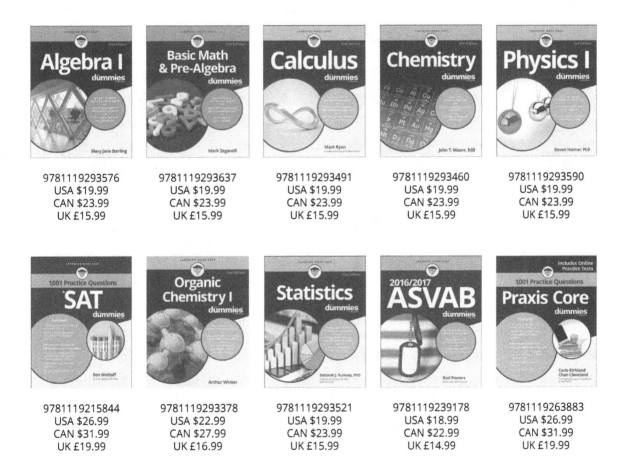

Algebra I dummies
Mary Jane Sterling
9781119293576
USA $19.99
CAN $23.99
UK £15.99

Basic Math & Pre-Algebra dummies
Mark Zegarelli
9781119293637
USA $19.99
CAN $23.99
UK £15.99

Calculus dummies
Mark Ryan
9781119293491
USA $19.99
CAN $23.99
UK £15.99

Chemistry dummies
John T. Moore, EdD
9781119293460
USA $19.99
CAN $23.99
UK £15.99

Physics I dummies
Steven Holzner, PhD
9781119293590
USA $19.99
CAN $23.99
UK £15.99

SAT dummies — 1,001 Practice Questions
Ron Woldoff
9781119215844
USA $26.99
CAN $31.99
UK £19.99

Organic Chemistry I dummies
Arthur Winter
9781119293378
USA $22.99
CAN $27.99
UK £16.99

Statistics dummies
Deborah J. Rumsey, PhD
9781119293521
USA $19.99
CAN $23.99
UK £15.99

2016/2017 ASVAB dummies
Rod Powers
9781119239178
USA $18.99
CAN $22.99
UK £14.99

Praxis Core dummies — 1,001 Practice Questions
Carla Kirkland, Chan Cleveland
9781119263883
USA $26.99
CAN $31.99
UK £19.99

Available Everywhere Books Are Sold

dummies.com

dummies
A Wiley Brand

Small books for big imaginations

9781119177173
USA $9.99
CAN $9.99
UK £8.99

9781119177272
USA $9.99
CAN $9.99
UK £8.99

9781119177241
USA $9.99
CAN $9.99
UK £8.99

9781119177210
USA $9.99
CAN $9.99
UK £8.99

9781119262657
USA $9.99
CAN $9.99
UK £6.99

9781119291336
USA $9.99
CAN $9.99
UK £6.99

9781119233527
USA $9.99
CAN $9.99
UK £6.99

9781119291220
USA $9.99
CAN $9.99
UK £6.99

9781119177302
USA $9.99
CAN $9.99
UK £8.99

Unleash Their Creativity

dummies.com

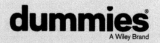

CPSIA information can be obtained
at www.ICGtesting.com
Printed in the USA
LVHW021655150322
713511LV00011B/255

9 781119 790464